Papers *from the* Headmaster

By Richard A. Hawley

Boys Will Be Men: Masculinity in Troubled Times. Eriksson, 1994.

Hail University! A Century of University School Life. University School Press, 1990.

Mr. Chips Redux/Miss Dove Redivivus: In Praise of the Teaching Life. University School Press, 1988.

The Big Issues in the Passage to Adulthood. Walker and Co., 1987.

Seeing Things: A Chronicle of Surprises. Walker and Co., 1987.

Drugs and Society: Responding to an Epidemic. Walker and Co., 1987.

St. Julian. Bits Press, 1987.

A School Answers Back. American Council on Drug Education, 1984.

The Headmaster's Papers. Eriksson, 1983. Bantam, 1984. Revised Edition, Eriksson, 1992.

The Purposes of Pleasure: A Reflection on Youth and Drugs. Independent School Press, 1983.

With Love to My Survivors. Cleveland State University Poetry Center, 1982.

Papers *from the* Headmaster

Reflections on a World Fit for Children

by
Richard A. Hawley

Paul S. Eriksson, *Publisher*

Forest Dale   Vermont

Luke 18:16.

"Let these Children alone.
Don't get between them—(£2.81.)
and ME.

Order date. 16th May 2011.

Mark 10:16.
Gathering the Children up in
His arms, JESUS laid His hands
of Blessing on them.

LORD & Master Who has Called us, All our days to follow Thee
We have heard Thy Clear Commandment 'Bring the Children
(Thee)
C Mark 10:14/Luke 18:16.) Unto ME."

Manufactured in the United States of America

10 9 8 7 6 5 4 3 2 1

Library of Congress Cataloging-in-Publication Data

Hawley, Richard A.,
    Papers from the Headmaster: Reflections on a world fit for children / by Richard A. Hawley.
        p. cm.
    Includes bibliographical references.
    ISBN 0-8397-6488-X (hardcover)
    1. Education—United States. 2. Education—Social aspects—United States. 3. Popular culture—United States. 4. Child development—United States. I. Title.
LA210.H44 1996
370'.973—dc20   96-20349
                                                       CIP

ACKNOWLEDGMENTS

Grateful acknowledgment is made to the following publications in which some of these pieces originally appeared: *The Roxbury Latin Journal, The Cleveland Plain Dealer, Character, Northern Ohio Live, The Anglican Theological Review, American Film, The American Council for Drug Education, Phi Delta Kappan, The Atlantic Monthly, Independent School, Orion, The University School Journal.*

For Paul Nelson, my teacher.

CONTENTS

Preface   ix

PART ONE   A Culture No One Asked For   3
1. Toward a Better Age   4
2. Vulgarity and What We Need   26
3. Concert   29
4. Sex, Violence, the Usual   40
5. Some Thoughts on the Pop Jesus   44
6. Privacy and Dignity   61
7. Television and Adolescents   65
8. Some Unsettling Thoughts About
   Settling in with Pot   74
9. Legalizing the Intolerable   95
10. The Bumpy Road to Drug–Free Schools   103

PART TWO   Looking After the Children   118
11. Read for Your Life   119
12. Mr. Chips Redux   123
13. Teaching as Failing   129
14. Odds and Ends: ToThose who March to the Beat
    of a Different Drummer if Any   142
15. Miss Dove Rediviva   160
16. About Boys' Schools   169
17. Bring Back Chips   187

PART THREE   True Stories   196
    18. Seeing Things   197
    19. Boys' Stories   209

PART FOUR   A Bully Pulpit   232
    20. Three Hopes for School   233
    21. A Good Student   246
    22. Peaceful Confrontation   251
    23. Inherent Responsibility   254
    24. Real Thanksgiving   258
    25. A Self Worth Esteeming   263

Index   269

A Prefatory Note to the Reader

I have spent the twenty-eight years of my working life, all of it, in the company of high school boys. Given the nature of the school where I teach, I begin each day in an assembly full of boys. I spend the subsequent periods in a swirl of boys swarming past me on the staircases, or seated quietly nearby in nooks in the library, or clustered about me in a classroom, or seated around me at lunch as we dine "family style."

The boys are expressive. Sooner or later each of them is likely to disclose who he is, what he cares about, how well he is thriving. They reveal wonderful idiosyncrasies too numerous and too particular to relate. They also reveal a few general characteristics and attitudes. In this regard, they serve as a barometer—in my opinion, a crucial barometer—of the culture in which they are embedded.

I have a feeling anybody who is reasonably responsive to children would like the boys of my school. But to live among them in close proximity, to share, literally, the world they live in, one cannot help being concerned on their behalf.

The concern has nothing to do with their general health, which is excellent, or their intelligence, which is promising. The concern is that the public, commercial culture they experience is failing them. More specifically, it frightens them and disillusions them. It frightens and disillusions them every day.

The boys of my school watch, listen, and read about celebrities who have apparently committed murder but who seem to escape justice because police involved in the case are vicious bigots. Cameras closely scanning the faces of athlete heroes reveal unmistakably the filthiest curses on their lips or, in the case of the World Series, those lips parting to spit tobacco juice on the floor of the dugout. The least of these athletes, my students learn, earns a million dollars a year. Increasingly, though, they are likely to go on strike for more money or more flexible personal options.

As the boys of my school grow into the wonder of sexual feeling, they learn that sexual expression is deadly, that it transmits unviewably hideous symptoms and diseases. They learn that sex is dangerous, that it is never safe, only that certain precautions make it "safer." Yet everywhere, whether in prime time T.V., movies, pop music, or commercial advertising, these boys are invited, enticed, dared to have sex.

All inhibitions on sex have fallen away, yet sex is always dangerous, often a crime, never a wonder and a joy. Heartthrob film stars are arrested for soliciting sex acts from street walkers, for videotaping sex acts with children. They appear on television where they are applauded for talking about these acts, while on adjacent channels call girls and lap dancers and cuckolds and teenage girls who sleep with their fathers are talking about their sex experiences. It is assumed that the incumbent President has had a succession of sexual infidelities, that past Presidents have had even more. A veteran senator leaves office in the wake of charges that he has throughout his career imposed himself sexually on the women with whom he works. My boys read about the video pornography purchased by a candidate for the Supreme Court. Despite so much revealed sexual expression and boundary pressing, the discovered sex is always embarrassing, always trouble. And the act itself is deadly.

No one, anywhere, is secure. No one is likely to live. On the way out of a state assembly in which he pleads for peace and conciliation, a prime-minister is brutally shot to death. A federal office building in middle America is blown up by an alleged "militiaman" allegedly hostile to centralized authority;

because he feels this way, dozens die in the bright light of day—including children enrolled in a day care center. The World Trade Center is bombed. A jumbo jet blows up over the Atlantic when a terrorist's bomb is detonated. A documentary-looking film about genocide in Poland during World War II wins Academy Awards, while in Yugoslavia and Somalia uncountable thousands of targeted peoples are herded together and executed en masse. A woman jogging in Central Park is savagely beaten, slashed and disfigured with a knife, left for dead. U.S. servicemen stationed in Japan lure a school-girl into their van, tape her mouth closed, bind her, brutally beat her, then rape her. Children, parents, shoppers, neighbors tending their lawns are shot to death by "drive by" killers. Citizens driving the streets of the nation's cities are increasingly accosted in traffic, yanked from their cars, beaten senseless, shot through the head.

This is gruesome news. A quarter century ago it would be called "tabloid stuff." But today it is the only news my boys see, hear, and read. There are only tabloids. "Tabloid" journalism is targeted to children. it is broadcast at times when children are most available to tune in.

Without question, the very culture sketched above is the culture in which and against which late twentieth century children attempt to think and learn. Unlike most of their parents, late twentieth century children remember no other or better culture. They see no decline, no difference.

But they are themselves different. They, without knowing it, are changed. They are four times more likely to take someone's life than their parents or grandparents would have been. They are eight times more likely to kill themselves than their parents or grandparents would have been.

My point—and the point of collecting these essays—is that our children, those we bear and those we school—are finding it hard, many of them impossibly hard, to see the point of living like this, of living at all.

It is neither myopic or naively nostalgic to say we have created or allowed a public, commercial culture that is toxic to children and, through them, to us all. There will be no helpful reckoning or change until we face this fact.

It is perhaps past time to look some humiliating and unattractive realities in the eye. It is in this spirit that I offer the following essays and reflections. They represent a quarter century's responses not just to cultural developments I have found especially jarring, but also to the way these developments have been pitched to and experienced by children and emerging adults, including, once, me.

These pieces were composed, most of them, out of genuine interest in children and out of affection for them. My hope in collecting these essays is to invite a reconsideration of what has happened to our shared public culture so that we might improve it.

There is a moment in Quentin Tarentino's film, *Pulp Fiction*, that arrested everyone of my students who saw it. Two thugs sitting in the front seat of a car accidentally discharge a revolver which, literally, blows a third thug's brains out. The shock and horror of this grisly event are not discussed. In fact, the men in the front seat are unmoved—except by a nagging concern, played for laughs, about how to clean up the car. This is cool. This is irony in our age.

In the pages that follow, I attempt to look at and even to see through that kind of cruelty and fake detachment. It's long past time to do so, even if it requires a long hard look into the back seat.

R.A.H.

PART ONE

A CULTURE NO ONE ASKED FOR

A Culture No One Asked For

What American pundit or sage could have looked ahead, say, in 1950 and predicted the cultural preoccupations of the past fifty years? Imaginative futurists like Aldous Huxley, George Orwell, and B.F. Skinner sensed that mass information and technology would play some vastly transforming role, ominous in Huxley's and Orwell's vision, redemptive in Skinner's.

No one, however, had a clue that something like "political correctness" would fall like a blanket over the nation's universities, creating a climate timid about and respectful of all disenfranchised views, while regarding established ones with deep suspicion and contempt— of even the central values of civilized living: the objectivity of truth and the inalienable rights of all humans. Nor did anyone predict that the culture of adolescents would, with massive commercial assistance, become the dominant public culture.

Who, for that matter, predicted so rapid a disintegration of clear language and speech? And who foresaw at mid-century that we would live in a drug culture, in which central nervous system toxins, previously favored by the most marginal social elements, would make their way prominently and unashamedly into the American pantry?

The fact is that no one predicted these developments; largely unintended and unwanted, they have nevertheless created a problematic and too often impossible climate in which to rear durable children. The essays gathered together in this section consider the impact on children of some of the defining themes of our age. These are the very children, it must be added, who will decide, literally, what will become of us late twentieth century survivors in our old age. It is certainly none too soon to consider what we have done to and for the children who will be the stewards of not just our personal futures, but of our planet, in the years ahead.

1

Toward A Better Age

Without ever coming to terms with it, we are sick of it.

Political correctness. What possible gifts or training could prepare anyone, much less a humble schoolmaster, to isolate, classify, understand, and see beyond what late twentieth century westerners call "political correctness"? "Political correctness" is not an explicit doctrine, although its critics find it doctrinaire. It is not a policy, although it seems to spawn policies in bewildering profusion. It is not a party, although there seem to be legions, even majorities, of partisans. It seeks with aching sincerity not to offend, but in some form or another it has probably offended every person I know. Some claim our entire higher education establishment has succumbed to it, yet I cannot think of a single card-carrying adherent. No one seems to want to march under its banner.

Is "political correctness" possibly nothing? Or slightly more than nothing, is it merely an irritating attitude putatively held by those we do not like? As a mere attitude, does it matter much in the conduct of our lives and work?

Perhaps it might be useful at this point to observe it in practice.

Last November a religious conference was assembled in Minneapolis in honor of the World Council of Churches Ecumenical Decade in Solidarity with Women. The conference was titled "Re-imagining," and in light of what follows, I ask you to keep in mind that this was no fringe enterprise, that the conferees were there representing Christian churches, seminaries, and schools; Christian practices and beliefs. In the course of their Re-imagining, these modern women proposed the following things.

First, the Judeo-Christian tradition has been an unbroken

4

succession of bad news. One presenter, Ms. Chung Hyun Kyung, declared, "The Christian church has been very patriarchal. That's why we are here together to destroy this patriarchal idolatry of Christianity." Another presenter, Ada Maria Isasi-Diaz, added: "'Church'" is a human construct, the church is oppressive to women." Another dismissed for once and for all the theological notion of transcendence, calling it "that orgy of self-alienation beloved of the fathers."

The Re-imaginers had no patience with the Resurrection, which Aruna Gnadasan dismissed in the following way: "(The Church) centered its faith around the cruel and violent death of Christ on the cross, sanctioning violence against the powerless in society." Virginia Ramsey Mollenkott saw the crucifixion drama as cosmic child abuse: "I can no longer worship in a theological context that depicts God as an abusive parent and Jesus as the obedient trusting child...this violent theology encourages the violence of our streets and our nations."

This view struck a sympathetic chord with Dolores Williams, who told the conference, "We don't need a theory of atonement at all. Atonement has too much to do with death. I don't think we need folks hanging on crosses and blood dripping and weird stuff."

With striking ambition, the Re-imagining Conferees conceived a new God. They called her Sophia, and invoked her in this way: "Sophia Creator God, let your milk and honey flow. Sophia, Creator God, shower us with your love." With the deification of Sophia comes a new theology: "We celebrate the sensual life you give us...we celebrate our bodiliness, our physicality, the sensations of pleasure, our oneness with earth and water."

From this new theology were derived a number of highly specific prescriptions. First and foremost, in the view of Elizabeth Bettenhausen, the notion that "God created us to be perfectly heterosexual and monogamous" had to go. "How many of you (conferees)," Ms. Bettenhausen asked, "have actually talked to girls under the age of twelve about the specifics of the erotic pleasures of their bodies?" Frances

Wood opined that sexual fidelity was a form of "idolatry."

I could go on about the Re-imagining conference, but I won't. I offer the example of these re-imagining conclusions not as an instance of "political correctness" itself, but rather as an example of what happens in a *climate* of "political correctness." The distinction between instance and climate is important. My purpose here is not to resolve the religious issues raised in the Re-imagining Conference (although, God knows, somebody had better resolve them), but we would do well to examine the way in which these nominal heiresses of a particular spiritual and cultural tradition, Christianity, address that tradition.

Secure and confident among so many like-minded souls, the Re-imagining Christian women made assumptions about divinity, society, history, and sexuality that *only* like-minded souls could assume. Seeking to be taken seriously and respectfully, they spoke frivolously and disrespectfully of the tradition out of which they had emerged and, not incidentally, of those who live passionately by that tradition. Perhaps nothing more than this describes the era of "political correctness": the unargued and unproven assumption of the validity of one's most basic premises and the unargued and unproven rejection of the premises of those who think otherwise.

Our annoyance with what we feel to be "politically correct" utterance and practice is nothing more than the dissonance of unearned assumptions. These assumptions are offered—often righteously—to a larger community that has not and would not grant them.

As such, late twentieth century "political correctness" is just a contemporary example of ordinary bad thinking. Throughout history people have organized themselves around poorly worked out and even preposterous ideas. And because the goodness and badness of ideas is not always immediately apparent, civil societies, especially in the West, have tended to tolerate some degree of dissonance and contradiction.

Indeed the natural right tradition in western philosophy

has included the liberty to pursue solitary, unpopular, and even wrong headed beliefs and practices. Put very simply, the way we might put it to our own middle schoolers: freely pursuing our happiness means that we can make terrible, even fatal mistakes. Our freedom is a necessary but not a sufficient condition of our living well. To live well, we actually have to get it right.

I believe we are negotiating through the distinctive cultural gloom of the late twentieth century because we have misunderstood and lost confidence in the idea of natural rights. We have lost confidence not just in specific rights, but in the very *basis* of human rights. Modern men and women cannot affirm, as Thomas Jefferson did, that these natural rights were *endowed by a Creator.* And if they are not, where do they come from? Are they merely another cultural convention, relative to a particular time and circumstances, the product of the persuasive minds of the era? If so, they are not correct in any reliable, absolute sense; they are merely—yes, "politically correct."

So we warm to our subject. "Political correctness" is the offspring of consciously or unconsciously held moral relativism. Since, according to this modern view, there are no inalienable, cross-cultural, transpersonal rights or truths of any kind, any view is as good as another. We tend to pick and choose among alternatives not by their logical consistency, not their historical and political efficacy, not their demonstrated potential for redeeming our lives—but rather for, well, the way they *feel.* Yes. We base our preferences on how sincere and *nice* people are about what they are saying. In the era of relativism, in the era of "political correctness," we negotiate by style, we negotiate by attitude. Reason becomes feeble. We find we often do not like the way reason feels. We suspect that reason might be gendered—and gendered the wrong way. Once we begin to operate in this manner, we very quickly turn the idea of natural rights on its head. The idea that both genders and all kinds and conditions of people have inalienable rights, that human beings are inherently worthy and as such entitled to

and obligated to share in the common human enterprise—
goes up with a poof.

The modern woman or man, the relativist, asks *what* rights
and worth? Defined by whom? What common enterprise?
Whose enterprise? Jefferson's? Marx's? Why those particular
dead men?

So what is left? In the absence of absolute truths, we have
claims, competing claims, warring claims, any claim you can
think of: a claim that God imagined us; the claim that we
imagine God. We have the claims of pro-life and the claims of
pro-choice. We have the claims of Louis Farrakhan and the
claims of David Duke. We have the claims of men and women
against pornography, and we have the claims of pornogra-
phers. We have the claims that one is free to think and speak
freely; and we have the claims of those who believe another
person's speech must not make them feel uncomfortable.

So many claims. What construct, what criterion, what ideal
could possibly mediate among them in an age that considers
ideals—any ideals—an "absolutist" (and you may wish to
throw in "patriarchal" or "fascist" or "imperialist") imposition
of your values onto me and mine?

Again, there is nothing new in competing claims. Nor,
philosophically speaking, is relativism new. What is new is the
enthronement of relativism as a cultural norm: the (unargued
and unproven) assumption that there is no transpersonal
truth, right, or basis for obligation. Practically, this is very
important, because it is hard to negotiate for fifteen minutes
through our school or community affairs without an urgent
need to ground what we are doing in what is humane, decent,
proper, right. Assuming these terms are unknowable doesn't
help much when we are faced, say, with a sticky student lapse
that the student, her parents, and perhaps her parents' attor-
neys would prefer that we ignore. Doing well, trying hard,
being kind, respecting others and their things, doing your
own work, keeping commitments—these are values in action,
absolutes, without which there could be no school worth having. Yet even as we adhere to our values, our culture is deny-

ing any durable basis for doing so.

The enthronement of relativism frees relativists from any obligation to be consistent. And it is with a bold and self-righteous insistence that our era's relativists lay down their social and moral agenda. Never mind that there is no possible earthly or heavenly basis for relativist moral agendas, contemporary relativists feel strongly about a few things and demand that you take heed. Here, more or less, is the late twentieth century agenda:

1. Men are toxic. Acting alone, but especially acting together, they do terrible things to each other, to women, and to children.

2. The historical record is the record of the Patriarchs. It is a terrible story. New, better stories must be found.

3. All established religions are false and pernicious, believing that some things are fundamentally true and being the expressions of toxic men in patriarchal society.

4. Ethics and obligations are invented by individuals and groups who hold them.

5. There is no culture. There are only particular cultures.

6. Western culture is toxic. Western people should stop imposing their culture on others, which means they should stop practicing their culture. Western people should understand, tolerate, and if possible, adopt other cultures. No one should adopt western culture.

7. All sexual practices and expressions are valid and good. The full variety of sexual practices should be publicly aired, institutionally endorsed, and children should be educated to all the possibilities.

8. No sexual practice or expression should make any person feel uncomfortable.

9. Language is about language, not about experience, not about the world.

10. Nothing is knowable.

As you have no doubt already noted, the propositions listed above either negate themselves, negate the others, or both. Nevertheless, I suspect many of you have felt their presence in your lives. Perhaps you have tried to accommodate them in a spirit of conciliation and courtesy. Taken together, they are not a bad set of parameters to define what we mean when we use the term "political correctness."

Again, bad thinking is bad thinking, trendy bad thinking is bad thinking, and entrenched trendy bad thinking is still bad thinking. How did we land in such a spot? Is there a way past it? These, I believe, are good questions.

We have arrived in an era of "political correctness" not due to a sinister and well-orchestrated campaign on the part of "politically correct" advocates. As I have said, almost nobody knowingly wears the "politically correct" badge. Not a virus that has burrowed in and ruined things, "political correctness" is more like the malaise we suffer once things are ruined. There was little "political correctness" in the Age of Faith or in the Age of Reason. Neither faith nor reason would allow the ten propositions I listed earlier. "Political correctness," then, reflects an absence of a necessary good, a collapse: specifically, the collapse of faith and reason.

But how? Those are major collapses!

I propose, I hope not too grandiosely, that the cultural collapse that led to "political correctness" is nothing less than a fundamental misunderstanding of what democracy can and cannot deliver.

Late twentieth century Americans have conveniently put out of their minds half of what our founders had to say about liberty. They said that liberty was indeed a necessary good and even a natural right. But liberty was not a sufficient good; indeed it was a likely ticket to trouble. In *Federalist Paper Number Ten* Madison formed his famous double analogy that air is to fire as liberty is to faction. Air sustains us, but it also enables deadly combustion. Liberty sustains and energizes us, but also leads us, if we are not careful, to impose our selfish wills on others. Liberty then is no easy proposition. It poses an existential problem of the first order. It is tempting sometimes to suppress liberty in the name of order and convenience, but this is the equivalent of banishing air in order to promote fire safety.

There has to be a mid-way, a better way, between lethal combustion and airlessness, between anarchism and political repression. That middle way was the Constitution of the United States, a political instrument that *never* promised to banish selfishness, stupidity, and cruelty from public life. Instead, it proposed something much more modest—but hopeful: a labyrinth of process so deliberate, so infused with countervailing checks and balances and separations of powers that, while not impossible, it would not be easy for the selfish will of a given faction to rise to public policy or law. Schooled in the natural right tradition and in common law, the founders knew they were onto a good thing. But they also knew and stated that its goodness in practice would depend on sources beyond their invention.

The Constitution would depend on virtue. At least some critically placed players in the constitutional process would have to be selfless, prudent, deliberate, and wise. They would have to cultivate reason in order to decide what was fair and wise, and they would have to use the constituted instruments of government and the due process of law to be sure that justice be done. The Constitution would stand or fall on human virtue, just as the perfectly serviceable constitution of the Weimar Republic would stand or fall on human virtue. The founders, unlike our current "strict constructionists" or the A.C.L.U., did not make an idol of the Constitution or any of its provisions.

Not only did the Founders see that our Constitution, or any constitution, rests on certain moral absolutes, they saw those absolutes in clear relief. These were men of the Enlightenment. These were men who had looked at the wonderful complexities of nature itself and found law-like consistencies. They saw how to harness force and motion to make wheels turn and clocks tick. The solar system, the very universe, was a clock. Nature—the nature of things, the nature of everything—was becoming, thanks to reasoned observation, accessible. And while this science evolved, human virtue would be fortified by faith in an immanent God. Not just Jefferson, but virtually all colonials believed in the Creator who had endowed them with certain inalienable rights. Perhaps more than just an obligatory first week of required American history courses is necessary to drive home that America was a passionately religious foundation before it was a political theory. It was founded by fundamentalists. Faith preceded reason, science, and "political correctness" on our shores. The First Amendment could guard against the public establishment of any particular religious denomination with the same confidence it protected all religious worship from state encroachment—because the founders knew they lived in a policy of religious believers. In God they trusted.

This potted lesson in American political theory is necessary, I think, to help show how a robust affirmation of faith in the natural rights of all persons freely to pursue their happiness has devolved into a guarded hunch that anybody ought to be able to do anything. How, to put the question more clearly, did a republic founded on natural law, virtue, and faith become a civic culture which views nature as entropy, virtue as attitude, and which banishes expressions and symbols of faith from public places?

As it happens, there is a very clear account of how this happened. Remarkably, the explanation is 2,400 years old. It appears in Book VIII of Plato's *Republic*. For those of you who haven't read Plato's *Republic*, or haven't read it recently, let me supply a little background. The dialog is an account of a very long discussion between Socrates and a handful of friends about what is the best way to live. A number of plausible, but ultimately inadequate, theories of the good life are put forward, including the good life as good business; the good life as helping your friends, harming your enemies; the good life as whatever a strong party can get away with; and the good life as a social contract among individuals who realize that the pursuit of selfish ends, though natural, creates more misery than do social cooperation and compromise.

In the process of refuting these views, Socrates establishes an altogether different model of the good life. Since human beings are naturally interdependent and derive their ultimate satisfaction and meaning socially, he sets out to establish a theoretically just society. As Plato sketches it, society is a dynamic complex of different types of people who are educated to refine their economic and personal specialties for the common good. In this republic, there are three broad types of people, all of them valuable. There are the great mass of men and women who are driven principally by the appetites. But this is not a terrible thing, as the appetites, which after all energize us and drive us on to restore ourselves, are susceptible to education of a kind. Directed and moderated, appetites drive each person and society to great productivity. Plato's conception of the appetites is not the Freudian Id—unless somehow they become misdirected and inflamed.

Appetites will not be misdirected in Plato's republic because another type of person, less numerous but critically important, keeps the appetites and appetitive people on task. These are the guardians—soldiers, civil servants, police, magistrates, judges—whose defining feature is not appetite but spirit. They have the courage and will power to keep themselves and others in line, enforcing laws and necessary public policies.

Not all the guardians know, in the profoundest sense, what is right and just, but they believe in such a thing and are loyal to those essential souls who do know. This third and least numerous type is the philosophic ruler, who has been rigorously trained both intellectually and morally to seek only what is good in itself, never a mere personal benefit.

So to review: Each human type has a distinctive and socially essential capacity: appetite, spirit, and intellect. Moreover, each capacity can be trained to produce a related virtue. The virtue of the appetites is moderation; the virtue of spirit is courage; and the virtue of reason is wisdom. These three virtues working in social harmony produce a fourth and final virtue: justice.

The good personal life, as Plato sees it, is a simple reduction of this social scheme to a personal psychology. The individual psyche is composed just as society is. The appetites are first to appear and quantitatively the largest part of the soul, certainly of the emergent child's soul. With socialization and education, spirit will surface and, with practice, begin to moderate appetitive urges. Finally, a reverence for and a burning desire to access the *source* of what moves our spirits impels a few tenacious souls to learn the truth of things: formal truths like math and logic, and then the relationship between the material, changeable world and those formal perfections. People who develop this way are self-sufficient, mentally healthy, and equipped to live as well as humans can possibly live. And while it is tempting to liken Plato's triadic psychology to the Freudian triad of id, ego, superego, the comparison won't work. Freud's psychological model is a tension reduction machine. It is not grounded in any metaphysical scheme of value. It does not necessarily act in the person's best interest. By contrast, Plato's model is aligned with truth itself. Personal and social viability are the proofs of the Platonic pudding.

For example, if a shipwrecked Platonic psyche were stranded for days on a raft in the Caribbean, his appetites would crave drink, his reason would say "I must not drink because the salt water will dehydrate and kill me faster than otherwise would be the case," and the spirit would affirm reason and deny appetite. By contrast, a shipwrecked Freudian psyche in an adjacent raft would be thrown out of equilibrium by the dehydrated cravings of the id. The super ego, depending on its parental sources, might say "you'd better tough it out," while the ego tries to decide which demand is easier to please. The ego may begin at this point subtly to rationalize (a little salt water can't hurt," "what do the experts know," "who could really blame me in this heat") or it might erupt in a fit of desire and start to swill. Again, the goal of the ego in the Freudian scheme is to relieve tension. In that scheme ethical imperatives increase tension. They are part of the problem, not the solution. In the Platonic scheme, the goal of all these parts of the psyche is to advance the purposes and well-being of the organism.

Plato's psychology is compelling. However, it derives from a political scheme so idealistic, so removed from actual historical practice, and frankly so *undemocratic* that it embarrasses us. Philosophic rulers? Heroic willpower? Suppression of pleasure, sensuality, and forbidden delights? This doesn't sound right for the '90s. This doesn't sound like fun.

Our dilemma is that we really do want to be—and we want the children in our care to be—like that Platonic psyche in the lifeboat. We want the hard truth, the reasonable thing to prevail. We want that psyche to be courageous enough not to throw its life away. We want our urges to be disciplined enough to submit to reason. We want to live and to live well.

But Book VIII of Plato's *Republic* demonstrates that you can't live well if you turn that hard won psychological hierarchy over on its side. And this, Plato says, is precisely what democracy does. Democracy enshrines volatile liberty and uses it at once to decree false equalities, and here the real trouble begins. Democracy declares the equality of intellect and appetites, which becomes by that very declaration an enormous inequality, since appetites outsize intellect, outnumber intellect, and precede intellect into this world. Give appetitive and intellectual people the vote, and appetite wins in a landslide every time. But here one could not do better than simply to listen to Plato:

> In a democracy you are not obliged to be in authority, however competent you may be, or to submit to authority, if you do not like it; you need not fight when your fellow citizens are at war, nor remain at peace when they do, unless you want peace; and though you may have no legal right to hold office or sit on juries, you will do so all the same if the fancy takes you. A wonderfully pleasant life, surely, for the moment. There is a charm, too, in the forgiving spirit shown by some who have been sentenced by the courts. In a democracy you must have seen how men condemned to death or exile stay on and go about in public, and no one takes any more notice than he would of a spirit that walked invisible. There is so much tolerance and superiority to petty considerations; such a contempt for all those

fine principles we laid down when we said that only a very exceptional nature could turn out a good man, if he had not played as a child among things of beauty and given himself only to creditable pursuits.

Inflamed and sick democracies hate the cure, which involves a curtailment of liberty. Democrats won't stand for this and will vilify anyone who proposes it.

The parent falls into the habit of behaving like the child, and the child like the parent: the father is afraid of his sons, and they show no fear or respect for their parents, in order to assert their freedom. Citizens, resident aliens, and strangers from abroad are all on an equal footing. To descend to smaller matters, the schoolmaster timidly flatters his pupils, and the pupils make light of their masters as well as of their attendants. Generally speaking, the young copy their elders, argue with them, and will not do as they are told; while the old, anxious not to be thought disagreeable tyrants, imitate the young and condescend to enter into their jokes and amusements...A democratic state may fall under the influence of unprincipled leaders, ready to minister to its thirst for liberty with too deep draughts of this heady wine; and then, if its rulers are not complaisant enough to give it unstinted freedom, they will be arraigned as accursed oligarchs and punished. Law-abiding citizens will be insulted as nonentities who hug their chains; and all praise and honor will be bestowed, both publicly and in private, on rulers who behave like subjects and subjects who behave like rulers. In such a state the spirit of liberty is bound to go to all lengths.

Thus, sadly, sick democracies lack the genius of their own redemption. Just as overindulgence of an appetite results in a debilitating dependence, the democratization and liberation of all appetites finally requires a terrible antidote: despotism, the forfeiture of all liberty.

The truth is that, in the constitution of society, quite as much as in the weather or in plants and animals, any excess brings about an equally violent reaction. So the only outcome of too much freedom is likely to be excessive subjection, in the state or in the individual; which means that the culmination of liberty in democracy is precisely what prepares the way for the cruelest extreme of servitude under a despot.

That, I am afraid, is a pretty gruesome appraisal of democracy. You can see perhaps why the Athenian democrats finally found Socrates annoying enough to put him up on capital charges. But perhaps you can also see how fond Socrates must have been of his democratic countrymen to work so hard and to sacrifice so much on their behalf. At his own trial, in fact after his conviction and sentence, Socrates likened himself to a stinging fly on the flank of an ill-disciplined thoroughbred. Plato wrote *The Republic* a generation later when the Athenian thoroughbred had been hobbled past recovery.

Plato did not flog democracy because he was mad at it. He flogged it because it was mistaken. It was mistaken in the belief that liberty and the democratization of everything could sustain human life and sustain society. How lighthearted and easy, how serene and even hip life would be if this were the case.

But the redemption of even the best intentioned, well-meaning democracy takes more than this. It takes just what Plato says it takes: it takes a habit of virtue, it takes steel, it takes informed vision, and all of it in the service of the community. I don't need to return to the fountain of classical political theory to make this point. If you don't care for Plato's *Republic*, would you consider Frank Capra's *It's a Wonderful Life?*

That wonderfully acted and reliably uplifting film actually teaches a vivid lesson about democracies: what sustains them and what destroys them. Before anything like trouble emerges in Bedford Falls, we meet the people. Educationally, economically, and ethnically they are rather a mix. Except for one twisted miser, they are a likable lot: the principled old building and loan officer, his house servant, the druggist, the cabbie, the tavern keeper, the cop on the beat, the optimistic young entrepreneur, the fast and foolish young woman, tipsy old Uncle Billy. With humor, common sense, reflexive kindness, and occasional high spirits, the citizens of Bedford Falls more than muddle through. At the level of style and attitude, there are some very attractive things about Bedford Falls. Almost nobody is self-important or puffed up or inaccessible to the others.

And as you no doubt recall from the film, which has now been colorized and seems to be aired over the holidays every hour on every channel, Bedford Falls has both a savior and a nemesis. The savior is George Bailey, son of a wise and selfless man. From earliest boyhood George has been a striver, or heroic risk taker, a hard worker, quite literally his brother's keeper. He has dreams of seeing the world and then learning architecture so that he can shape the future along monumental lines. The needs of family, community—the needs of others—conspire to keep him at home, however, and we realize there would be no livable Bedford Falls without him.

The nemesis is a warped and wizened old oligarch named Potter, the richest man, the most rapacious creditor in Bedford Falls. He controls a good deal of the economic and civic life in town, and he is driven to control the rest.

But here is the peculiar part—especially from the standpoint of the relativist '90s. The pleasing tension between George Bailey the Redeemer and Potter the despot, with the lovable citizens of Bedford Falls hanging in the balance, does not resolve triumphantly and happily. Due to economic reality, sheer bad behavior on Potter's part, and the ordinary kind of bad luck we experience from time to time, democracy fails. Even George Bailey, democracy's compassionate and principled best hope, loses heart, turns surly, and is about to jump off a wintry bridge to his death. As he sees it, he has given everything he has to the democratic enterprise, but it did not give enough back to him. George has had enough of democracy's relative liberty, its winsome variety of life, and the ease with which willful malevolence can carry the day in an open society.

But George is saved and, for the moment at least, Bedford Falls is saved, although not by its own lights. As you recall, it takes an utterly trans-human, trans-democratic intervention to save the day. Through the efficacy of Mary Bailey's and others' prayers, George's predicament comes to the attention of the court of heaven. And from heaven an angel is dispatched, a rather marginal old coot of an angel, technically an angel-in-training, but one appropriate to a democracy.

The angel, Clarence, demonstrates to the despairing George a terrible and transforming truth. George is privileged to see, as Dickens' Scrooge is privileged to see, the world without him. In George's case, he is able to see a world without the virtue he so unselfconsciously provided. Perhaps Capra's most stunning achievement is his chilling rendering of a democratic community stripped of virtue. The vision is Pottersville, a venal, garishly lighted invitation to fast credit, sensual indulgence, jumpy music, and narcotic oblivion. And just beyond the lighted come-ons for the Pottersville sin palaces lie the dreary streets and grinding poverty of the citizenry. I mentioned that this cinematic vision was "chilling." It is chilling to me because it so closely resembles the Cleveland, Ohio, I departed to come here, and the New York City I passed briefly through on my way to these unreal heights.

When the politics of Bedford Falls were really correct—correct with no quotation marks around the word—democracy was not the cause. The cause was virtue. But virtue alone, even George Bailey's outsized helping, could not carry the day without a saving faith in divine justice and Grace.

I believe, despite the many darkly portentous things I have said, there is great hope that both virtue and faith may resume their saving work in the world. I believe it because my students respond instinctively and powerfully to *It's a Wonderful Life.* They also respond, if they are taught properly, to Plato's *Republic.* They cheer for George, and their eyes well up in the glorious scene when he is resurrected. They know in their deep interiors, in their souls, that virtue is virtue, that right is right. And what encourages me so much is that the culture into which they were born did not teach them this. That culture has taught them to see through historical personages, especially public figures, whom past ages have called virtuous. Their culture and many of their schools have cast a disapproving eye on religious practice of any established kind. That culture forbids public expression of the kinds of prayer that saved George Bailey's life.

With a little principled guidance on our part, children in school can not only see the value of faith and virtue in a free society, they can come to treasure those things, to live for them. But we are no help to children, as parents or teachers, if we cannot or will not affirm those things ourselves. If we are too timid to prescribe and affirm, if we limit our school mission to description, we turn over the prescriptive, moral part of education to those forces anxious to take on the job: that is, the multi-billion dollar youth products and entertainment industry; that is, anybody with a design on children's money, their bodies, or their souls. Gangsta rappers and Oliver Stone and the Gap are not reluctant to impose their values on developing children.

Happily, children respond to the truth when they are told the truth. But for contemporary children to learn the truth, some obstacles must be removed at once. For a start, we must stop deliberately distorting the historical record. We need, with humility, to acknowledge that there *is* a historical record, and we must do our best to compose it accurately and to interpret it honestly. This of course means an end to the battle of "centrisms." There can be no more "centric" historic, at least intentionally. When certain critics began dismissing standard approaches to teaching history as "Eurocentric," they meant that the narration and interpretation of some part of the historical record, of whatever era or region, was mistaken, skewed. The term "Eurocentric," whether applied to the treatment of Indian experience in North America or the origins of the African slave trade or the rise of classical Mediterranean culture, implied a criticism: that European emphases were falsifying the account, that European developments were given undue precedence. In other words "Eurocentric" is to historical study as "egocentric" is to personality; it is undesirable, false practice. The remedy should have been fairly straightforward: to correct the record and to document the corrections with verifiable evidence and arguments.

But no. Historians too are susceptible to relativism, and indeed many of them found the notion that there is no objectively true historical experience a liberation from all manner of confining scholarly obligations. If history is only what the record keepers say it is, the "it" becomes the subjective preserve of whoever is empowered to keep the record. Discard or disown records that make you feel uncomfortable, and—presto!—you can make a more pleasing history. And in just this way critics of Eurocentric history embraced its fallacious methods and created "Afrocentric" and other "-centric" histories, inviting by their example the utter Balkanization of historical understanding. For what could be more culturally stifling to an Ibo or a Masai or a Zulu tribesman than Afro-centrism? Bring on Ibo-centrism, Masai-centrism, or the "-centrism" of the unsung clans within the tribes, of the families, of each eccentric soul on earth. And please, please bear in mind that in despairing of ideologically "-centric" practices like Afro-centric history, I am not questioning the essential and valid pursuit of African history.

In their timid and woolly attempts not to be culturally arrogant or exclusive, American schools have taken the global lead in making a hash of historical understanding. And it is no small irony that this hash has been concocted by the very heirs and heiresses of the western line of thinking that implanted the notion of historical truth.

Once again, bad thinking is bad thinking. Bad historical thinking in the schools can be traced directly to a fuzzy, relativist interpretation of our historical moment. Here our National Association of Independent Schools must take special responsibility. In their National Conferences, publications, and suggested policies, American independent schools have generated a thick conceptual fog through the imprecise employment or two imprecise terms: "multi-culturalism" and "diversity." The only word to appear more frequently in independent school literature is "marketing."

"Multi-culturalism" and "diversity" tend to be used interchangeably, and what they finally come down to in the minds and words of their advocates is a kind of notional xenophilia. I say "notional" because this drive to teach the histories of non-western, underdocumented, and remote peoples doesn't go very deep. This is no golden age of historical scholarship of *any* culture or region. The real consequence of this blurring of scholastic focus in our schools is that, without demonstrating a knowledge of anything else, American school children now know less about western civilization and American history than do the children of Korea, Japan, Europe, or Australia.

The terms "multiculturalism" and "diversity" arouse pious feelings among independent school people for the wrong reasons. I have sat at the feet and heard from the very mouths of educators whose profession it is to monitor and facilitate student diversity and multi-cultural curricula. Their doctrine is that once schools are so constituted they will be good schools. But this is demonstrably untrue. There are excellent schools in Sweden, Japan, and Nigeria that are not diverse. Nor are the multiculturalists champing to go into Japan and Nigeria to break up those schools. And in nearly every large city in the United States there are wonderfully diverse schools that are a scholastic and moral disgrace.

I believe that the American independent schools have tried to parlay a sweeping, but value-neutral, demographic change in the national population into a moral achievement. The truth of the matter is that diversity has nothing to do with good schools. The truth of the matter is that all regions of the nation simply *are* more racially, culturally, and economically diverse than they were a half century ago. Since the talents and gifts of children are distributed among these diverse populations, *of course* schools should, and have, become more diverse. To do anything else would be downright bigoted, not to mention practically short-sighted. My school is racially and culturally diverse, very diverse, but that is because greater Cleveland is, and we are a school of greater Cleveland. The achievement of diversity at my school, and I suspect yours, involves nothing more than sensible, fair admission practice.

Doing this is not a monumental moral achievement. Moral achievement will be measured, as it always has been measured, by what we do with these diverse children once they are seated before us. And as I have said already, we must begin by telling them the truth, by creating a climate in which the truth is honored, a climate in which the best that humankind has said, built, done, and created is revealed and passed along.

If that is not possible in a climate that thinks in "politically correct" terms, then that climate has to go. In fact, the very words "politically correct," used that way, have to go. The term "political correctness" is what we today call highly nuanced speech. Indeed both words in the expression are uttered as if they are under heavy quotation marks. The quotation marks ironically negate each word, and each word ironically negates the other. The word "political" in the phrase means politically convenient or politically unfair. The word "correct" in the phrase means outwardly convenient but morally incorrect. And since this is what the term really means, I propose that it is not very good for us, and that it is even worse for children. To their great credit, children's speech is less "nuanced" than our own. To hear a morally shabby policy or action dismissed as "politically correct" raises at once in a child's mind the idea that "politics" is inherently shabby, that "correct" really means "convenient." We need, and children need, both words, "politics" and "correct," in all their un-nuanced, unambiguous power. We need, and children need, to conceive of and to revere correct politics.

The very notion of correct politics requires clearing out that ornery, self-contradictory cultural agenda I enumerated earlier and replacing it with propositions we can live by. This better agenda should really be a continuing and collaborative enterprise, but permit me a few personal suggestions, offered to all of you in a spirit of hope.

1. Established religions have guided and grounded men and women since the dawn of humankind. The relationship between Creator and Creation is the supreme fact and mystery. Religious practice deserves our deepest respect.

2. Historical experience is objectively knowable. To discover it, a respect for past peoples, for evidence, is essential.

3. Men and women are inherently valuable. The honest and reverent inquiry into what is distinctive about each gender and what they share in common is the most promising avenue to promote their mutual productivity and the pleasure we take in one another.

4. Ethics are discovered, not invented.

5. Culture is accrued human achievement. The best and most durable cultural products should be accessible to human beings everywhere.

6. Western culture has contributed distinctive and valuable things to humankind. The best of it should be accessible to human beings everywhere.

7. Sexual practices serve human needs and purposes; sexuality is not a morally isolated, socially privileged dimension of life.

8. Sexuality and gender are both mysterious, deeply rooted, and powerful. As such they should be regarded reverently. Adult sexuality should not be imposed on children.

9. Language is about experience and the world, not about itself.

10. The truth is knowable, and human beings yearn to know it.

I don't know if you find that agenda agreeable. I certainly hope you do. Even more than that, I hope you find it valid. But if you do, beware that you are in for hard work and no small trouble.

Because if that agenda is in any measure correct, the prevailing agenda, the agenda of relativism, is incorrect. No matter how widely endorsed, how well supported in the polls, how entrenched its adherents, mistakes are mistakes. As C.S. Lewis pointed out, if you are adding a long column of numbers and you make a mistake early on, no amount of correct computing afterward is going to get the sum right. It can be humiliating—or better, humbling—to go back to where we were before, to where we made a mistake and to begin again.

But if the future of the children in our charge is going to add up to anything, we may have to do just that.

One final point—actually, an anecdote. I teach high school seniors parts of Aristotle's *Nichomachean Ethics*. Until I started thinking through some of the issues I have raised here, I could never seem to figure out why, after Aristotle made his elegant, seemingly air-tight case for the practice of virtue as the only means of achieving happiness, he shifts jarringly to a discussion of a particular virtue, courage. Why courage? I wondered. Why courage right then?

Slowly but surely I have come to realize that identifying the mistakes and foibles of others, in addition to feeling rather exhilarating, is fairly easy. A little less easy is forming a better agenda for life and learning, but school heads are obligated to do this by their calling. And of course it feels very grand, very prophetic to prescribe lofty new, or ancient, measures.

But step down from your podium and try to correct a single faulty practice, alter a single child's or colleague's behavior, stand by a single unfashionable truth, and you will have, as I said, trouble. You will have enemies—you will have your hands full.

To progress from an era of "political correctness" to an era of correct politics, for our own sake and for the sake of our children, is going to take great convictions and great courage.

Be brave.

This essay is from an address delivered before the independent school heads of New York and Connecticut. The quoted material was from a report by Diane Knippers in an essay, "Re-imaging God," which appeared in Crisis, September, 1994. The Republic of Plato, *F. M. Cornford tr., Oxford.*

2

Vulgarity and What We Need

A friend of mine who works with aphasic stroke victims reported to me a fascinating, and sometimes hilarious, dimension of his profession. Damage to the speech centers of his patients' brains rarely eliminates all of their language. The vilest, "dirtiest" words and phrases are left intact.

This stroke effect, while often temporary, has resulted in some astonishing experiences for my friend. An elderly, diminutive matron, unable to open the window near her bed, smiled seraphically up at him and said, "This f—er won't move." Down the hall, a distinguished old gentleman indicated that his evening meal tray could be taken away, "Finished!" he said. "Finished! Would you please shove it up your a—?" Often, late at night, my friend would walk the length of the darkened aphasic ward and hear an eerie bedlam of the foulest imaginable imprecations: a twilight realm where disembodied graffiti find voices, a locker room from hell.

The stroke patients are often horrified witnesses of their own utterances, their eyes wide as they attempt to ask for a sandwich—but hear themselves requesting excrement. But on the brighter side, stroke victims improve. As they regain mental function, including speech, they tend to reconfine their most obscene and ugly language to the lower reaches of their linguistic cellars.

There is less consolation, however, for people, especially children, whose most offensive linguistic gestures have never been so confined. On the proverbial street, and even in elementary school corridors, speech once understood to be offensive and disgusting may be becoming commonplace.

This is a development to be taken seriously. It poses a real harm.

Civilization is maintained—and may even advance—as instinctive impulses are suppressed, deferred or transformed into humane and socially necessary behavior. Crucial to both of these developments is effective language.

We need language, first to name things. Once the names are affixed, we can begin to distinguish one thing from another, true things from false things. Next, we need language to describe the true relationships between the named things. If we fail in either of these undertakings, we fail to read the world correctly. Socially, things go wrong. Personally, we become stupid.

Repetitive cursing—whether profaning the sacred or wallowing in sexual and excretory slang—diminishes human experience by failing to meet the necessary obligations of language: true naming and true relating.

Repetitive cursing is also offensive—one had better hope!—and while this is a secondary concern, it bears some comment. Cursing offends because it forces listeners to hear, conceptualize and visualize things they do not wish, in most interpersonal settings, to hear. Cursing casts a crude, visceral mood onto the subjects to which it refers and onto the people in earshot of the speaker.

The worst outcome of offensive cursing is that the wrong words and the wrong feelings are summoned up to describe experiences that need more complex, more nuanced language. Vulgarity suspends speaker and hearer alike in a realm both vague and unpleasant. It represents a sad inadequacy in adults and a serious danger signal in children.

Unthinkable words in the mouths of babes have become commonplace in an era of trash talking from the commercial icons of sport and entertainment. Here the vulgarity is marketed—to children—as somehow specially "authentic," rebellious and boundary testing.

And vulgar speech does press a boundary: the boundary separating civility and primitive impulse. This is the world's easiest boundary to press. Pressing the opposite boundary, the boundary between ordinary speech and eloquence, is very hard.

Children are not born with an innate disposition to curse. If anything, they have a tropism for that true naming mentioned earlier. The foul-mouthed lines in the mouths of youthful actors in current films are scripted by adults.

Adults—parents, teachers, writers, broadcasters—need to understand and to love language. They need to discipline themselves to speak it well. When enraged and overcome, they need to hold their tongue; when inspired, to find their voice.

There is of course a place, a modest place, for vulgarity in public discourse. Sometimes it is funny. Sometimes it adds an evocative realism to accounts of vulgar people. But even these limited uses of vulgarity depend for their impact on a better, more expressive parlance. Without the latter, the former cannot amuse or instruct. Cursing is inherently parasitic.

In the beginning, St. John wrote, was the Word. The end, it is fair to say, will be wordless. We will end neither with a bang nor a whimper, but, words failing us, with an obscenity.

3

Concert

Last summer my wife and I agreed to accompany two other couples to a James Taylor concert at Blossom Center, an enormous, partly covered, open-air amphitheatre (seating about 18,000) in the rich green countryside between Cleveland and Akron, Ohio. Blossom Center likes to offer a summer program of light classical and pops concerts by the Cleveland Orchestra, interspersed with pop-rock blockbusters such as Barry Manilow, Bette Midler, and numerous groups with names like "The Astral Rats" or "Three Arse Pig" or "Carrion." As one might imagine, the two kinds of performances attract distinctly different crowds, the twain rarely meeting on purpose. The orchestra crowd is quite uniform and tame. Indeed, except for the odd, tell-tale leisure suit, these listeners, quietly glad for Brahms and starry summer nights, would have been appropriate to a corresponding musical evening of the Victorian or Edwardian era.

The pop-rock blockbuster crowd is less easy to transpose historically; one could not do so confidently before 1965. The general tone is still decidedly Sixties, or Suburban Indian. Although somewhat on the wane on schoolyard, campus, and shopping mall, the patched denim, tee shirt, and leather goods ensemble continue to be standard dress when the young assemble for their own purposes *en masse. En masse* is itself a quality crucial to the youthful concert experience. Through the combined influences of the political rally and the Rock Concert, the youth of the past decade have found, as those attending the Roman Games and Hitler's Nuremburg Rally once found, that crowds are a kick. Psychologists and participants alike testify to a kind of euphoric rush experienced when a crowd member loses particular identity and becomes something collectively "larger than life." Arguable claims can be and have been made that some such experiences are life-enhancing.

The apogee, or at least the stereotype, of this experience among contemporary youth was the Woodstock concert, an object of much national attention, including a feature length documentary movie. At Woodstock, because thousands of individuals managed to assemble in a meadow in upstate New York at roughly the same time, a novel achievement was proclaimed by the promoters and by many of the star attractions: all those faces out there represented something spiritual: a Woodstock Nation. What was achieved and what felt spiritual was the crowd itself; a crowd which had overwhelmed the promoters' plans to collect thickets and to provide toilets; a crowd which, however short of food or drugs, managed to survive; a crowd most of whom could neither see nor hear much of what was proffered in the way of entertainment, "but there we were—*incredible*—all of us, just out there!"

It is increasingly clear that what motivates an individual to become part of a large crowd is the experience of crowdedness, not the prospect of seeing or hearing or doing something. Some of the medieval crusades revealed a surprising willingness on the part of all manner of people, with only the most dimly understood pretext, to combine massively, pick up stakes, and head vaguely off on foot for months of grueling discomfort and hostility. Take away the transcendent purpose and the dynamic elements—movement, hostility, and the intergenerational mix of young and old—and you have the Big Concert crowd. These significant elements of the Big Concert are essentially the same whether it is held outdoors or in an urban concert hall.

The pretext of our little Woodstock at Blossom Center was James Taylor. James Taylor is definitely in the pop-rock blockbuster category, but his appeal, given the category, is relatively broad: those in their twenties and early thirties who grew up on the Beatles and campus folk music to young teens of the present. While there is some evidence that people throughout this age range buy James Taylor records, my own casual experience suggests that his big concerts are attended almost exclusively by young teens of the present. At the time of the concert in question, I did not know this, and so it happened my wife and I (29 and 32 respectively) and four friends (each of them 40) found ourselves completely and, considering the Center's parking arrangements, irrevocably immersed in youth. We all liked the reedy resonance of James Taylor's voice, liked his timing, and liked the sure poetry of his best lyrics. I don't think we were, at our ages, much interested in those themes that caused some critics to call his music "identity crisis rock," although we were certainly able to understand the adolescent appeal of the tall, passive, winsome figure of James Taylor crooning his childlike entreaties for someone to "take his hand" so that he can "keep his head together."

In an attempt to beat the traffic and in general to make more of an occasion of our outing, we arrived early and ate a leisurely picnic supper on the Center's massive lawns. While having our picnic, we became aware, and then certain, that we were "out of our element." More than anything else, except possibly one man's bald head, our dress set us apart from the crowd. In the eyes of scores of kids on adjacent blankets we were strictly "orchestra crowd." I'll wager that in the course of the evening each of us questioned himself or herself at least once about the appropriateness of liking James Taylor at mature life, but I'm sure we allowed little of this to show; rather we resolved through what seemed a very long supper to be bright and with-it and receptive, not Establishment squares, but anthropologists.

In the Woodstock tradition, the nation grew and grew. We read often enough about how mobile we all are. Still it is instructive to witness first-hand how easily even fourteen-year-olds can get ten, twenty, or even a hundred miles from home. Most of this crowd drove cars whose insignia revealed Cleveland or Akron residence, but Columbus (90 miles thence) was represented, as were New York State and Michigan. How, practically speaking, does this happen? Are there really households in Columbus or Ann Arbor or Buffalo in which a teenager bounds into the kitchen at breakfast and says, "Hey Mom and Dad, I wonder if I could use the car for most of the day. There's a big James Taylor concert tonight in Cleveland. A bunch of us got tickets at Record Carnival—the last ones! What d'ya say? I can easily be back by 5 a.m."

My own experience working with adolescents and their parents, (as a Dean in a private school) however, suggests that a verbal exchange of any kind is increasingly unnecessary to a youth's decision to leave the house by car. These days even parents who are outwardly strict and stern show only the most passive resistance to the two main attractions of contemporary adolescent social life: the unchaperoned "party" and the concert. Because the idea of the latter still stirs up in many parental minds vague associations with the old-fashioned symphonic concert, and because of an unarticulated but dangerously misguided notion that anything big and public can't be too awful, the parental deference to concerts is almost complete. Increasingly parents will, without detectable embarrassment or irony, call me at school to excuse the lateness of a son who got back awfully late from a concert, or to ask that he be excused early from sports or some other school commitment so that he can make the concert on time. (All excuses and requests are declined—previously on impulse, now on principle.)

There is something about these school/parent exchanges which arouses an uneasy thought: something more than ignorance or disinterest may be at work when children are tacitly or otherwise allowed to join the (perhaps primal) horde of the concert; I seem almost able to detect in these calls from parents a trace of *approval* in their tone—possibly an incompletely suppressed remnant of their own prehistoric drive to assemble in multitudes for orgiastic or ritual purposes—and in their peculiar resistance to speaking or thinking clearly about what actually might go on at a concert.

A half hour or so before Taylor was supposed to perform we began as part of an organic movement of thousands to make our way from the grassy picnic site to the amphitheatre. The panorama of this process was dramatic. The movies have taught us to see that great numbers moving at different rates over uneven terrain look, at a distance, like viscous liquid; it is true. Many of us, too, have beheld from the cavalry/movie seat perspective the awesome and oddly pleasing spectacle of one row, then another, then *still another* row of resolute Indians surfacing weightlessly over a distant rise. Better at a distance, I think. From the shoulder-to-shoulder standpoint, one gets a good deal of vulgar talk—certainly the most assignable consequence of the past decade's liberations—and maybe even a bit of roughhouse. Along each walkway leading to the amphitheatre are tidy little wooden signs saying ALCO-HOLIC BEVERAGES NOT PERMITTED. Unenforced. A friendly usher I questioned later told me that the staff was instructed not to question or otherwise prevent customers' drinking and smoking. He said the signs provided a basis for removing anyone who might get badly out of hand, which (he smiled) was very seldom. Whatever the truth of this, the policy certainly did not prevent customers from getting drunk. Clumsy drunk. Horse-laughing, isn't-it-hilarious-I'm-so-out-of-control-drunk. Is this *more* unattractive among adolescents? Hard to judge from the 20-40 perspective, but it's unattractive enough.

Our seats under the vast, irregularly vaulted enclosure were dead center, about fifty yards back from the stage. Nothing about the appearance of the stage itself suggested that a performance of any kind was imminent. There was, rather, the suggestion of some electronic problem being investigated or recently abandoned. Thick black electrical cables draped loosely from overhead, others were strewn across the stage floor, linking microphones and guitars to amplifiers and to enormous, megalithic gray and black speakers stacked on top of one another like blocks. Why, I wondered uneasily, was all this apparatus necessary for James Taylor who sings in the ordinary manner and who plays an ordinary acoustical guitar? My question was answered and certain fears confirmed when three or four scruffy men, each of them very short, disengaged themselves gradually from the wiring littering the stage—a progress which at first gave me the incorrect impression that they were some sort of work crew—and took up instruments in preparation to play. These presumably supporting musicians established at once that, thousands of spectators or not, they were preoccupied with solemn, private concerns, in relation to which any regard for "show business" was out of place. Perhaps this attitude of preoccupation has evolved over time as a defense against the chaotic roar of rock crowds interested only, if interested at all, in the main attraction. That roar was certainly all about us as we took our seats: under the roof rackety volleys of salutations across aisles to remotely seated acquaintances; on the darkening slopes beyond, a hoarse, impatient wall of sound, more variegated and less peaceful than a waterfall.

Then all of a sudden James Taylor—no doubt about that size as the youthful James Arness face—was at the microphone. He wore close-cropped hair, a faded tee shirt, and a pair of baggy work pants. Waves of recognition began moving in irregularly concentric fashion from the stage out over the enclosed seats and beyond into whatnot. Not very audibly over those waves Taylor, himself preoccupied, said something in praise of the work of the little musicians, introduced them by name, mentioned their forthcoming record, and left the stage. The former noise level restored, the musicians looked at one another sharply, as if sending danger, and began to play. The hardest rock. Their first penetrating chord served in some way as a signal for everyone in attendance who had brought marijuana to the concert to light it up and pass it around. It was at this moment that I realized that the distinctive smell of burning marijuana, a drug which is illegal in Ohio, has become as familiar to me, a non-user, as the smell of McDonald's hamburgers.

The music, I'll have to say, was really terrible. Deafeningly, pulsingly monotonous. More helpless than defiant, I stopped my ears, not to shut out the sound, which was impossible, but to diminish it as much as I could. As conversation of any kind was now inaudible, there was nothing to do but sit and watch the peculiarly sacramental passing of marijuana cigarettes and pipes. The pot was, I suppose, taken in an attempt to intensify or otherwise improve the musical experience of the evening, but if, to any extent, it was taken to defend against— to "turn off"—this warm-up performance, the ill-will was amply returned by the performers. Seldom, and then only suspiciously, did they turn to face the audience. More typically, one of the guitar players would cross mid-song to one of the others or to a piece of equipment, ostensibly to check something—although I suspect for emotional support. When they weren't crossing or checking, they were usually hunched over, back-to-audience, as if straining to hear something very subtle in the workings of one of the mammoth speakers. This stage behavior said to us, "I'm not having a very good time, so I won't look at you. And since I have registered indifference before you did, I win."

But the audience wasn't watching and was listening only in the restricted sense of being unable to do otherwise. When a piece ended, there was no applause—not even silence—only the instant restoration of the pre-concert roar. It was literally as if, despite the chest-thudding volleys of sound that were produced, nobody had been on stage. For an hour or so while this performance was or wasn't going on, I took an interest in a young girl sitting in the row just ahead of us. In the context of her row she seemed to me appealingly prim and nicely turned out in pressed dungarees, a simple white blouse of the kind that is still sometimes part of parochial school uniforms, and a very effective bob of hair in the Dorothy Hamill manner. She looked quite young—thirteen or fourteen?—and certainly younger than those sitting around her. What interested me about her was her lack of animation; in fact, not once did I see her turn her elegant little head or smile or speak, and I was paying fairly close attention during the whole concert. Her immobility made it impossible to tell whether she was somebody's date or friend or little sister, although she was fixture enough in the social matrix of her row to be offered the wine jugs and joints that were passed back and forth. Since this passing never ceased in the two hours I observed it, she must have been affected in some way by what she consumed, so I can only suppose that her blank, sealed off expression was the *effect* of her intake, not a sign of paranormal imperviousness. Even later during the main attraction she did not, except for a mechanical raising of substance to lip, flinch or stir. I found myself wondering how the sights and sounds around us were being processed in her deep interior. *Were* they being processed? Was the deep interior switched on? Onto what? Would her parents ask her how she liked the concert? Would she reply?

The dispirited little back-up band never really finished; James Taylor simply entered and joined them. So quick and unobtrusive was his entrance that it went unnoticed by much of the audience for most of his first number, then a big hit. When the recognition came, it came as it had done the first time: noisily and unevenly, so that even the relatively contained crowd beneath the enclosure never came to any kind of general attention. The audio-technicians responded to this by turning up everybody's volume. Between songs Taylor looked a little disconcerted at the din beyond the lights, but as looking a little disconcerted is an integral part of his persona, the din persisted. Although he himself did a fair amount of crossing and checking the equipment on stage, his reaction to the crowd was markedly different from that of the warm-up group; he never looked any meaner than puzzled, and seemed determined to put out his program of songs frontally and efficiently. Most of his guitar introductions and bridges, which I like very much, were lost to noise, but all that I was able to hear clearly seemed, except for the harshness and excessive percussion of the accompaniment, remarkably faithful to his records. He "reached" his audience, I suppose, to the extent that those in the first ten or twelve rows would briefly arise and howl delightedly at the opening bars of every song (*every* song) before falling back into conversation.

A sensation roughly translated as *something is wrong!* kept rising to my consciousness. What was it? There was J.T. up there performing roughly the way one might have imagined, and here was this crowd, more unruly than one had expected, but not by this time especially strange or posing any danger. Yet I was bothered—seriously bothered—by a sense of nothing cohering. It was not that an unpleasant relationship had developed between performance and audience, but that no relationship had developed: two discrete human activities, only incidentally violating the other's air space. Arresting but not engaging; aversive but not boring; *angst*. And the unmoving possibly bionic presence of that young girl in front of me didn't help matters much.

What she might have focused on, had she been able and had there been one, was the stage picture. James Taylor standing anywhere is tall and focal. But he is less so set against a warehouse of speakers and wires. Add to the picture the random crossing and checking of the sullen little side-men and the composition blurs. I wonder if even the engineers responsible believe that sudden washes of different colored light have an assignable effect on such a stage picture. Perhaps to those under the influence of drugs, these lighting changes are dramatic, but without drugs they serve as a kind of ironic commentary or what they illumine: a spookily aquamarine James Taylor picking an inaudible riff on his guitar suddenly turns garish crimson as he steps gingerly over the cables to talk to his drummer. The failure to create, or even to attempt, a stage picture is yet another way of escaping the demands of performance. Again, the logic here, so perfectly expressed by the posture of the side-men, is "if I don't commit myself to playing for your attention, I cannot be accused of failing if I don't get it." Which was fine with the girl in front of me.

Taylor concluded the concert with a blues-rocker from an early album. It was by far the most rackety number he performed, and in it he made some uncharacteristic concessions to the crowd: he embellished the original lyrics with a low obscenity or two, and at one point he made a comic gesture in

the direction of his genitals, presumably to emphasize a suggestive line of lyrics. These concessions roused the crowd as
much as anything else had done, but our little party took off
for the parking lots. Either because they wanted an encore or
because they had no other plans, most of the crowd stayed
put. As we made our way up the grassy slopes to the exits, I
took a backwards glance at the stage. James Taylor had
returned, and the crowd had done a strange thing: practically
all of them were holding lighters or matches up over their
heads—an eerie, rather impressive spectacle in the dark, a
sign too that I perhaps underestimated the performances's
impact on the crowd. But as I pointed out this flickering display to my friends, an usher volunteered that "They always do
that, it's been going on for a couple of years." That explanation made sense. Those little flames were a statement of self-
affirmation on behalf of the crowd for the benefit of the
crowd: "Even in the dark, just *look* at all of us."

It was good to get away, but there was little of the exhilara-
tion of having escaped from a hostile or boring confinement.
We had not really enjoyed ourselves, even as anthropologists.
In the quiet of the drive back home my mind turned, depressingly, to the ways the concert experience had imprinted itself
on my own students, many of whom, it turned out, were in
attendance at that very concert. The imprint is especially clear
in their approach to organizing outings and 'dances': entertainments which eschew format of any kind, including any for-
mality or care in dress; entertainments which are considered
duds unless the crowd is big enough to assure anonymity and
the music is loud enough to eliminate communication. It is
important to these entertainments that the site be unadorned,
preferably ill-lit or unlit—except for 'light shows' (see com-
ments above). At such entertainments when the amps are up
and the speakers booming, chaperones (rarely volunteers)
have no effect, much less a repressive effect. Where there is no
focus, there is no responsibility. Nor any fun. At such entertainments, whether at the school level or the concert level, no
one has ever gotten to know anybody else, nobody has fallen

in love, nobody has grown in conversation or poise. At such entertainments one assembles into a crowd for the purpose of enduring. With or without drugs, one learns that assembly requires becoming impervious.

4

Sex, Violence, the Usual...

For years before I actually sat down to watch *Fatal Attraction*, I had been puzzling over the formula that drives such stories. Why, I wondered, must the erotic impulse, which is in so many ways wonderful, be linked to pain, danger and death?

Of course I select *Fatal Attraction* practically at random. *Basic Instinct* would serve as well, as would *Body Heat* or *9 1/2 Weeks* or *Sleeping with the Enemy* or even *Risky Business*, which is a kind of *Fatal Attraction* for children. In fact, unless my own local video store researches deceive me, there is an unviewably burgeoning array of "erotic suspense thrillers" touting irresistible sexual liaisons devolving into what the video-carton rhetoric is likely to call "the unspeakable": violence, mayhem and murder.

Perhaps it is not too late to step back and ask: Excuse me, but are these stories true? Are erotic attractions fatal, brutal and frightening? Given the power of the emotions and sensations involved, sexual liaisons may well be dangerous at times, but to tell the truth, they are more often not. Yet we have these films, these stories—and this decidedly unsatisfactory social and sexual climate. Has the commercial arts establishment possibly put something over on this twentieth century?

The glut of stories portraying sex and violence as the *yin* and *yang* of erotic life has become an emblem of our era, an orthodoxy. It wants to tell us that we have struggled free of our inhibitions and sugary sublimations so that we can at last face our true erotic/violent selves. Accepting this notion fortifies, and perhaps even explains, the obsessive decadence of a David Lynch (e.g. *Blue Velvet*) or Ken Russell (e.g. *Whore*).

But maybe there is a simpler explanation: that by depicting *two* adrenaline-releasing activities, eroticism and violence, a film may give audiences a double, and therefore bigger, jolt of unsorted-out feeling. Bigger may feel somehow more profound, but may be a mere accretion of feeling: a sum, rather than an insight.

The idea that the impulses to sex and violence are linked in our deep unconscious lies at the heart of modern psychotherapy. Freud postulated that the cosmos itself is shot through with two elemental forces, eros and thanatos, the impulse to sex and the impulse to death. Eros and thanatos erupt like twin fountains at the dark core of the human psyche; they are the source of our instincts. They are seen, in combination, in every human action. When we eat, we incorporate the foodstuff into our mouths, savor it, then we bite it, chew it, break it apart. A linebacker sacking a quarterback is both embracing him and assaulting him. Not only do eros and thanatos combine, each can also supplant the other; one's very ardor, when it is frustrated or when it exceeds a certain pitch, can be transformed into aggression and rage. In the Freudian scheme, lover becomes rapist. Love kills. We have heard this story. The price of Romeo and Juliet's consummated love is death. As the song goes, you always hurt the one you love.

But do we? More to the point, do we want to or have to? Isn't there merit to the notion that a kind of warmed-over Puritanism is at work in believing erotic attractions are fatal? Sixties visionaries stated this position clearly in the slogan, "Make love, nor war." At the heart of this claim is the possibility, or at least hope, that making love and making war are separable. One might even opt for a love-making approach to life, casting aside war-making altogether.

This theme was driven home with sledgehammer righteousness in the 1978 antiwar film *Coming Home*, in which a disabled veteran (Jon Voight) and a bimbo-in-transition (Jane Fonda) achieve self-realization in the course of learning to pleasure one another sexually. The bimbo's soldier husband (Bruce Dern) has made too much war to make love properly, and so his cuckholding is represented as just; there is nothing left for him but despair and, ultimately, a solitary walk into the sea.

A far more honest portrayal of the tension between sex and violence was conveyed in the movie version of Ken Follett's World War II thriller, *Eye of the Needle*. Here a good woman Kate Nelligan) does not want or need war at all, but she needs, for reasons the film makes generously clear, sex; her embittered husband has been sexually incapacitated in a car accident. Sex and violence are indeed amply set forth in the film, but they are not opposed in the usual way. Sex is shown to be better than violence; the sexually honest, and only reluctantly violent, person wins.

More recently a number of serious erotic films have decided to explore sexuality rather on its own terms, muting the violence and tension. *The Unbearable Lightness of Being* and *Henry and June* are serviceable examples. In both films, the principals like sex, have sex on their minds a good deal, and do it in ways that either promise or remind one that sex is an agreeable activity.

But here a thorny aesthetic question arises. Do these films engage any humane concerns? Do they sustain any viewer interest apart from the voyeuristic pleasure of watching gorgeously filmed flesh? A robust chorus arises: *So what? Bring it on!* Which may be fine—but certainly no endorsement of the above-named films.

The fact is that straight pornography—sans the art-film's period costumes, labored political and literary overlay—delivers the goods, all of them. In this regard nonviolent pornographic films are better than *Unbearable Lightness* or *Henry and June*. Well, bring on pornography too, our era seems to be saying.

But I should conclude with a word of caution, not about pornography, but about hitching one's spiritual wagon to an erotic star. The ancient and durable story of Dionysus tells us that the erotic quest is total. You can't do it a little. You can't do it some weekend. You have to give up your life to it. There are rumors of ecstasy, but from what you can actually see, Dionysians seem only to get sick or ruined.

And there's a worse outcome. Crabby Allan Bloom, in the

course of debunking the modish academic fashions in his *Closing of the American Mind,* hints that the ultimate outcome of ever more explicit sex will not be the unleashing of any monstrous erotic beast; to the contrary, he says, we may open the sexual closet door all the way only to find some auntie's domestic cat.

Perhaps we need to worry less about sex consuming us in some horrific (and pretty interesting) way—and still less about whether we will overdo it and lose interest. We should perhaps worry, as the late John Cheever did, that we will lose touch with our natural reverence for the erotic. The saddest commentary on contemporary culture, Cheever told an interviewer once, was that people might find sex funny.

Cheever himself didn't. He found it mysterious, maddening and unspeakably beautiful. He and many of his characters were drawn to it like moths to flame. Not in itself, but in its place in the human scheme, he worshipped it.

5

Some Thoughts on the Pop Jesus

Those who survived the sixties—and many great men and women did not—found the experience disruptive, nervous and in many respects formless. The balance of simple, subconscious trust in the correctness of liberal-democratic political principles, if not in their day-to-day application, was withdrawn, leaving the bipartisan political system with both its faces blank. 'Law and order' was no longer a desirable social condition but just an ideology, full of fear and resentment against the opposed but similarly structured ideology of 'peace and freedom.' Values were words; the fact was anxiety. Affluence—indisputedly, there was affluence—did not seem to help. The newly affluent vacillated between wanting more, which was socially disruptive, and wanting to secure their holdings, which was also socially disruptive. The more established affluent demanded 'options': free schools, group encounters, open classrooms, more various narcotic and sexual stimulation, rural real estate and, oddly, *tolerance;* tolerance of the Black Panthers and tolerance of the status quo.

Certainly the distinctive characteristic of life in the sixties was youth-obsession. (Some have argued that this was no obsession at all but a straightforward response to the sheer numbers of youth inhabiting the land.) Why did the Beatles of Liverpool induce the middle aged brokers of Chicago to drop their sideburns below their ear lobes and to wear flared trousers? Of course it must be kept in mind that an obsession does not discriminate between love and hate. The Chicago police working the 1968 Democratic National Convention showed us the darker side of youth obsession. Yet what a strange event that was—terrifying surely, but surely no mystery. Naive protestations aside, we all seemed to *understand*

44

that televised beating in Chicago; our lasting response was determined by whether we identified with those who were giving or getting it. But again, why, throughout the messy turbulence of the decade, did the plight and style of youth so dominate the culture? It is tempting, depending on one's own ideological investment, to explain the phenomenon in terms of the explicit issues and symbols of the decade. Accordingly, youth emerges as the victim (or demon) of an unjust (or just) war. The novel (or depraved) behavior of sixties' youth is seen as the inevitable response to cultural repression (or permissiveness). Such explanations, while providing plenty of partial and particular truths, lack generality.

It is perhaps not too general to suggest that something is missing in a society whose adult members become so uncertain of their own callings that they come to rely anxiously on the lights of their untrained children. To such a society youth is not merely attractive, it is the hope of salvation. Youth is 'in process' and therefore has potential, a future. Youth is untried and therefore uncorrupted. Inexperienced, youth is *forgivably* weak and inept; youth cannot fairly be held responsible. Youth is sensitive rather than competent—but no less attractive for the incompetence, if the examples of Hamlet and Holden Caulfield are anything to judge by. Of course youth is full of doubt and pain, particularly as it is transformed through what Erikson has called Identity into maturity. But doubt and pain—as when forsaking the sweetness of childhood to face an uncertain and demanding maturity—can, in the right historical circumstances, harden from an inevitable, temporary condition of adolescence into a lasting world view. It is always an instructive sign of the times whether the Hamlets of the land are preoccupied in mooning over the imponderables, or, hang it all, are getting down to the business of becoming proper princes. It is instructive of the present that the King Marks of the land are preoccupied in mooning over Hamlets who have disappeared 'underground' where, perhaps, they are making primal screams.

Which brings us, still mixed up, into the seventies, where all is as it has been—except for Jesus, who keeps cropping up everywhere. He's gone a bit youthful, and occasionally he comes across more Dionysian than seems appropriate, but undeniable he is back. (Mere commercial exploitation of yet another fad? Decidedly not. It is important to remember that the producers of wall posters and those who are responsible for the garish stage setting for *Jesus Christ Superstar* have clearly jumped onto a bandwagon whose surprising velocity has not been accelerated by such baggage.) Significantly, the Jesus invoked by pop culture is no mere extension of the drug-inspired 'mysticism' of the sixties. No 'Eastern' figure, no guru surrogate, the Jesus, like the Jesus of the synoptics, is worldly and unpretentious. Occasionally he is moody. As in the scriptures, he is a teacher by example. He not only saves, he helps out, and his help is sought straightforwardly, perhaps impiously but certainly without hoop-la. What Jesus is most often asked to do these days is to guide uncertain youth to certainty: the classical problem of identity. Clive James has accused the very popular folk singer-composer James Taylor of having founded the *genre* Identity Crisis Rock, and indeed Taylor is a lost or wandering or drifting first-person in his gentle music. What he asks of Jesus is, literally, to keep his head together. In *Fire and Rain* he sings

> Look down on me Jesus
> You've got to help me make a stand
> You've just got to see me through another day,
> My body's aching and my time is at hand
> I just can't make it any other way...[1]

Another folk-rock performer, Tom Rush, who had previously specialized in remaking traditional folk songs and themes, echoes his younger colleague in asking for help in resolving personal problems:

> The sun she dies to quietly
> So sure of resurrection

And I am dying on the street
Crying for connection

And Jesus you've got to help me this time
Sweet Savior I'm lost and I'm blind
Too weary to weep, too crazy to sleep
The hours and the cold are the company I keep...[2]

(Behind this lonely appeal is the fact that the singer has lost his girl.)

There is no novelty in youth's seeking emotional comfort, but there is some novelty in their seeking it in a fresh conception of Jesus, a conception that has not grown out of the teaching of the institutional church. For new converts the importance of the contemporary Jesus depends neither on his historical roots nor on any theological scheme that places him comfortably in the world of thought. The pop Jesus, if he is to be known, must be known as his devotees—his fans?—know him. This does not imply that their Jesus is an invention; he may be a discovery. To know this Jesus, then, one must know those who know him: the young. This is an undertaking that seems to be on many people's minds.

I

It has been maintained above that the contemporary Jesus did not evolve out of the Sunday Schools, communicants' classes, Christian youth groups or from any other such likely source; but as surely as he exists, he has evolved. The contemporary Jesus, like the historical Jesus, emerged at the end of a string of similar but distinctly different forerunners. And like the historical Jesus, the contemporary Jesus has entered popular consciousness via the most popular media, media which are themselves a pop vernacular; like the Nazarene, the contemporary Jesus is a current event. He makes his way in and out of institutional church services, strengthened by his ecstatic reception there, oblivious to the derision of established churchmen jealous of their feeble prerogatives. Just as in the

gospels, his power does not (like pop art's) lie in its uncon-
ventionality; he fulfills rather than negates the ancient law. We
know him through the media, but no medium is the message.
Long before he made the scene, the febrile twanging of guitars was attended by tolerant but unmoved congregations.

In the months between President Johnson's abdication and
the Democratic National Convention in 1968, Mel Lyman, at
one time a contributor to Jim Kweskin's Jug Band and then
editor of the 'underground' Boston-Cambridge paper *Avatar*,
disclosed to his readers that he was Jesus Christ. This disclosure was greeted with exasperation on the part of his practical-
minded left-wing readers. Some hailed the move as a terrific
put-on but grew uneasy as they became aware that Lyman was
dead earnest about being Jesus. Many of his readers from
coast to coast, especially the girls, accepted the news of his
calling uncritically, even enthusiastically. But the Boston-
Cambridge underground dispersed, moved on, recruited new
ranks, and forgot. In his Jesus role, Mel Lyman churned out
abrasive obscenity-laden poems in which America would
imminently be razed to the ground. The poems aroused little
interest. Mel Lyman did not amount to much as a Christ figure, but his gesture, along with other similar, less pretentious
gestures, served to provide the kind of backdrop to the contemporary Jesus that the Dionysian cults had been to the historical Jesus.

To be sure, Dionysus is among the most compelling and
persistent of the mythological archetypes. Like Jesus, he revi-
talizes his followers through the miracle of death and resurrection. But where Jesus offers grace, Dionysus offers erotic
release. Embodying in an unstable unity the paradox of passive femininity and violently aggressive masculinity, the
Dionysian figure has dominated pre-Jesus pop culture, particularly in the realm of rock music. Mick Jagger of the Rolling
Stones is able to titillate his public by appearing to them alternately as a drag queen and as Satan. The late Jimi Hendrix
made much the same appeal with equal effect. The appeal of
the hippies and, formally, the Yippies, has been a Dionysian

appeal. Usually the violent wishes implicit in the Dionysian appeal are vented in the ritual posturings of the Dionysus-figure; thus, for example, until the novelty wore off, rock groups liked to conclude their performances with a showy demolition of their instruments and equipment. Occasionally the violence is not displaced in ritual and comes to the surface in such acts as the public murder that concluded a Rolling Stones concert in California or, still more gruesomely, the Tate killings. When it is actually realized, this kind of violence—along with the internal violence of drug abuse that has killed cult idols like Hendrix and Janis Joplin—alarms the practical sensibilities of cult members and potential cult members. As Don McLean puts it in his runaway hit, *American Pie*, a brief history of rock:

> And there we were all in one place
> A generation lost in space
> No time left to start again
> Come on Jack be nimble, Jack be quick
> Jack Flash sat on candle stick
> 'Cause fire is the devil's only friend
>
> And as I watched him on the stage
> My hands were clenched in fists of rage
> No angel born in hell
> Could break that Satan's spell
>
> And as the flames climbed into the night
> To light the sacrificial rite
> I saw Satan laughing with delight
> The night the music died...[3]

When the promise of ecstasy gives way to the realization of horror and despair, initiates come to look for what Dionysus cannot provide: grace.

This seeking after grace is dramatized, although by no means intentionally, in the 'tribal love-rock musical' *Hair*. Almost by the choice of its name alone, *Hair* was destined to

give form—story—to the Dionysian impulse that had so clearly arisen among sixties' youth. Hair, progressive school masters are now inclined to argue, *is not the issue,* but either they
are faking or they are deluded: hair *is* the issue—a point the
cast of the show is delighted to drive home:

Hair that's long like Jesus wore it
Hallelujah I adore it
Jesus' mother loved her son
Why don't my mother love me?

Hair! Hair!
Long as I can grow my hair...[5]

Before it was anything else, long hair was a cult symbol of
the unisex paradox. Wearers and viewers alike came to accept
it as a badge of liberated libido. Indeed for many cultists life
did become more erotic—and certainly more openly erotic;
for others, just wearing the badge was erotic enough.
Pervading *Hair* is a many-layered approval of erotic life: out-
ermost is the message that sex activity in general, for its own
sake, is good; there is the social message that sex should not
discriminate as to race; and there is the Dionysian message
that freed libido seeks both masculine and feminine objects.
Hair persistently stresses this latter theme, joining each explic-
itly homosexual posturing with the suggestion of its wicked-
ness; thus, a middle aged transvestite is made to sing the message:

I would just like to say
That it is my conviction
That longer hair and other flamboyant affectations
Are appearance and nothing more
Than the male's emergence from his drab camouflage
Into the gaudy plumage that is the birth right of his sex...

(Finishing the song, the lady throws open her fur coat,
revealing, alas, a man clad in jockey shorts.)

But the deepest and most erotic message of *Hair* is never articulated; it is communicated by dance, posturing, and the manipulation of common symbols. Stated, the message would be something like 'eros leads to the unknown, to the depths, it defiles all sacred things, it kills.' The performance tries mightily to take us into the unknown: the Age of Aquarius. The rite of passage is marijuana; the celebrants are "Walking in Space," singing "in this way we rediscover sensation." And of course the Dionysian impulse is iconoclastic: the troop mockingly assembles a human crucifix in order to deliver the message: ·

> Sodomy, fellatio
> Cunnilingus, pederasty
> Father why do these words sound so nasty?
> Masturbation can be fun...

And so, for an hour or two, the *Hair* troop goes its tribal way, but the going gets rough. In addition to workaday problems like unrequited love and being drafted into the Army, the tribe falls into a kind of collective despair: "facing a dying nation, a spinning paper fantasy, listening to the new-told lies...." But if this is merely social criticism, it is very odd, for *Hair* dramatizes no "dying nation"; the drama consists wholly in the life of the tribe. It is more than just suggestive that no representative of the straight world or of the State figures directly into the show. The invisible hand of the State touches the tribe only to extract one member, cut off his hair, and to return him, dead, a casualty of "the dirty little war." The return of the sacrificed member's body to the tribe is not the cause of their despair; rather it coincides with their despair and heightens it. The death arouses no fresh wrath or feelings of vengeance for the State. Confronted with the cold fact of death, the tribe is simply lost. Over and over they raise the haunting chant:

> Let the sunshine

Let the sunshine
Let the sunshine in

The plea is answered, characteristically, by a manipulation of symbols: the sacrificed member is raised up in the arms of his fellows in the position of Christ on the Cross; over his head is placed a simple crucifix. A tragic mood is transformed unmistakably into a triumphant one.

But why? What kind of triumph is it? Surely it is not a Dionysian triumph. The victim, in contrast to some of his comrades, is not characterized as an especially Dionysian type. Nor is it a triumph of the Dionysian *theme*, for the sacrifice, far from confirming the Dionysian principle, is not really related to it; the boy was not killed because he was a hippy but because he was a soldier. The tribe's mode of living is not confirmed by the death. They cannot be imagined to be better off as a result nor even able to avoid the draft themselves. But such literal speculation ignores the concluding spectacle of the show: the figure of the crucified Christ is held up by his ragged comrades, who demand

Let the sunshine
Let the sunshine
Let the sunshine in.

II

The hint or promise of Christ literally redeems the performance of *Hair*, but in order that the promise be fulfilled, Jesus would have to be given substance; that is, he would require his own story. Of course the story of Jesus is already a collective myth, complete with weekly ritual tellings and authorized texts. But the tribesmen crying out for light in the finale of *Hair* have no use for the established Christian tradition. The rationality, the self-conscious good will, the order, and the reserve of the established church offer nothing to the young Dionysian seeking grace. This is not to say that the life and teaching, death and resurrection, of Jesus offer nothing. The Dionysians recognized the power of Jesus' myth, but to realize that power, they had to remake Jesus' story and thus make it their own.

The contemporary Jesus was defined in the musical production of *Jesus Christ Superstar*. An immensely popular recording, its popularity preceded its commercial exploitation and succeeded in spite of it. Neither words nor music are unsophisticated, but their communication requires no sophistication.

Jesus Christ Superstar is the story of the passion and death of Christ. The general narrative is true to the scriptures. As Superstar, Christ differs from the biblical Christ mainly in showing rather more common humanity: he tires, gets discouraged, is overcome with doubt, is capable of passionate rage. Yet, this Jesus is no anti-hero. His moods are mitigated by sweetness and optimism; overall the moods serve to dramatize his courage. While only slightly more interesting than the sympathetically portrayed Judas, this Jesus is very compelling. To the authorities he sings.

> Why be concerned about the clamor of the crowds; if they were completely silenced, then nature itself would continue the song.[5]

Superstar is a genuinely passionate passion because it succeeds, as Kazantzakis succeeds in *The Last Temptation of Christ*, in convincing us that to be fully human and to submit consciously to a great but tragic destiny involves suffering. God's will be done, yes—but we are not allowed to forget that Christ has a will of his own. The authors dramatize Christ's dilemma delicately and simply, as in his soliloquy on the sacrament of the last supper.

> Jesus relates that an end caused by friends is more difficult to bear. He is sensitive to their indifference that the bread and wine could be his body and blood. Yet the reality is pro-

nounced; it is his body and his blood by which he hopes to be remembered in future suppers.

Or again, alone in Gethsemane,

knowing he surpassed all expectations, Jesus notes how his once-inspired zeal is now replaced by sadness and weariness. The three year ordeal seems like thirty.

If *Superstar* is, as it has been maintained, a worldly but overall faithful interpretation of the Gospels, what does it have to say to the Dionysians? It seems to say a number of things. Foremost perhaps is that its Jesus, like the historical Jesus but unlike the Sunday School Jesus, shares in many respects the life style of contemporary cultists; for while there is no documentary support to suggest that Jesus ever indulged the appetites of the Dionysians, it seems likely that at the time of his active ministry, he did live communally, nomadically, and was economically dependent on the largess of others. Moreover, Jesus speaks the common speech, eschews materialism, and shows concern for *personal* relationships over institutional and collective ones—followers are exhorted to love their neighbors, not the Movement. In many points of style, Jesus is hip. But while being hip makes Christ acceptable to the Dionysians, it does not of itself make him an object of special interest. The key to the appeal of the contemporary Jesus is that he is what every uncertain adolescent at one time fancies himself to be: the persecuted rebel. But unlike the Dionysian rebel, Jesus is innocent, pure, entirely just. His moral superiority puts him 'one up' on his persecutors and this posture is always appealing to those approaching adulthood as 'outsiders'—as former children. Here it helps that in addition to being hip, Jesus is occasionally cool. He parries the legalistic thrusts of the churchmen with a winsome ease: 'render unto Caesar,' whatever else it is, is cool. Similarly, in *Superstar*, when one of his followers takes up his sword in anger at the betrayal in Gethsemane, the captured Christ admonishes

> swords are no longer useful, the gig is up. Remarking on their obsession with violence he advises, "Hereafter, 'stick to fishing.'"

Cool indeed from a man on the way to his execution.

Superstar makes Christ attractive to contemporary youth by employing their own musical idiom to dramatize their archetypal situation: the persecution of the rebel-hero. It is appropriate that the contemporary Jesus should emerge out of *Superstar*,[6] a passion. The passion stresses the doubt, betrayal, suffering and death of Jesus—only part of the story, but the part that matters to the Dionysians and, through them, to the culture at large. It is inevitable that, in taking someone to ourselves—whether it is a friend, a lover, or Jesus—we start with only 'part of the story,' the part that has attracted us. At present we are sensitive to Jesus' suffering; other ages responded more to the miracles. Ultimately we are eager to have the whole story.

The whole story includes the ministry—the work—of Jesus. Indeed sympathy for the Christ of the passion is heightened by knowing his message and how he conveyed it. In the wrong hands, the ministry of Jesus can be made to appear alternately dreary and sanctimonious, a result not, as it sometimes supposed, of too many tellings but rather of too many heartless tellings. In the hands of John-Michael Tebelak, who conceived and directed *Godspell*, the teaching of Jesus is made to do what has apparently never occurred to institutional religious instructors: to delight the hell out of you.

Although it uses contemporary musical idiom—a mixture of pop, rock, and folk—*Godspell* is not cool. Nor, on the other hand, is it square. The show's immense appeal lies in its ability to coax, by dint of sheer good nature and enthusiasm, both the Dionysians and their enemies to come out from behind their respective cools. Incredibly, the show succeeds. It is said that it succeeds best in the London production where, in the person of David Essex, Jesus is irresistible for being so happy. In *Godspell,* Jesus is a jester, full of tricks in the manner of certain precocious and healthy little boys, and his apostles are clowns. Sticking scrupulously to the Gospel of St. Matthew, the parables are acted out in antics that are both imaginative and infantile. The show consists almost entirely of uninterrupted play. As children Christ's entourage are able to dramatize the human inclination to sin—all children make mistakes—without suggesting that they are any less worthy, attractive, or lovable for having done so. Thus, romp after romp, *Godspell* exhilaratingly makes the Christian point: God (and clearly Jesus) must love these incorrigible children.

As in *Superstar, Godspell* takes Jesus to his crucifixion. Suggested simply and movingly, this is the only gloomy sequence in the show, but without so much as a break in the score, Christ is resurrected and the troop is in high spirits, developing what is at first a hopeful, then a confident, "Long live God" into a jubilant "Prepare ye the way of the Lord." The show concludes with the rock reprise:

> Day by day, day by day
> Oh dear Lord three things I pray
> To see thee more clearly
> To love thee more clearly
> To follow thee more nearly
> Day by day...

(Many of the show's songs, like the one above, take their lyrics from traditional Anglican hymns and anthems.)

III

It is obvious, but perhaps not unnecessary, to state that the contemporary Jesus makes the impact that he does because he is needed. Affluence and even the aspiration to affluence show diminishing power to satisfy. Regardless of whether one probes into the right or the left of the materialist dialectic these days, one is likely to find tired justifications of tired enterprises. The apparent passion of the young Left is really the Dionysian passion, which becomes political only occasionally and coincidentally—and then only to achieve the Dionysian aim of defiling the sacred things, i.e., conventional political forms. As such, Dionysian youth is more a challenge to the Communist Party than to either the Republicans or Democrats; the latter are dull, the former repressive.

What is needed is a Superstar, and Jesus is proving adequate to the part. His example is a critique of materialism. He is simple; we are complex. Our experience is broad and bland, his is deep and rich. And again, he's hip—and what's more impressive, he's always been hip. Just right. But in order for this to continue to be so, his story must be told truly. Variety is always invigorating, provided there is vigor in what is being varied.

Not every attempt to invoke the contemporary Jesus is successful. Leonard Bernstein's elaborate new Mass is decidedly not successful. Its defenders (not many of them appear to be critics) would of course argue that as it is a mass, not a gospel, it must not be compared to the likes of *Jesus Christ Superstar* and *Godspell.* But while certainly the *Mass* has far more grandiose musical intentions than its pop forerunners, it is like them in seeking to portray the ordeal of Christ. Jesus does not appear as such in the *Mass,* but the performance proceeds as a youthful Celebrant, formally in the process of celebrating mass, undergoes an ordeal parallel to that of Christ. The Celebrant is overcome by doubt and despair, then is resurrected by love and hope. Bernstein's spectacle is not a mass. One takes mass; in the Bernstein piece, one observes the drama of another person's mass. That drama shows the familiar outlines of the ordeal of Christ, but lacking a real Christ, it lacks power. The Celebrant is a hero of sorts, but he is no Jesus; he lacks the genius of his own redemption. Also—and this is perhaps a technical rather than a thematic point—the Celebrant, despite his longish hair and plain clothes, lacks the common touch. One can listen to the singing of David Essex's Jesus in *Godspell* and reflect, without regret, that this voice had

best not attempt *Der Meistersinger.* On the other hand, when
Alan Titus (the Celebrant) manfully intones

> Sing God a simple song
> Make it up as you go along
> Sing like you like to sing
> God loves all simple things[7]

one wishes in vain for that voice to break training.[8] The principal disappointment, though, is not how he sings, but that he
is not singing as Jesus. (Some listeners maintain that the principal disappointment is that Leonard Bernstein combines too
many musical *genres* and idioms and as a result has produced
a messy, uninteresting pastiche. Such claims are best left to the
aestheticians.)

The *Mass* does not give us Jesus or even a satisfying Jesus-fig-
ure, but it does articulate, through its 'street people' and cho-
ruses, the pathos of existing without him:

> Your body's always ready, but your soul's not there
> Don't be non-plussed
> Come love, come lust
> It's so easy when you just don't care.

Elsewhere:

> Oh, I suddenly feel every step I've ever taken,
> And my legs are lead
> And suddenly I feel every hand I've ever shaken
> And my arms are dead
> I feel every psalm that I've ever sung
> Turn to wormwood on my tongue
> And I wonder
> Oh, I wonder
> Was I ever really young

Elsewhere:

When the thunder rumbles
Now the Age of Gold is Dead
And the dreams we've clung to dying to stay young
Have left us parched and old instead...

When my courage crumbles
When I feel confused and frail
When my spirit falters on decaying altars
And my illusions fail...

I go on right then.
I go on again.

There is much of this rhetoric of disenchantment in the *Mass,* so much in fact that it is fair to challenge: *why* go on again? Why, for that matter, is the Celebrant resurrected from his despair? The *Mass* provides no answer. For all we are shown, the players embracing one another at the conclusion of the mass could be putting up a brave front in the face of utter despair. This is no answer, nor, probably, is it the intention of those who conceived the *Mass.*

The answer lies in the personality of Jesus, the person wailing in *Superstar,* laughing in *Godspell.* Without a personality Jesus can communicate no message to men. It is a nice historical touch, now, that 'alienated' youth have given body, appearance, and personality to Jesus. They have found him, not made him, and they have found him contemporary. Otherwise we might have been stranded in this crowded, loveless decade with no hope beyond the rumor of a miracle.

[1] *Quoted by permission of Blackwood Music, Inc., 1650 Broadway, New York City.*

[2] *Quoted by permission of Music Administration Corp., 75 East 55th Street, New York City.*

[3] *Quoted by permission of Unart Music Corp., 729 Seventh Avenue, New York, NY.*

[4] *Quotations from* Hair *are by arrangement with United Artists Music Co., Inc., 729 Seventh Avenue, New York City.*

[5] *Passages from* Superstar *are paraphrased because permission to quote from its lyrics for purposes of "theological interpretation" is not given.*

[6] *Again, the recording or the concert performance, not the spectacular adaptation for the stage that would follow in New York. The stage version is not just less effective, it is critically different. For example it renders the resurrection miracle literally (and with a silly grandeur) while the concert version leaves one wondering at the tomb.*

In contrast to Superstar, *listeners who have not seen* Godspell *performed are often indifferent to the cast recording.*

[7] *Copyright 1971 by Leonard Bernstein and Stephen Schwartz. Used by permission of G. Schirmer, Inc.*

[8] *Stephen Schwartz, who wrote these and all the lyrics for the Mass, also did the lyrics for* Godspell. *It is likely that only a trained voice could manage Bernstein's demanding music.*

6

Privacy and Dignity

With respect to intimate and unpleasant personal experiences, it recently occurred to me that I know more about Bill Clinton and Dan Quayle than I do about my mother and father. I am serious—and I have been on good, close terms with my mother and father for forty-seven years.

We have come to accept paparazzo intrusiveness as a journalistic norm. We are used to seeing lists of a presidential candidate's former houseguests and their alleged habits, computer printouts of a Supreme Court justice's video rentals. We assume that we can, and shortly will, know anything about everybody. More tellingly, we have learned to assume the worst. This development matters; it is not at all like a dietary fad or some dismal development in fashion.

The natural impulse to find out other people's troubles and secrets has throughout history been tempered by a higher impulse: sympathy. Sympathy combined with respect (a still higher impulse) bids us to avert our eyes from another's embarrassment or nakedness, to resist reading someone else's personal mail.

The prevailing abandonment of natural decency makes perfect commercial and psychological sense, but it is nevertheless a monumental cultural loss. It ought to alarm us, to beg some hard questions, the first of which might be: Who or what ever conferred a "right to know" anything about another person's non-criminal conduct?

I do not want to know that Clarence Thomas watched pornographic films, still less which ones—and I am sure I'm not alone in feeling this way.

There is no such right to know; there is merely a prurient desire. The problem would be simpler and its solution nearer at hand if the task were simply to protect private persons from nefarious invaders. But private persons are half the problem.

We live in an eerily confessional—but one hopes passing—era in which every possible personal problem or horror is on view for public consumption. A virtual parade of Donahues fronts a booming television industry exposing crimes, sins, abuses, addictions and every imaginable sexual practice of obscure private persons hungry to confess.

The history of ideas includes the history of bad ideas, and here we might pick a bone with the late poet Sylvia Plath and legions of other "confessional" writers to follow. In her later works, the manic and undeniably interesting poems that preceded her suicide in 1963, Plath entered what some critics considered "new mental territory," a lucidly hysterical realm where, at last, it could all hang out: daddy hang-ups, sexual intimacies, masochistic fantasies, murderous hatred.

Poetic license notwithstanding, the narrator of these poems, her father, her husband, and her baby are easily identifiable. Plath's former husband and the rest of her family were hurt and embarrassed, not to mention *exposed* for the rest of their lives, by Plath's confessional writing. But because her suicide lent her work a kind of grotesque and final sincerity, her confession is, in effect, unanswerable.

The price is high, but late twentieth-century celebrity is achieved through the ultimate surrender of privacy. Posthumously abetted by her psychiatrist's willingness to share her most intimate secrets, Plath's friend and colleague in poetry, Anne Sexton, followed her lead: tell all, then end it all.

Which is not to say that private confession has no public place. St. Augustine, Rousseau and many other luminaries confessed in ways that expanded the very boundaries of consciousness. But a line should be drawn between confessing for insight and confessing for sensational effect. The former is profoundly self-effacing; the latter, self-indulgent.

The line between illuminating personal disclosure and mere gossip is fairly easy to draw. The former somehow improves our understanding of the human condition; the latter does not. The brothers Tobias (*This Boy's Life*) and Geoffrey Wolff *(The Duke of Deception),* in their own distinctive voices, told very private and, at times, self-abasing tales of their coming of age under neglectful and abusive parents—but so acute is their telling that we learn something important about the legacy of abuse and neglect. This is a public good.

In this vein, a beautifully written memoir, *Class,* by newcomer Geoff Douglas, is due this fall from Henry Holt. It tells the story of a poor little rich boy, and without ever raising his voice in complaint, Douglas helps readers understand dimensions of childhood anxiety and loss readers of *Mommie Dearest* could never imagine.

The same line dividing humane confession from vulgar exhibitionism also divides essential biography from journalistic voyeurism. The only good to be derived from publicizing the personal is the improvement of persons. That's right; no one needs to know that Princess Diana is sicking up her meals. Moreover, it's *bad* for us to know. Glutted with extraneous stories, we lose our capacity for real ones.

Our understanding of public persons is shaped by the stories told about them. One's capacity for such stories is finite. In the very best of circumstances, it is difficult to reduce journalism to what we need in order to think clearly and act wisely. It is hard to understand complexities like the federal deficit, global ecology and the social dynamics of poverty and crime. It is harder still to grasp a public figure's considered responses to these complexities. It is a sign of our times that the public has massively quit trying. Voter turnout is at its lowest level in years.

Complexities are, well, complex. The essence of public issues is elusive. But style, a largely private matter, is easy. We take in a subject's bearing, hairdo and attire at the speed of light. Before we have a clue to the substance of a public person's political or moral position, we sense an attitude: Clinton as aging frat brother, Perot as cracker, Bush as bumbler.

Legions of citizens who themselves had never given a thought to whether potato ends in *e* or *o,* much less placed that kind of knowledge in a political category, took a positive pleasure in the Vice President's televised embarrassment.

My ten-year-old daughter knows about Quayle's "potatoe" gaffe. Knowing about it—and the hundred other nonessentials she has been told and shown about the national candidates—*is the reason* she does not know a single point on which, say, Governor Clinton differs from President Bush. What she needs to know has been displaced.

In gaining public access to the realm of privacy—millions have viewed and reviewed . . . President Bush getting sick and passing out over dinner—we have become politically stupid.

But the public cost of losing privacy is, if anything, exceeded by that paid by persons whose privacy has been taken away. Real loss of privacy is devastating. We feel it more deeply than anything discussed behind our back at parties or aired in a court of law. In our privacy lies our very soul.

In a telling, if strange, digression toward the end of *Bonfire of the Vanities,* Tom Wolfe drew on obscure Amazonian anthropology to make the point that when the community has sufficient access to an individual's inner life, the inner life disappears. Invasion becomes infestation, and finally the person's soul, like that of Wolfe's hapless Sherman McCoy, is displaced by whatever the public says it is.

This is a distinctively modern way of dying. These dead are everywhere around us. These dead do not rise up in indignation. They do not even cry out for help. But, for the time being, you and I can. We can live the way Socrates told us philosophers should live. We can mind our own business.

7

Television and Adolescents

Ever since its novelty wore off in the fifties, we have all known, really, that television in its commercial form wasn't up to much good. This isn't to say that millions of people don't still depend on it, but dependency is hardly a sign of virtue. Except for Marshall McLuhan's grab-bag theoretics, few claims have been advanced for the improving effects of television. In fact, recently there has been a flurry of publishing activity, most notably Marie Winn's *The Plug-in Drug*, about television as a cause of downright mental erosion. But what I think Marie Winn and others need is a concrete, closely observed, and intensely felt illustration of the larger thesis.

Television has a way of intruding into our lives, and last year it intruded into my life and into the life of the school where I work in a way that many of us there will never forget. We had all taken our seats for morning assembly. The usual announcements were read, after which the morning's senior speaker was introduced. Like many independent schools, ours requires each senior to address the student body in some manner before he graduates. Since public speaking is not a widely distributed gift these days, the senior speeches are infrequently a source of much interest or intentional amusement.

As the curtains parted, we could see that the speaker had opted for a skit. On the stage were a covered table and a number of cooking implements. Out stepped the speaker wearing an apron and chef's hat, which very quickly established that he was going to satirize one of my colleagues who has a national reputation as a gourmet chef. Since this colleague is also a man who can take a joke, the prospects for the skit seemed bright. But not for long.

At first, I think almost all of us pretended that we didn't

hear, that we were making too much of certain, possibly accidental, double entendres. But then came the direct statements and a few blatant physical gestures. Then it was clear! This boy was standing before 500 of us making fun of what he suggested at some length was the deviant sexual nature of one of his teachers. The response to this was at first stupefaction, then some outbursts of laughter (the groaning kind of laughter that says, "I don't believe you said that"), then a quieting, as the speech progressed, to periodic oohs (the kind that say, "You *did* say that, and you're in for it").

When he had finished, there was a nearly nauseating level of tension afloat. As the students filed off to class, I made my way backstage to find the speaker. It had by now dawned on him that he had done something wrong, even seriously wrong. We met in my office.

He expressed remorse at having offended a teacher whom he said he particularly liked. (Before the conference I had checked briefly with the teacher and found him badly flustered and deeply hurt.) The remorse was, I felt, genuine. But something was decidedly missing in the boy's explanation of how he came to think that such a presentation might, under any circumstances, have been appropriate. He hadn't, he admitted, really thought about it, and some of his friends thought the idea was funny, and, well, he didn't know. When it occurred to him that serious school action was in the offing, he protested that in no way had he intended the sexual references to be taken sexually—they were, you know, a joke.

I pointed out to him that the objects of such jokes have no way to respond: To ignore the insinuation might affirm its validity; on the other hand, to object vigorously would draw additional attention to the offense and sustain the embarrassment connected with it. I pointed out further that sometimes innocent parties *never* regain their stature after being offended in this manner, and that the injured party was, at the very least, in for a terrible day of school.

The boy became reflective and said, "Was it *that* bad? You can see worse on 'Saturday Night Live.'" I told him I doubted this, but if it were true, and were I in a position to judge, I would be in favor of expelling "Saturday Night Live" from the air. He left the office, and subsequently endured the appropriate consequences.

For my part, I resolved to turn on "Saturday Night Live," and when I did, I realized the student had spoken truly. The show's quick-succession, absurdist comedy spots depended for their appeal on establishing an almost dangerous sense of inappropriateness: exactly that sense created by our senior speaker. To me, for some years a lapsed viewer, it seemed that both the variety and specificity of sexual innuendo had developed considerably since, say, the once daring Smothers Brothers show of the sixties. What struck me more, however, was how many punch lines and visual gags depended on suddenly introducing the idea of injury or violent death.

I happened to tune in the night a funny caption was put over the documentary shot of Middle Eastern political partisans being dragged to death behind an automobile. Was this funny? I asked my students. They said it was "sick" and laughed. Does this kind of fun trivialize crisis? Trivialize cruelty? Inure us to both? Or is it, you know, a joke?

The right things were said, I think, to our students about the boy's speech. But I can't say the situation improved. Not more than a couple of weeks later, a speaker garbed in a woman's tennis dress took the podium and began to talk humorously about the transsexual tennis player Renee Richards. I can't think of a subject harder for an adolescent to discuss before an adolescent audience. Rarely noted for their confidence and breadth of vision in matters of human sexuality, adolescents are unlikely to be objective, sympathetic, or (let me tell you) funny about so disturbing a phenomenon as sex change. This particular boy, whose inflection is very flat and whose normal countenance is especially stony, managed to convey almost a sense of bitterness in making his string of insulting and, in his references to genitals and to menstruation, awfully tasteless cracks.

So there it was again: the inappropriateness, the tension.

This time the injured party was remote from our particular world, so the hastily arranged conference with the boy turned on general considerations of taste and judgment. This time, however, the speaker was recalcitrant: We could disapprove of his speech and discipline him if we chose, but we ought to know that we could hear the same thing on television.

At that moment something clicked for me. Not only did my brief exposure to "Saturday Night Live" convince me that, yes, I would hear the same thing on television, but I was suddenly struck with the realization that he was using television as an arbiter of taste—that is, *as an arbiter of good taste.* I began to see in this premise a common ground upon which he and I could at least argue. Both of us were in agreement that what is broadcast over television ought to be acceptable; our point of disagreement was his feeling that broadcasting something over television *made* it acceptable. Alarming as such a feeling is to me, it is not hard to see how it has developed over the past few decades.

Until the middle sixties, with the exception of the very earthiest plays and novels, the values of home and school and the values of the popular culture were fairly continuous; if anything, radio, television, and motion pictures were more staid than real life. Of course, all this would change very quickly—not because change was requested or even consented to, but because it wasn't, perhaps couldn't be, resisted. And suddenly there it all was at once: the most embarrassing expletives as common speech; every imaginable kind of sexual coupling depicted in ever increasing candor; obsessively specific wounds, mutilations.

These formerly unacceptable kinds of stimulation made their way more easily into the relatively insulated world of print and film than they did into the more communal world of the television set. Television is typically viewed in homes, and what is communally seen and heard must be communally integrated, or there will be friction. Since American households—set-holds?—share this communal experience for an estimated two to seven hours per day, the potential for friction is considerable. This is why, on grounds of taste, criticism of television programming tends to be more bitter and more relentless than criticism of books and films.

Television foes and partisans alike continue to advise, with some reason, that those who object to certain programs ought not to watch them. But given the impossibility of monitoring the set at all hours, control over the amount and quality of viewing is difficult to maintain even in principled, surveillant households. Too, some viewers will insist on being their brother's keeper. Not everyone who is convinced that what is beaming over the national airwaves is inhumane, unscrupulous, or scurrilous is going to fight to the death for the networks' right to be so.

For many people, television is no longer on the polite side of real life. This is an obvious observation about a novel development, one whose consequences are only just dawning on us. A realist or an existentialist may argue that the unflappably suburban world of "Father Knows Best" revealed none of the complex, ambivalent, and other irrational forces at work in real families: But it is hard to argue that "Father Knows Best" in any way contributed to those dark forces. On the contrary, it is possible to argue—although one hesitates to carry it too far—that the theme of Father Knowing Best serves as a psychologically soothing backdrop to the prickly dynamics of real family life. And while today's most highly rated shows suggest that the prevailing seventies' theme is Nobody Knows Anything, there are still apparently enough viewers who like Parents Knowing Best to support series like "The Waltons" and "Little House on the Prairie."

Sometimes the theme is compromised in a typical seventies' manner, of which "James at 16" provides a good example: The parents are cast very much in the Robert Young–Jane Wyatt mold, but their son James is, to borrow a phrase, kind of now. By far the most interesting thing he did was to lose his virginity on prime time. The 15-going-on-16-year-old boys I work with, many of them at least as sophisticated as James, typically hold on to their virginity a bit longer, until the disposition of their sexual feelings is under surer control. The best clinical evidence maintains that the process of bringing newly emergent sexuality under control is inherently delicate and troublesome. James's television plunge planted the anxiety-provoking notion in the mind of the adolescent viewer that he was sexually lagging behind not only the precocious kid down the block, but the Average American Boy character of James. (One was allowed to be less anxious when Father Knew Best.)

Why shouldn't television make people anxious? say the producers of programs that make people anxious. After all, the *world* is anxious. (An awfully self-serving position: Programs that arouse anxiety are relevant; those that don't are enjoyable.) Before long, this line of argument begins to lay claim that programs which bring up irritating subjects in an irritating manner are performing a valuable social mission. Norman Lear, the producer of comedies such as "All in the Family" and "Maude," makes such a claim. According to the Lear formula, a controversial topic will be raised, tossed around for laughs, then either discarded or resolved. Resolution occurs when one of the characters tolerates or forgives the controversial person or practice, while some other character, usually a combination of lovable old coot and ass, does not.

As many critics have pointed out, this is only apparent resolution. Nothing much really happens to a racial or sexual conflict when it is laughed at (a device that is supposed to soften outright slurring and stereotyping), discarded, tolerated, or forgiven. The idea that "if we can joke about it this way, we have taken a humanitarian stride" is mistaken. There is plenty of evidence, particularly among the student population, that, for one thing, race relations are more strained today than they were a decade ago. No one would want to claim that racism among youth disappeared during the politically active sixties; however, a claim can be made that when a student was confronted then with having made a racial slur, he seemed to be aware of having violated a standard.

Who is to say that Archie Bunker hath no sting? More and more television comedians, in the manner of Don Rickles, seek *only* to sting. It is really an empirical question, not a matter of taste, whether or not it is harmless, much less healing, to denigrate everybody, including oneself. A hit song by Randy Newman insults small people; this is no parody of unkindness or bigotry, but the real thing. My students understand it perfectly and parrot it enthusiastically. Rebuked, they grimace in exasperation. Nothing in their youthful experience tells them that bigotry is a sign of cultural regression ("It isn't bigotry; it's, you know, a joke"). They prefer to see whatever wicked delights crop up in the media as a progressive casting off of prudish inhibitions. According to such a view, progress is whatever happens next.

Toleration of the intolerable is always worrying, but it is especially so when it takes place among the young, in whom we want to invest so much hope. Tolerating the intolerable is part of a dynamic, not a static, process; the intolerable, when it is nurtured, grows.

Which brings me back to the senior speeches. Two so thoroughly inappropriate presentations in a single year represented a high count for us, so we were not ready, at least I wasn't, for the third.

This time the talk was about a summer spent working on a ranch, and the format was that of a commentary with slides. No apparent harm in this, but there were a number of factors working against the speech's success. The first was that the speaker was renowned for being a card, a reputation the welcoming ovation insisted he live up to. Second, he had not adequately rehearsed the projection of the slides, so that they tended to appear out of order and askew, the effect of which was to provide a subtextual comedy of visual nonsequiturs. Third, he chose to capitalize on the audience's nearly unrestrained hilarity by playing up certain questionable references.

The speaker made a fairly good, not too inappropriate crack about a slide which depicted a bull mounting a cow— "Sometimes the corrals get so crowded we have to stack the cattle on top of one another." But he chose to exploit his ref-

erences to the gelding of bulls. There were, in all, four jokey
and brutal evocations of this process which served to keep the
image of bull genitalia before our minds for quite a few minutes. Since laughter had already been spent, the castration
jokes were met with a kind of nervous applause. Bolstered by
this, the speaker closed with a coda to the effect that he would
be available after assembly to anybody who wanted tips on
"cutting meat."

Since I happened to be in charge that day, I sent him home.
It seemed to me, in light of the various reprisals and fore-
warnings connected with the previous speeches, that this particular performance, though perhaps less offensive in its specific references than the other two, ought to be the last straw.
The speaker had clearly exceeded anything required by either
schoolboy or cowboy saltiness. He had created an anything-
goes atmosphere, and then he had let it go—for which he was
applauded. "That was great!" said the boy next to me on the
way out of the auditorium.

That morning and afterward scores of students, most, but
not all, of them civil, hastened to let me know that they felt it
was unfair to have sent the speaker home. Not one of them
failed to remind me that I could see worse on television. Had
I never seen "Saturday Night Live"? That afternoon an opinion poll went up requesting signatures from those who disap-
proved of the action I had taken and, in an opposing column,
those who approved. Within the hour, hundreds expressed
disapproval, only one approved.

For a day or two at school there was an animated atmosphere of martyrdom (the speaker's, not mine), but it dissipat-
ed rapidly, possibly because the right to make castration jokes
from the stage was not, as a cause, very catalytic. The banished
speaker, a very likable boy, returned, was received warmly, and
apologized not at all cringingly.

In the calm that has followed, my colleagues and I have
taken pains to stress to our students, especially at the com-
mencement of the new school year, that whenever somebody
addresses an assembly, it is a special occasion. Speakers are

expected to observe definite standards when they speak or perform; audiences are expected to be courteous and restrained. Humor at someone else's expense is out, unless it is prearranged with the party lampooned, and even then it ought not to be inhuman. Excretory and copulatory humor is out; it's too easy. Preparation is important. Being persuasive is important. Being controversial is important. Being funny is a delight to all, though it is harder than it looks.

Perhaps these expectations are high. However, schools, especially parochial and independent schools, are gloriously unencumbered in setting such standards: Schools are often chosen for the standards they set, the difference they represent. One of the things schools have an opportunity to be different from is television, for although we are all wired into it and it feels public, like the law, it is actually private, like a door-to-door salesman. We don't have to buy the goods.

Since children who watch a fair amount of television will quite naturally assume they are being told and shown the truth, it seems to me crucial that they are exposed to models who view it selectively and critically, who judge it by criteria other than its potential to engage. My own experience has been that students are surprised, but not hostile, when television programming is harshly judged. I think they may even come to like the idea that they themselves, at their discriminating best, are in the process of becoming people television ought to measure up to.

8

Some Unsettling Thoughts About
Settling in with Pot

The seventies, some of my friends like to argue, will be remembered as the decade in which the novelties that erupted in the sixties got sorted out and integrated into the general culture. Certainly one of those novelties was the emergence of drugs, especially marijuana, out of urban slums and bohemia up into the light of suburbia and the middle class. And as everybody knows, the pre-sixties' view of marijuana was preposterous: pot was naively linked to addictive drugs such as heroin and morphine; pot was believed to trigger violent and promiscuous behavior; one way or another, pot was assumed to lead unerringly to personal ruin. But the reckless Aquarians of the sixties, in their drive to "expand consciousness," smoked pot like mad and put such myths to rest. Or did they?

In the sixties and early seventies the suspicion that pot is harmless (or "no worse than" numerous legally available substances such as alcohol, tobacco, coffee, candy) received massive attention in the media. Arlo Guthrie said "There's no such thing as a bad joint" on the Johnny Carson Show. John Lennon told the press that pot was "a harmless giggle" when he was arrested for possessing some. It became stylish—nearly monotonous—to record songs about marijuana and other highs. Norman Mailer began to smoke pot at public forums and on T.V.; Peter Fonda and Dennis Hopper *pretended* to smoke it during a David Frost interview. In 1970 the federal government empaneled a National Commission on Marihuana and Drug Abuse, and in 1972 its report, "Marihuana: A Signal of Misunderstanding," stated baldly that there was little or no danger that could be shown to result from the experimental or intermittent use of the kind of mar-

74

ijuana that was commonly processed in the United States. There was, however, a caution that "Chronic, heavy use may jeopardize the social and economic adjustment of the adolescent."

So with pot readily available, relatively inexpensive, and easy to cultivate, with youth's heroes endorsing it and the national government at best ambivalent, pot has managed to sneak into the American pantry, although not quite in plain view. And the momentum continues. Pot has lost its "counter-culture" identification; jocks and burn-outs alike smoke openly out of doors and at concerts of all kinds. State legislatures are increasingly busy working out ways to "decriminalize" possession of the drug. In Oregon the law places marijuana possession in a category between a parking violation and a misdemeanor. In enthusiastic support of such measures, "smoke-ins" are staged in the public gaze on the public squares of major cities.

What to make of this.

What I made of it, being in the profession of teaching and counseling adolescent boys, is that the inclusion of pot into the popular culture is of an altogether different order from the inclusion of some harmless, if unredeeming, trend such as bralessness or new dietary habits. Having graduated from college amidst the first great wave of casual marijuana use and having been enrolled in or teaching in schools since that time, I have seen much that has shaken my initial predisposition to accept the sixties' verdict on pot. Some college friends who began smoking pot enthusiastically have, by their own standards, lost their social and career bearings and have not yet regained them. But even more troubling, and a persistent factor in my work, are students who, due to smoking pot twice a week or more, lose their learning momentum, impair their social and physical development, and are enervated and depressed in the process. The regularity with which pot-smoking students suffer dramatic personal and academic reversals and the uniformity of their affect suggest to me that something beyond individual set-backs or family trouble is at work.

I have seen and continue to see once-bright students whose speech and thought patterns are fuzzed, whose memories are alarmingly poor, and whose lack of engagement in former relationships and former activities cannot be explained by simple adolescent lassitude. I am seeing, if anything, more of such students now than I did five years ago, and increasing numbers are in the first two years of high school. A development like this in the otherwise docile seventies is unsettling and has provoked me to find out about pot beyond what I might find in the papers or education journals. Could the popular culture *and* a National Commission be wrong? Could the examples of Arlo Guthrie and Norman Mailer have thrown us all a curve?

The answer, if the international medical community is anything to go by, is an emphatic yes. Pot is very probably *worse* than the makers of the now camp 30's classic "Reefer Madness" wanted us to believe, and it is worse in ways that few of the twenty-odd million users in the United States wish to be aware of. The best and most careful research has been completed and published in the scientific community since 1970 and has, outside of *Reader's Digest*-like synopses and the occasional reference or press blurb, come to public attention very rarely and very vaguely. For instance, a couple of years ago there was a buzz in the student world—half in fun, half in fear—that pot smoking made boys effeminate, even gave them a feminine bust. That particular correlation, incidentally, is not fanciful and comes in part from the research done by Drs. J. W. Harmon and Menelaos Aliapoulios at the New England Deaconess Hospital in Brookline, Mass. These men first reported their findings in the *New England Journal of Medicine*. Later more conclusive research was abstracted and printed with pictures in medical journals. Remote ripples reached the national press, and the news, usually reduced to a few stark, sweeping statements, was received as news of other low-intensity but engaging oddities (multiple slayings, hijackings, carcinogenic food) is received by all of us every day. Yet there are no words adequate to describe the horror—something like what I imagine to be the way a pious monk of the middle ages might respond if he suddenly beheld the Devil in the mirror—in the faces of the tenth graders to whom I showed Dr. Harmon's material and pictures of amply buxom *gynecomastial* young men, patients whose common denominator was that they showed no inclination to *gynecomastia* prior to their heavy pot smoking.

But few of our nation's youth, particularly those who take drugs, can be found poring over medical journals. Moreover, most of them and most of us are used to taking seriously very little of what is transmitted by the popular media. For again, in less than a generation, those media have told us that pot is dangerous and criminal, then spirit enhancing, then harmless, then maybe harmful, then trivial in the eyes of the law. Thus we find ourselves in the odd position of being at once saturated with drug news and woefully ignorant about drugs. By way of illustration, the following is a rough but overall fair transcription of a public forum I attended in my community last week:

In what seemed to me an unusually tardy response, a number of interested residents and concerned officials convened at the Episcopal Church to take stock of "the drug scene" in the local schools. The high school had conducted a survey which showed that about half the students used pot and/or alcohol intermittently, a picture which conforms almost perfectly to the national pattern of drug use among the young.

The principal felt the survey was valid.

The president of the student council revealed that some students had exaggerated their drug use, while others had understated theirs, but that the counterbalancing distortions rendered the survey "about right."

After a half hour of such exchanges the group resolved to make up a booklet of facts about drugs and mail it to each community family.

A woman who worked for a local "head help" emergency phone service was skeptical about the usefulness of a book of facts, since the kids on the street already "knew so much" about drugs. The area businessman disagreed; he felt the booklet would acquaint the parents with what the various drugs look like, which would be the first step in preventing their use.

The director of community relations closed the meeting, citing "a lot of terrific in-put," and called for another at a date to be established.

This meeting, I suspect, is not unrepresentative of thousands that have taken place across the country in school auditoriums, church basements, and civic buildings. It is not hard to imagine the local newspaper's account of the meeting; I can see with perfect prescience the quotation marks around the colorful words of the area businessman. Nor is it hard to imagine what the "book of facts" will be like and what its impact will be on the community's health and welfare.

The reason the "basic facts" about a drug like marijuana are not likely to be clearly communicated to the general public is that those basic facts involve a thoroughgoing understanding of the drug's properties (relatively easy), of the complexity with which neural cells interact (very hard) and of the changes undergone when drug and cells meet (also very hard). Hard but not impossible. Dr. Gabriel Nahas, research professor of anesthesiology at Columbia, Consultant to the United Nations Commission on Narcotics, and possibly the leading international authority on what pot does to human cells, spoke for his Swiss, Canadian, Jamaican, and American fellow researchers when he published his "Patho-Physiological Effects of Marihuana Use in Man" in *Private Practice* (January, 1975). In this article and in his articles and books which have followed, Dr. Nahas is not wildly theorizing but summarizing the most well established research in the world on the physiological effects of pot, research which indicates unequivocally that marijuana interferes with the metabolism of cells responsible for replicating ourselves genetically, for sexual performance and for the growth of sexual tissues, for long and short term memory, for thinking, for making us immune, and for regulating our hormonal activity in general. In simple terms, the cell processes most subtle and most responsible for the development of human personality are affected adversely—damaged—by marijuana. Strong stuff, but it is unwise to ignore it. Even the federal government acknowledged the importance of the new research and documented much of it in the Senate's hearings on "The Marihuana-Hashish Epidemic and its Impact on United States Security" (U.S. Government Printing Office, 1974). This alarming document is a far cry and just two years from the gently probing National Commission's "Marihuana: A Signal of Misunderstanding." It is instructive to consider the kinds of evidence sought and stressed when an internal need of government, and not just its external image, is at stake.

Since the National Commission's 1972 report, clinical studies have dramatically refuted practically all of the former's most hard edged contentions: that marijuana does not cause chromosome damage or other mutagenic effects, that marijuana has no medically significant effects on organs or tissue. Like so much sixties and early seventies marijuana study, these "no danger" findings were based largely on a study of Jamaican cane farmers who were habitual marijuana smokers. As Dr. Nahas and others have pointed out, this study is now widely discredited in the scientific community on the grounds that (1) almost half the cell cultures prepared failed to grow at all, (2) the cells were analyzed only two days after culture, when the chemical active in the drug is known to be active three times longer than that, and (3) too few cells (twelve to fifteen per patient) were analyzed to prove anything conclusively. On the other hand, at the Swiss Institute for Cancer Research, Drs. Cecille and Rudolf Leuchtenberger's more careful research on the effects of marijuana's active agent (THC) in cultured human tissue indicates that our most crucial genetic materials, RNA and DNA, are definitely altered. Moreover, Dr. Robert Kolodny and his associates at the Reproductive Biology Research Foundation in St. Louis have documented, and Dr. Nahas and associates have confirmed, a marked decrease in sperm count among young men who used marijuana several times a week for a period of six months. In Britain Dr. Malcolm Gordon Campbell of Bristol Royal United Hospitals has used air encephalograms to document brain atrophy in the regular pot users (age 18-28) he has tested. And while Dr. Campbell's study is controversial, the work of Dr. Robert Heath on the effects of marijuana on the waking brains of men and animals is not. Heath was the first to indicate, through the use of electrodes planted deep in the brain, that marijuana (although not tobacco, alcohol, or amphetamines) produces discharges in the phylogenically ancient limbic system of the brain. These discharges occurred as the patient experienced his "rush" in the process of getting high. The implications of these findings are profound, since limbic activity once aroused tends to persist unaltered long after the triggering stimulus is gone. The limbic activity stimulated by marijuana intoxication is accompanied by a diminished ability to form concepts, to appraise situations, to reach judgments.

Any consideration of the long range effects of having marijuana at the national population's fingertips requires a careful look at evidence pointing to damaged genetic material. In the African and Asian subcultures which have the longest tradition of chronic cannabis use (usually hashish), clear behavior changes—the "anti-motivational syndrome"—and physiological deficits have been documented for over a century. It is important to know, Dr. Nahas reminds us, that in those cultures the drug has been used exclusively by males, so that the effects of THC-related interference in developing embryos would not be likely to register. But in a society like ours, in which both sexes are likely to indulge, there is danger, as pot, among its other biochemical abilities, is able to pass through the placental barrier of pregnant women.

The research into the effects of marijuana is often technically subtle, and it is carried out in several specialized branches of medical and social science, but there is much about these cautiously articulated findings that is downright obvious—or should have been obvious—to the least scientist among us. We all know, for instance, that people generally smoke pot to change themselves, to "get high." And we all know, or ought to know, that when we change our feelings, we are changing cells—there is no other way to feel. There has been since pre-history an almost grail-like search for some substance, some practice, some kind of understanding that will get us delight-fully high without undesirable side effects, like delirium tremens, paralysis, or death. Prayer, study, adventure, sex, and substances have for millennia been popular means of attempt-ed transcendence, but the impulse to prayer and meditation is less than universal; study or mastery takes a long time; adventures are costly and uncertain; sexual ecstasy is gone in a flash, and setting it up requires a mutuality or conditions of dominance that are not always easy or even possible to achieve. The most time-honored "substances" are alcohol and opiates, although they deliver many—millions—into the maw of those undesirable side effects mentioned above. In the six-ties the case was made, especially among the young, that pot was a superior substance: non-addictive, in most preparations not uncontrollably hallucinogenic, cheap, plentiful, and *with-out undesirable side effects.* Granted that the distinctive feature of pot as a drug is the user's inability to perceive clearly its most important effects, why weren't more users suspicious? Did they think, if they thought at all, that here at last was a mar-velous—even improving—euphoria-food, ingested or inhaled as brownie or smoke, metabolized as quanta of joy? If pot was such a substance, and since its cultivation and use among sev-eral subcultures has been documented since antiquity, why was it opposed? Anybody so opposed must be opposed to joy itself. Here again one is reminded of the way the generalized Establishment was painted during the sixties: pro-work, anti-play, pro-thing, anti-person; pro-machine, anti-nature. The Establishment created Viet Nam, strip mining, pollution, My-Lai. The youthful response created Haight-Ashbury, rural communes, organic farming, and a new spiritualism. So sim-ple and inadequate a dichotomy as I have just caricatured actually prevailed to a significant extent for about five years in this country. As of this writing, it is still possible to feel resonances from that period; soon the sixties will feel like history.

But pot was no euphoria-food, although, like alcohol, it is still used as if it were. Pot is an extract of varying potency made from dried parts of the female Indian hemp plant *(Cannabis sativa).* The potency of this extract is determined by the amount of hallucinogenic material in the plant itself and in the particular part of the plant processed; North African and Indian *cannabis* plants are most potent (hallucinogenic), and the pure resin of the plant is the most potent part. The kind of cannabis grown in North America is about a third to a tenth as potent as that grown in India and North Africa. The most potent preparations are called hashish and are as hallucinogenic as synthetic drugs such as LSD or psilocybin. Most American preparations are less potent and are called marijuana or pot or dope or weed or stuff or, my favorite, shit.

Unlike alcohol, which is water soluble and, after its relatively gross ravaging of cells, metabolizes out of the human system in a day (side effects very unambiguous), the active chemical in pot, delta-9 tetrahydrocannabinol (THC), is fat soluble and stores itself very efficiently in the fat sheaths lining the cells of our nervous system where it is not metabolized away for about a week. Consequently, a person who ingests even moderate amounts of pot—say, one joint—twice a week is *building* the level of stored THC in his nervous system.

Getting high or "getting off" on marijuana occurs when the THC is carried by the bloodstream to the brain and sufficiently interferes with various cell functions to produce an altered feeling state. The functions most immediately affected are various systems of suppression. Suppression is the process in which neural cells keep extraneous impulses and information at bay so the brain can attend to the practical business of keeping the organism operating. Suppression is a tricky concept, and it does not conform to the common sense conception of the brain as a mass of gray matter that *does* things. Actually much, if not most, brain activity is bound up in not doing things—metaphorically speaking, flicking switches off and keeping them off. When suppression systems are working properly in reasonably mature human beings, we are able to unscrew the cap of a toothpaste tube, apply the paste to the brush, and brush our teeth. When suppression is interfered with, the tube, the cap, the brush bristles may become over-poweringly interesting and complex in themselves; their textures, taste, and smells register simultaneously and are beheld with wonder or stupefaction. The latter response is common in infants up to twelve months old, but it is not at all a good sign in adolescents and adults—in fact it is the neurological opposite of "mind expansion": critical amounts of hard-earned discrimination are lost, and it is bad for the teeth. Similarly, our ability to suppress—disregard particular stimuli in order to see complexities, wholes, the point—is what makes us able to extend our taste in music from rhythmic banging to, perhaps, Mozart; in art from spangles of bright color to, perhaps, Monet. By now a decent enough interval of time has passed for us to call the emperor naked or at least a spade a spade the next time we hear a rhapsodic account from somebody old enough to know better who tells us that, pot-saturated, he "really heard" or for the first time "really understood" some rudimentary form of artistic expression. We must learn to say, "It wasn't the first time. You heard it that way when you were two." Losing our suppression does not make the world more wonderful; it makes us more stupid. But here a voice from the sixties says, "But two is better than thirty. Glorious polymorphously perverse infancy is all." One has to smoke a lot of pot to persist in such a belief.

Many of the other suppression-interference aspects of the marijuana high are well known: the satiety function of the hypothalamus is immobilized so that one is hungry, although one's stomach is full; the suppressers that stop laughter after an appropriate interval are out of commission, so that with insufficient stimulation, laugher goes on and on—medical science calls this reaction "fatuous hilarity." Sequencing ability is impaired, as are memory, time sense, and depth perception, all of which augur poorly for highway safety. Heart rate increases, the whole body is mildly anesthetized, and psychomotor skills are diminished.

Mood is altered in some interesting ways. Dr. Robert Gilkeson who is the consulting psychiatrist to the Cleveland Independent Schools and who has a specialty in neurology-psychology, has an interesting hypothesis about the rate of paranoia so commonly reported by disturbed and ordinary pot smokers. According to Dr. Gilkeson, the forebrain (top layer) anxieties are immobilized by THC, but the suppressers of midbrain (inner layer, archaic) fear are altered with them. Thus the high paranoid might be *feeling* a prehistoric sense of dread and danger but, due to cortical impairment, is unable to express it or otherwise defend himself against it; Dr. Gilkeson even suggests that an EEG test of such a person would fail to register this kind of fear. It is at least plausible that a maladjustment of the forebrain-midbrain relationship, which is in effect the relationship between our present selves and our evolutionary precursors, may help to explain the severe psychoses experienced by a minority of several-times-per-week pot smokers.

These severe mental disturbances are not, according to the popular verdict, supposed to happen, but they do. Landmark studies by Dr. Helen Kaplan at Metropolitan Hospital in New York, Drs. John Talbot and James Teague who worked with Viet Nam veterans, Harold Kolanski and William Moore who worked with Philadelphia adolescents—and others whose names, like Dr. Nahas', are not household words—confirm that severe psychotic reaction may follow heavy marijuana use and that such reactions occur in individuals who have had no previous history of mental disorder. In the past four years seven pot-dependent students of my acquaintance have committed themselves, or been committed, to the mental wards of Cleveland hospitals for detoxification and long-range psychotherapy. Reading Kolanski and Moore's touching case summaries in *The Journal of American Medicine* ("Effects of Marihuana on Adolescents and Young Adults"), I realized that the profiles of the seven I know were interchangeable with theirs. I recognized the same dramatic reversals in personal performance, the same enervation, the impulse to self-destruction (Kolanski and Moore report four suicide attempts in 38 patients studied; I report two out of seven). I observed the same grandiose delusions such as messiah obsession or the belief that one is able to exercise occult powers. I have seen the same continuing loss of intellectual capacity, and I have no reason to believe this loss, like the specific neurological damage confirmed by their abnormal EEGs and by their reported "flashbacks," is not permanent.

The experience of being high on marijuana tends to dissipate itself within a few hours, with or without an interval of sleep, and blend fairly smoothly into a normal state of mind. Because one experiences the drug this way, one tends naturally to consider the high to be the sum total of the drug's effect. But this view is mistaken. The THC has by no means completed its assignment and, again, won't do so for a week. During that time RNA and DNA synthesis are slowed, the system's hormonal instructions are altered, and immunity is down. A number of medical experts suggest that the acclaimed lack of hangover is actually a very gradually distributed hangover; instead of temporary nausea and a splitting head, the weekend pot smoker may feel edgy and irritable at school or work by mid-week. Heavier users may feel deeply and chronically depressed. Although such states of mind are by no means limited to pot smokers, they correspond strikingly to the reactions of my own pot-smoking counselees. The neural reaction that distorts one's sense of time—an almost universal experience among those high on pot—continues in less obvious ways days after the drug is ingested. When RNA is not synthesized in the brain, experience fails to become memory; in other words, learning does not happen. A tendency to insomnia and decreased dream activity are also characteristic of regular pot use. Dr. Gilkeson tells me that he likes to hear about the onset of vivid dreaming and nightmare from his drug-referral patients, because that is a sign they are cutting back on their dope.

Anyone who is in regular contact with older children and young adults needs no technical jargon or medical proof to recognize the post-high effects of chronic pot use. Although the specialist might put it that "cognitive gaps are filled by pauses or memorized phrases," almost anyone can recognize the fragmented, repetitive, "like"-plagued discourse of the "head" or "burn-out." Such souls have become a new youthful stereotype of whom George Carlin does a funny imitation. Many thousands of contemporary youth do the unfunny real thing. Being "spaced out" means the cell processes that manage speech and thought are impaired.

The experiments of Drs. Melges, Tinklenborg, Hollister, and Gillespie at Stanford have correlated the ingestion of THC with an inability to sequence operations serially and to relate a step in a sequence to the goal of that sequence. Those two mental processes—sequencing and relating parts to wholes—are essential for school success from the elementary grades onward; rather more importantly, they are essential to living an effective, comprehending life. The national Scholastic Aptitude Tests (SATs), which have declined consistently for the past eleven years, also measure these processes, and although one would certainly be vilified for suggesting that pot smoking is spoiling the nation's SAT scores, poorer explanations have been offered. Does anyone really believe that pot smoking has *no* effect on the academic development measured by tests? That pot has an *improving* effect?

The Electroencephalographs (brain wave recordings) of my former students who have been hospitalized for marijuana dependency are all abnormal. These tests measure the intensity of electrical activity in the brain under a number of different conditions: eyes closed and relaxed, eyes open and relaxed, answering simple questions, calculating, solving problems, etc. A normal EEG shows slow wave activity in relaxed states, faster wave activity in attending, problem-solving states. A normal subject who is relaxing and then asked to spell his name backwards will transmit slow waves while relaxing, faster waves while attending the problem and solving it. These faster (beta) waves are an electrical description of concentration, cognition, and execution. Beta activity is mobilized when one works out an equation, makes an executive decision, figures out how to change a tire. It is the diminished ability to put out beta waves that shows up abnormally in the pot-smoker's EEG. So in a true sense pot does serve to relieve anxiety (beta activity), but at a cost of reducing effectiveness. Seeing the use of pot this way helps to illuminate the connection between the personal, school, and vocational problems of young people and their decision to use pot.

Although users themselves are *unable* to see it this way, pot inhibits one's ability to feel stress—the stress of being challenged by school or work, the stress of measuring up to peer and adult expectations, the stress accompanying particular difficulties and losses. Because pot changes the user and not the stressful situation, the stressful situation is likely to remain stressful or to get worse, an occasion for more pot or, perhaps, for some stronger anesthesia. In this syndrome, I believe, lies the real seductiveness of pot. Users will say nonsense, or something more terse. They will say that the appeal of pot is the euphoric quality of the high and that they prefer this state to the boredom of their situations without it.

My own experience compels me to generalize that a need to dispel boredom has rarely—and something in me is straining to say "never"—driven a young person to regular marijuana use. In a number of respects, adolescence is awful, but it is not boring. If anything, it is too dramatic. In working with pot-dependent kids, it is an unusually dull psychologist or parent or friend who can't, after a ten minute interview, recognize the prominent features of Avoidance behind a child's mask of Boredom. Show me a maddeningly passive, bemused, couldn't-care-less pot-head, and I'll show you somebody avoiding something that scares him. This is not to say that there are no valid grounds for avoidance and fear, but it is to say that only when the objects of the fear are recognized for what they are and no longer veiled by pot and its cultural supports will the individual be able to come to terms with his problems and to continue his growth. The youth who feels anxious and lost and scared in a badly coordinated complex of relationships and responsibilities is showing *a healthy response* to that badness. If he uses his wits and reflexes, makes some errors, endures some trials, he will grow. If he anesthetizes himself instead, we lose him, and if we get him back at all, the best evidence suggests we get him back with diminished capacity.

It is no accident that a consideration of the social impact of marijuana has led to a consideration of the nature of adolescence. For even if marijuana had no effect of any kind on human cells and tissue, it would be necessary to argue that adolescents should steer clear of it. I can think of few experts who would disagree that alcohol is the worst drug in the country—worst for taking lives, causing misery, wasting potential—but many of these same experts allow that pot is worse for adolescents. If one accepts, as to an extent one must, that adolescence is a kind of temporary *malaise*, then one comes to see pot as a perniciously appropriate tonic. It has already been suggested that adolescence is dramatic; it is also, in a certain sense, violent. In adolescence, the bridge between the onset of puberty and adulthood, individuals experience the most profound physical upheaval they will have after infancy. Only the first years of life produce more rapid growth. In the turbulent course of adolescence every cell in the body is changed. The brain signals the pituitary gland to begin secreting hormones that will give boys and girls the physical apparatus and capacity of men and women. When these physical developments have abated, some time between the mid-teens and early twenties, males and females look more like adults than children and can, if pressed, reproduce their kind. This is all that can be said with confidence about the emergent adolescent.

From the inside the adolescent feels embattled. With the onset of sexual maturity, infantile waves of feeling about authority and about love objects are aroused anew. Erotic and aggressive feelings, powerful and half-understood, lead to uneasy relations with what may have recently been a congenial adult order. Being at the same time insistent and inappropriate, these new drives, whether expressed or contained, give occasion to frustration and moodiness. Even if he is spared the particular humiliation of awkwardness, acne, or alarming smells, the adolescent has no grounds for trusting himself physically.

The turmoil from within is matched almost simultaneously by unnerving challenges from without. Because they are big, adolescents are expected to act big, like adults. They are expected to be diligent about their schoolwork and other business for the sake of the future, although the present is practically unmanageable. Sexually, they are supposed, these days, to be "responsible," the explicit meaning of which must be divined from the utterly dishonest television and movie portrayals of enthusiastic, even prolific, teen-age lovemaking. Parents, following their primordial pattern, dread the sexuality of their children, are themselves aroused by it, and usually end up by ignoring or vaguely condemning it. And then, because this is the seventies, adolescents are given a media immersion into the *varieties* of sexual orientation, regardless of how securely their own are locked into place.

The adult order which adolescents are expected to join often greets them with less than open arms. There are ceaseless reminders of how few jobs are actually available in any field and of how long and arduous and chancey is the road to those few positions. This much established, adolescents are enjoined to work enthusiastically and hard for the future. Add to this picture the frequency, more than it is amusing to concede, of adult models—parents, teachers, employers—who are visibly stunted or inadequate or joyless in their roles, and there you have it: the adolescent's-eye view of The Future.

The natural adolescent escape route, of course, is into a world of pure peers, the world of what Erik Erikson calls "cliques and crowds." But even though a temporary refuge in exclusive peerhood is to a degree healing and maybe inevitable, peerhood isn't all roses and denim. It is in and around the cliques of adolescent peers that the put-down, especially among boys, becomes almost the standard medium of communication. And in spite of the intense conformity of adolescents in groups, someone is always irritatingly distinguishing himself athletically or academically, thereby threatening the delicate equilibria of lesser achievers. Someone, too, is always a step ahead sexually or has qualified for the Olympics or has read Proust. So even among fellow tribesmen, it's a jungle out there, although *a recognizable, appropriate jungle*. At a time when self-esteem is usually fragile, the challenges are intense, and the stakes are high. One can emerge a star or "O.K." or, just as easily, a nerd, a loser, a fag, a grind, a brown-nose, a spaz, a snob, a greaser, a prole.

All adolescents need to feel physically adequate, to feel a secure family base (although their expressed indifference to family is common), to share vigorous relationships, and to achieve visibly in some socially valued field of endeavor. If one or more of these crucial components of self-esteem is lacking in adolescence, the resulting anxiety is acute and defenses are thrown up quickly. Those with difficulty in algebra or in writing clearly begin to find school ridiculous, a drag. The frustrated or modestly endowed athlete begins to find gung-ho jocks laughable. Those isolated socially begin righteously to isolate themselves further, because "that activity/school/town is nothing but a bunch of cliques." These common defenses can quickly become full-blown syndromes of self-defeat as one proves the validity of his complaints about the world by taking care to remain an injured party. Parents and teachers and counselors often get manipulated into this syndrome by urging the injured adolescent to try out for the team, have some friends over, see the teacher for extra help—well intentioned advice which, if followed, would pit the adolescent face to face with the anxiety he has taken such pains to avoid.

The adolescent dilemma and defenses sketched above are to some extent the common and, at best, temporary experiences of everybody. But throw pot into the dilemma and the prospects dim for growing out of it. Pot diffuses the anxiety and initial depression that naturally follows inadequate performance and inadequate defenses. Pot smoking, in other words, becomes the defense. As such, it may even masquerade as a kind of achievement in itself. When this happens, the pot group takes its place alongside the jocks and the student politicians and the drama group.

So pot, in its dark way, seems almost to have been designed for adolescence. If adolescents were down-to-earth rational hedonists, the straight medical-pharmacological story on pot—say, in the schools—might be an effective deterrent to its use. But adolescence is a notoriously irrational time. And many of us who come out against drugs can only represent, given our ages and positions, that dubious Future mentioned above. Most kids inclined to use pot regularly are not interested in facts. And despite what a number of educators think, they're not much interested in adolescent psychology, either. Facts and psychologies that endanger defenses are effortlessly avoided, especially with the help of pot.

What to do?

This is what to do. We have an obligation to children we love and to something no less profound than the character of civilization to interfere with what is, after all, a relatively recent cultural trend and one which does a variety of harm and no good whatsoever. We know that it is futile to barge onto the scene like the cops, mad and frustrated. What we can do is to change the climate in which marijuana and other drugs are used. We do this by updating our drug information and learning the facts, especially the gross, unavoidable facts of what we *see* in our own children and students. We must also, without withdrawing our affection and support, confront adolescents with their own destructive defenses; and we must by all means stop reinforcing those defenses by becoming dramatically afraid or pious about the whole business. Adolescents love to play the leading role in such drama and welcome supporting players who wring their hands or who make condescending attempts to "rap" about "where it's at." We must keep in mind that few adolescents know anything about drugs beyond what it feels like to take them—sometimes not even this. If anyone seriously suggests that kids "learn" about drugs from "street knowledge," silence him. Street knowledge consists of how much drugs cost, their whereabouts, their nicknames, and what they may look like. Due to such knowledge, crude poisons are sold under catchy names like "angel dust" in every big city in the country. Deferring, as some civic groups continue to do, to pushers, users, and even ex-users for "the real story" is rather like deferring the question of the place of the automobile in America's future to a panel of used car salesmen.

Neither propounding good information nor identifying defenses will, of themselves, deter kids from using pot, but these measures will alter the climate of use in one important way: kids will see parents, teachers, and other authorities modeling a control of facts, respect for evidence, and a capacity for analysis—not a bad model to store away for post-adolescent consideration. The patterns of drug use among the young will be most effectively altered when practical, unambiguous *consequences* are established. A school policy stating that students will be dismissed who attend under the influence of drugs or who exchange drugs on the premises will dramatically alter the drug climate; the use and exchange of drugs will decrease. Dismissing a student whose behavior adversely and seriously affects the whole school is, in my experience, usually a bad thing for the offending student, but, if communicated properly to the community, a good thing for the school. If a school adopts an unambiguous policy such as the one stated above, a student considering using drugs at school has an opportunity to make a meaningful choice. And if the student making that choice has been made to feel valuable himself and has had explained to him the reasons supporting the policy, he may even perceive that the school has done something rare: it has, out of concern for him, taken a stand.

At home the procedure is even more basic. In the scores of drug-related disciplinary and counseling sessions to which I have been a party over the past five years, not *once* has the family of the culprit or client had a previously stated policy about the use of drugs—not even the relatively crude, "If I catch you using ———, I'll. . ." Drug use, like sex, is a subject apparently too feeling-charged for some families to talk about comfortably, but the costs of not doing so are high. The family is a far more powerful factor than the school in an adolescent's decision-making; the relationships are more intense, and accountability is more direct. Most kids who do not use drugs that are readily available do not do so because of the climate of consequences established at home. Parents too timid or too preoccupied to sit down with their children for the purposes of discussing drugs and establishing rules governing their use are creating a climate in which experimentation and then regular use are likely.

Of legal consequences, not much of interest can be said. The enforcement strategy of existing marijuana laws has for the past decade been directed at suppliers rather than users. This emphasis, in its logic if not its specific intention, reveals a concern about a burgeoning commercial activity outside the state's taxing structure, but not much concern about the effect of the drug on users. In fairness to state and local governments, the best public information about drugs has not until recently been very good, and the practical obstacles to prosecuting possession are many and great. Some states have attached drug education programs to first-time possession convictions, but however well-intentioned, such programs do not have the controls to alter behavior, nor do they, as a kind of consequence, alter the climate in which drugs are used. The movement on behalf of states to decriminalize possession may ease the embarrassment of enforcement officers who have to watch helplessly as existing laws are violated massively in public places, but no other good can come from that movement. As a symbol, decriminalization brightens the green light for experimentation and casual marijuana use; the decision to use pot becomes less dramatic, and the conviction that pot is harmless gets public support. As a strategy of prevention, decriminalization is self-defeating; increasing numbers of criminal suppliers will arise to meet the demands of the new markets opened up by decriminalized possession. It is, I think, safe to say that tinkering with marijuana laws will influence the nation's drug problems about as positively as revised divorce laws have influenced marital problems.

Marijuana isn't going away. Channels of supply are well established. For the purpose, I think, of providing us suspense, a general reader publication like the *New York Times Magazine* will publish a step-by-step account of how a big deal is completed between Mexican growers and a Colorado distributor. The proprietors of with-it stores like to display prominently packets of papers used for rolling joints; sometimes a whole establishment, or "toke shop," will be given over to pipes, toking scissors, and other drug apparatus—complete with maybe not-so-young "different-life-style" proprietors who enjoy confronting the maybe not-so-frequent raised eyebrow.

Although it is youth-specific in its most serious effects, although it effaces memory and the ability to attend, although it produces irreversible cell damage and learning deficits, although it halts motivation and the ability to comprehend complexity, pot has made our scene. We will in all likelihood read tomorrow that "The verdict is still out on pot." We will find it for sale.

We will, it is said, buy anything.

9

Legalizing the Intolerable

Laws that restrict the use and supply of psychoactive drugs have been devised for the same reason that laws have been made to prevent the discharge of toxic chemicals into public waterways or to keep known poisons out of food. There would be little public debate about keeping substances like marijuana, heroin, crack, and powder cocaine out of the public pantry if these substances, in addition to their several toxic effects, did not also deliver sensual pleasure.

Because various chemical preparations—whether stimulants, depressants, or hallucinogens—have the capacity to elicit powerfully reinforcing (for many, irresistible) pleasures, users are driven to repeat the drug-taking experience. Among adults, mental acuity, human relationships, commitments, job performance, and general health decline as drug use becomes chronic; among children, drug use retards or eclipses critical maturation and learning altogether.

The biological and medical impact of drugs on healthy functioning has never been more clearly understood. If substances that do *not* pack a pleasurable payoff were known to wreak the kinds of health and social havoc that psychoactive drugs have done over the past 30 years, we would arise as one to banish the culprits. At massive public expense, we have removed asbestos from school ceilings, boiler rooms, and plumbing closets, because we believe it to be toxic. Asbestos has not impaired even 1% as many people as have lost their learning, their health, and even their lives due to the availability of illicit psychoactive drugs.

Again, the confusing issue is pleasure. Because pleasure-inducing drugs create a deep and powerful desire in users to have more, drug use appears, at first, to be a choice. Choices and preferences are the birthright of a free person, of an educated citizen. And so, one specious line of argument goes, drug use should be protected as an expression of individual liberty.

But as drug abuse professionals, drug-dependent people, and their families know, drug use ultimately effaces the capacity to choose; freedom of choice, along with health and performance, may be lost altogether. There is no constitutional right protecting drug use or any other form of self-destruction.

Physicians, drug-abuse counselors, school teachers, guidance staff, and the families of drug users—people who work closely with drug-impaired individuals—tend to oppose the legalization of drugs. Those favoring legalization are more likely to view the problem abstractly and statistically. Moreover, they are likely to come from university campuses—typically from academic departments, rather than from campus health facilities that work with drug users face to face.

Politically, legalization appeals to those who see it as a "non-judgmental" and "non-confrontational" solution to a massive and staggeringly complex social problem. It is comforting to maintain that drugs, drug use, and drug commerce are not the real problem; that, instead, an antiquated, perhaps puritanical "system" (designed by a benighted opposition party) is the problem. Make drugs legally available, allow the government to control and inspect them, and the nation will save and make billions of dollars, jails will be cleared of socially harmless persons, the mob will be outflanked, and the mayors of the nation's great cities can get back to business without crippling harassment from the press.

Why is this view so comforting? If the "system" is at fault, then no wrenching interventions need be undertaken, no political enemies made, no costly and dangerous law enforcement measures risked. If the system has been the culprit, then there has been no real crisis of values or commitment or courage in schools or workplaces or legislatures over the latter decades of this century. The error has been merely strategic.

But this kind of thinking will not stand up to the evidence. The performance of American schools has sunk to crisis levels in the very years in which illicit drug use became epidemic. It is important to remember that harsh drug laws did not cause the youthful drug epidemic of the 1960s and 1970s.

As the distinguished epidemiologist Nils Bejerot has made clear, the American and European drug epidemic of the 1960s was generated in the same way every other drug epidemic has been generated: social norms were challenged and altered by a sufficiently large norm-breaking population. In the case of the U.S., that population was the World War II baby boom as it reached college age, with the attendant freedom and mobility provided by campus life. When antidrug norms were successfully challenged—first by college students, then by adolescents generally—and when the norm-breaking was supported by popular culture, particularly its films and music (I'll "get high with a little help from my friends"), conditions were met for an exponential increase in formerly marginalized behavior: an epidemic.[1]

The peak years of illicit drug use on the part of students were *preceded* by a softening of drug laws in some states and municipalities. Typically, that change might have been the "decriminalization" of possession of small amounts of marijuana.

But by the mid-1970s—as the epidemic was approaching its 1979 peak—forces concerned about the effects of drug abuse began to find their voice. A national parents' movement was started at the grassroots level and was loosely coordinated by the now international Parents Resource Institute of Drug Education (PRIDE) in Atlanta. Drug-abuse professionals, public and private educators, and pediatricians also began to close ranks in opposition to drug experimentation and use. As a result, many states rescinded their "decriminalization" measures and stiffened drug penalties. A drug-free schools movement was initiated and still persists, and drug-abuse prevention efforts have been stepped up in the armed services. There have also been continuing efforts in the private sector to promote drug-free workplaces, and such media gesture as Partnerships for a Drug-Free America have sought to rebuild a consensus that drug use is harmful and wrong.

In sum, the past 30 years have seen a weakening of the norms prohibiting drug use, then an epidemic of illicit drug use, followed by a growing attempt to restore antidrug norms. At present, there is reason for guarded optimism that the antidrug measures are producing an effect. The use of marijuana and powder cocaine is down significantly from a decade ago (although levels of use are still unacceptably high).

From an epidemiologic standpoint, the news is even better: students are more than twice as likely as they were 10 years ago to believe that smoking marijuana poses a serious threat to their well-being.

As Jean Piaget, Lawrence Kohlberg, and their contemporary disciples have taught us, nearly all preadolescent children—and many people throughout their lives—hold the law as their highest moral standard. Even for those "higher stage" intellects who think about the principles of justice that laws are designed to promote, the law stands as a lofty, politically critical standard for personal decision making.

For children whose conceptual capacity does not yet enable them to entertain abstract principles of justice, the law is the ultimate guide to what is right and true and fair. The universal values we share—truth telling, keeping commitments, not injuring others without cause—are supported by laws. When liars, perjurers, cheats, vandals, and killers are legally punished for violating those values, children learn a concrete, yet profound, lesson concerning right and wrong.

It was Aristotle's view—and it is a durable one—that we should habituate children to right action, so that when they are mentally able to understand why, say, honesty is the best policy, they will be in effect conforming a socially necessary, already accepted fact; they will realize in a new way what they already know. Laws help us and our children to become habituated to right action.

When laws are openly ignored, when lawmakers themselves

break laws, or when laws permit repellent and harmful behavior, children are confused. They lose confidence not merely in the value of law, but in the value of any social standards.

Chemicals that retard, distort, or destroy healthy maturation and learning are harmful to children. Laws against using and trading such chemicals are consonant with the values we encourage children to embrace. Laws allowing even regulated use of these harmful substances undermine those values.

The legally available substances most comparable to illicit drugs are alcohol and tobacco. Each of them annually claims more lives and generates more pathology than all the currently illicit drugs combined. Moreover, unlike the illicit drugs of choice, tobacco has negligible psychoactive effects, and alcohol is typically consumed in such a way that users can monitor its intoxicating effects. Moreover, alcohol and tobacco, the drugs first and most frequently used by children, are legally available to adults. Adding more toxic and more dramatically psychoactive drugs to the legal marketplace will inevitably increase the use of those substances by children.

Legalizing and thus socially validating the use of psychoactive drugs would in effect "renorm" them in a more comprehensive way than the youthful counter-culture managed to do in the 1960s and 1970s. History reveals that legalization of drugs accelerates new use and contributes to a larger population of chronic users—never the reverse. In Great Britain, where laws were changed to enable heroin addicts to receive the narcotics they required on a prescription basis, the number of users doubled every 16 months between 1959 and 1968.[2]

By contrast, when states energetically enforce antidrug laws and policies, illegal drug use is reduced and eliminated. Internationally, tough laws and tough enforcement have been the *only* effective measures against drug abuse. Through such measures the Chinese government eradicated its centuries-old opium traffic in just two years, from 1951 to 1953. Cocaine use was similarly curtailed in Western Europe in the early Thirties, and the Japanese successfully reversed an epidemic dependence on amphetamines between 1954 and 1958.[3]

Advocates of legalization like to compare antidrug laws to the 13-year period of Prohibition. Yet looked at closely, the analogy with Prohibition actually undermines legalization arguments. Frequently portrayed as a triumph of Puritanism and conservatism, Prohibition was actually a progressive, strongly feminist movement. Women, politically disenfranchised and unable to establish credit or to gain access to many lines of employment, suffered most from fathers' and husbands' alcohol-related brutality and domestic irresponsibility. Sentiment in favor of Prohibition grew steadily from 1846, when Maine voted itself dry, to 1919, when the 18th Amendment and the Volstead Act were passed.

Without question, Prohibition failed. Enforcement provisions were hopelessly meager, and alcohol continued to be marketed and consumed illegally—especially by middle-income and wealthy people. However, overall alcohol consumption did dip considerably between 1920 and 1933, and the incidence of alcohol-related illnesses, such as cirrhosis of the liver, declined dramatically.

If one accepts that Prohibition was not the answer to the nation's alcohol problems, one must also accept that repealing Prohibition has proved to be an even worse answer. Today, an estimated seven adults in 10 use alcohol. Of approximately 110 million American drinkers, about 10 million are estimated to be problem drinkers. Alcohol-related accidents are the number-one cause of violent death in the U.S. Drunk drivers are responsible for half of all highway deaths; every year 25,000 Americans die as a result of drunk driving, more than half as many as were killed in the entire Vietnam War. High percentages of sex offenses and other violent crimes are committed under the influence of alcohol, as well.

Once again, alcohol is a legally vended, proof-controlled, tightly regulated "minor depressant." Yet there are those who wish to make the likes of high potency cannabis, LSD, and powder and crack cocaine as accessible as alcohol.

If you tell my physician friends in Cleveland who volunteer

to treat the growing legions of crack-impaired babies that drug abuse is a victimless crime, you are likely to get punched in the eye.

Legalize drugs, and certain busts and scandals may disappear from the newspapers. But the drug problem will not go away; it will persist and grow. Drugs impair the healthy functioning of users. *That* is the real drug problem. That is why there is no historical instance of an enduring society in which any of the substances currently controlled has been legally available for long.

We have never known more clearly what drugs do to those who use them. Caring people tend to act, to intervene. Those who confront drug use and attempt to curtail it are met with anger, fear, and cynicism by those who are so deeply enmeshed in the drug culture that they cannot imagine an alternative. Working to rid one's family or school or community of drugs will invariably lead to vilification, frustration, and periodic defeats. Confronting the consequences of drug abuse always produces bad news and bad feelings, at least in the short run.

Like antidrug activists, drug laws remind us of a standard that is not being met. Getting rid of the standard is like shooting the messenger who bears disturbing news.

It is past time for all of us—school-people foremost—to declare our values with respect to drug use and its related social consequences. The fact of the matter is that the availability and use of drugs are incompatible with healthy child development and with learning.

Moreover, we have reached a moment in history when exercises such as this one—airing the pros and cons of legalization in a "debate" format—may actually contribute to the problem. Whatever the strength of the contestants' arguments, the message of the subtext is stronger: "experts" disagree. But experts—at least advocates for children—don't disagree.

There is a point at which the editors of the magazine, *Kappan* must decide where they stand on the availability of drugs to children. When I pointed this out to the editor who commissioned this piece, I was told, "We have always trusted our readers to come to their own conclusions."

But is this magazine really as value-neutral as that? Will there be a debate on the pros and cons of using children for the sexual gratification of adults? Will pro-Semites soon square off against anti-Semites in the pages of the *Kappan*?

I doubt it. I believe that the editors have resolved these last two issues to their ethical satisfaction; yet drugs hurt children as surely and as intolerably as sexual abuse and ethnic and religious discrimination do.

Legalizing drugs is the shallowest and weakest of responses to the nation's drug problem. It is an attempt to redefine the problem, so as to feel less bad about the data. But the data of failed lives and failed learning should make us feel bad. Legal failures are still failures.

I don't think we need to debate this topic anymore.

[1] *Lloyd D. Johnston, Patrick M. O'Malley, and Jerald G. Bachman,* Drug Use, Drinking, and Smoking: National Survey Results from High School, College, and Young Adults Populations, 1975-1988 *(Rockville, Md.: National Institute on Drug Abuse, 1989).*

[2] *T. Bewley, O. Ben-Arie, and I. P. James, "Morbidity and Mortality from Heroin's Dependence," British Medical Journal, 1981, p. 725.*

[3] *Nils Bejerot,* Addiction and Society *(Springfield, Ill.: Charles C Thomas, 1970).*

10

The Bumpy Road to Drug-Free Schools

At an appropriate distance, the President's stated intention to create drug-free schools "by the year 2000" appears to be impeccable. Supported and articulated by a new Cabinet-level officer, former U.S. Secretary of Education William Bennett, the antidrug commitment even seems to be bearing some fruit.

According to the best and most long-standing survey of drug use among the nation's high school students, conducted by Lloyd Johnston, Patrick O'Malley, and Jerald Bachman,[1] the level of drug use in general continues to decline. Moreover, the 1989 figures show that the use of certain substances—marijuana and powder cocaine, in particular—is down significantly.

These encouraging findings require some qualification, however. The national high school survey does not include the 15% to 20% of high schoolers who drop out, a population especially "at risk" for drug abuse. And while the survey breaks down patterns of drug use by region, it is not structured to provide information to answer the questions school officials would most like answered: Do a school's concerted efforts to create a drug-free environment produce measurable, visible results? Or do vaguer out-of-school factors shape the drug scene?

However encouraging we may find the documented decline in certain forms of youthful drug use, there is clearly no cause for excessive optimism. The new, lower levels of use are still destructively high. Forty-four percent of last year's high school seniors reported having tried marijuana; 15 years ago, the reported percentage was about the same, 47%. In 1975, 9% of the seniors surveyed reported having at least tried cocaine;

last year's figure was over 10%. Last year, about three out of a hundred seniors reported having used cocaine during the previous month; about 17 out of a hundred reported having used marijuana. Distributed evenly throughout a school, these figures suggest that five or six students in each classroom might be drug impaired; the same might be said of two starters on the varsity football team, several members of the cast and crew of the school musical, and so on. Toss into the mix the fact that one in three students reports having been drunk (five or more drinks in a row) over the past two weeks, and you are not even within screaming distance of a drug-free school.

The public, including the nation's students, has grown inured to the idea of "the drug problem." There is the wearying impression that we have heard all the cautionary lessons . before. For the current generation of children, there has "always been" a drug problem. But the fact of the matter is that there *hasn't* always been a drug problem, at least not in American schools.

Drug-addled children and drug-riddled schools are a phenomenon of the late 20th century. Prior to 1964, drug use by school-age children was negligible to nonexistent in the literature of pediatric medicine, public health, law enforcement, and education policy. Within a decade, youthful drug use was epidemic, possibly the most distinctive feature of the rise of the counterculture.

Profound spiritual and political explanations have been advanced to account for the growth of the youth culture of the Sixties and Seventies, but perhaps the most persuasive explanation has to do with the sheer number of postwar baby boomers who entered adolescence between 1965 and 1974. Whole complexes of social life—suburbs and malls—were erected to house them and provide for their needs. New, streamlined schools were constructed; later, mega-universities were expanded to accommodate enrollments by an influx of baby boomers. For several consecutive years there were more Americans under than over 25 years of age.

This mass of youth grew up in conditions of unprecedented affluence and mobility. Expressed on such a scale, the ordinary tension between adolescents and the adult order felt ominous and system-threatening. Hair grew long, conventions of dress changed dramatically, new looks and new voices dominated the popular culture. This new youth-driven culture said yes to spontaneity, impulsiveness, and sensuality; it said no to discipline, tradition, and moderation. The media, captivated by so much novelty, tended to impute certain ephemeral countercultural attitudes—for example, "Make Love Not War"—to the young generally. But only in the media did the youth of America grow ideologically radical. In 1968, the first year in which 18-year-olds were able to vote in a Presidential election, they cast their votes predominantly for the Republican candidate, Richard Nixon. In fact, they supported him more strongly than their parents did.

By the late Seventies, the counterculture generation began to abandon the outward trappings of adolescence and became more conventional, more conservative, and the critics claimed, more self-centered. This change might be called the birth of the "me generation." But while long hair, bell-bottomed trousers, and ideological slogans were quickly abandoned, the production, distribution, and use of psychoactive drugs was left firmly and massively in place, especially among schoolage children.

Because drugs act on and alter the nervous system, they cannot be discarded along with Nehru jackets and love beads. Drug use is not merely a matter of attitude or style. Only when children make a "threshold" choice to try a drug can they be said to deliberate objectively. Once the drug has interacted with the nervous system—including perhaps an overwhelming neurochemical discharge of pleasurable sensations—the drug's effect becomes part of all subsequent deliberations. When a person proceeds from casual use to dependency, the drug becomes the primary determinant of decision making. The young people of the counterculture tended to abandon many of their one-time preferences, but the use of illegal drugs persisted.

Illicit drug use among children reached peak levels between 1978 and 1980. In 1978 and 1979, for example, more than one high school senior in 10 reported using marijuana *daily*. By this time, the public manifestation of the problem could no longer be ignored. Research scientists and physicians began to make an unambiguous case against the use of psychoactive drugs, especially marijuana, which had previously been represented by advocates as a relatively mild intoxicant.

The public momentum away from "recreational" drug use and away from drug use of any kind by children began in the mid-Seventies with a passionate but loosely organized collection of grassroots gestures. Research scientists, such as anesthesiologist Gabriel Nahas and pharmacologist Carlton Turner, were invited to an informal annual conference in Atlanta to explore approaches to stemming the burgeoning epidemic of drug use. These early Parents Resources In Drug Education (PRIDE) conferences were conceived and chartered by a Georgia State University physical education professor, Thomas Gleaton, and an Atlanta parent and doctoral candidate in English literature, Marsha Manatt Schuchard. By the late Seventies the PRIDE organization was drawing in national authorities on the prevention of drug abuse.

PRIDE also captured the attention of the White House drug advisors, the U.S. Congress, the armed services—and especially of schools and their parent/teacher associations. By the early Eighties the PRIDE organization had become international in scope, and its annual conference came to include the U.S. attorney general, First Lady Nancy Reagan, and celebrities and entertainers opposed to drug use.

Only a few Americans are likely to know or care much about the origins of the PRIDE organization, but it is worth noting that PRIDE began as an expression of educational and parental concern about drug-related losses among schoolchildren. Its earliest support came from an eclectic group of scientists and intellectuals, men and women who shared no particular political agenda. A movement later labeled as "conservative" and "right wing" by pro-drug lobbyists and by *Playboy* was in fact launched by independent progressives during the Carter Administration. It is this movement to which Nancy Reagan and the slogan "Just Say No" became affixed in the Eighties. The first lady discovered and embraced the antidrug crusade; she did not by any means create it.

The effects of pleasure-inducing toxic chemicals—i.e., drugs—on the human nervous system and the ensuing effects on behavior are so complex that its hard to describe them simply and clearly. Cannabis alone is composed of hundreds of biological substances. The nervous system is composed of billions of neurons and even more neural connections. So much complexity and subtlety does not lend itself readily to bumpersticker epigrams. However, all things considered, "Just Say No" isn't a bad start.

In an open society, firm policy and behavior-directing norms follow from a strong social consensus. For example, there is now a strong social consensus that people who behave in odd ways should not be labeled as witches, and, even if that label is applied, those so designated should not be burned. This consensus was a long time coming. While it might be demonstrated that recent progress has been made in restoring a social consensus that drug use is harmful to healthy human functioning, a number of obstacles are slowing the momentum.

That specialized knowledge is required to understand drug-related pathologies and losses has already been noted. However, misunderstanding also results from the inherent inability of even very intelligent nonaddicts to understand the phenomenon of addiction or drug dependency. Nonaddicts *feel* in control of their choices and decisions. They *know* they could pass up an opportunity to use an intoxicating substance. Nonaddicts project this assumed control onto others, including addicts. They are likely to ask, How *could* a person drink or smoke crack cocaine on the job? The nonaddict has no experience of losing control of decision making. The addict asks the opposite question: How could a person pass up an opportunity for intoxication?

Nonaddicts frequently respond to drug-related issues in one of two equally problematic ways. "Conservatives" may want to blame or punish the addict for making destructive choices, an approach that is ultimately futile because, with respect to drugs, an addict has no choice. "Liberals" are inclined to believe that informed choices can be made about drugs and that only destructive behavior, not mere drug use, should be proscribed. Liberals do not understand the causal, frequently one-way relationship between drug use, loss of decision making, and destructive behavior. Confronted with actual addicts or with data documenting destructive behavior, many liberals tend to blame a repressive system that reduces people to such miserable circumstances that drugs are a freely chosen, though destructive, alternative to those circumstances.

Drug use is reinforced by a more powerful (and more toxic) neurological "reward" than that derived from other forms of delinquency, such as vandalism or shoplifting. Drug use is thus built more deeply and permanently into behavior. Addicts know this; nonaddicts usually do not. Still, most people are not addicts, and it is this majority that establishes the norms regulating the use of drugs.

A related misunderstanding adds further confusion to drug-related decision making: a rhetorical emphasis on the civil rights and civil liberties of drug takers and would-be drug takers. There is no constitutional or other traditional right safeguarding the production, distribution, or use of drugs. Intoxicants have been openly regulated—and, in many instances, prohibited—throughout the history of civilization. New knowledge about some intoxicants—e.g., cocaine—has altered policy and attitudes, just as knowledge about alleged witches has altered policy and attitudes. But taking drugs has not historically been included among the protected human prerogatives: to speak freely, to worship as one chooses, to assemble, and to participate in public decision making.

Theorists from Plato to Lawrence Kohlberg have suggested

that the law—that is, what is deemed lawful—is for most children and many adults the highest ethical criterion. Schoolchildren tend to back up decisions and arguments with references to what rules and laws say. Children are troubled and confused by perceived ambivalence about what is right and lawful: laws that are not enforced, laws violated by those assigned to uphold them, "expert" disagreement over the validity of laws.

Confusion and, ultimately, bad decisions result when children see signs outside a concert hall stating "no alcoholic beverages allowed" but then enter to find open drinking and drug taking. Youthful commitments to abstain from alcohol and drugs are undermined when a Supreme Court nominee or the mayor of the nation's capital admits to drug use.

Arguments to legalize drugs run powerfully against the consensus that drugs are destructive to individuals and to society. The law has mandated that asbestos is to be removed speedily and at massive public and private expense because it is toxic. Drugs cause exponentially more deaths, pathology, and loss of productivity than asbestos does, yet prominent and "expert" voices periodically argue for their legalization. This is confusing.

Apart from undermining the conviction that drugs are bad for people, the notion of legalizing drugs is fraught with difficulties and contradictions. The appeal of legalization seems to lie in a strange conjunction of hedonism, frustration, and a brittle adherence to market economics. Proponents of legalization assure that, once drugs are legally available, drug-related crime will, by definition, be reduced or disappear. But in reality this is wildly unlikely, unless the government wants to vend and tax heroin, crack cocaine, "ice" (methamphetamine), LSD, and PCP along with Marlboros and Jack Daniels. Few legalization advocates want to see *all* drugs licensed and offered for sale. But unless that is what happens, the really potent stuff, the deadly stuff, will be produced and sold illegally.

Nationalizing and legitimizing an addictive vice may or may

not alter courtroom traffic and prison occupancy, but it will certainly not alter the effects of toxic chemicals on the health and conduct of human beings. *That* is the real drug problem, not the legal status of suppliers and users. Advocates of legalization are remarkably silent about projected consequences.

What does history teach us? Alcohol and tobacco are regulated by the state and are legally available. Of the two, only alcohol is psychoactive enough to be meaningfully analogous to the current illicit drugs. Together or separately alcohol and tobacco cause a thousandfold more deaths and illnesses annually than all of the illicit drugs combined. Once more, alcohol and tobacco are less psychoactive than illicit drugs, they are legally regulated, and their use is embedded in long-standing social conventions. *Still* they are the greatest killers and debilitators. Should other, more potent toxins be added to the legal pantry? Historical experience suggests that legalization is a deadly idea.

Historical perspective is not emphasized much in drug policy deliberations. To the extent that the historical record is scanned at all, it tends to be scanned badly. The impact of drug saturation on highly developed cultures—cannabis on Moslem culture in the medieval centuries, opium on Chinese culture in the 19th century—has been all but ignored. The "lesson" of Prohibition has been read as the failure of a repressive, puritanical assault on a sturdy American convention, resulting in 14 years of booming organized crime.

In fact, Prohibition was the culmination of a populist, progressive reform movement that had been building in individual states for decades. It was a close cousin of the reforms that led to cleaning up the meat industry and to countless public health measures. Prohibition reflected the sentiments of a majority of the nation's women who, without votes, commercial credit, or access to professional credentials, felt that they had suffered too long, both physically and financially, at the hands of drunken men.

Whatever its obvious failures in design and execution, Prohibition did not exacerbate the nation's *drinking* problem, the problem it addressed. The consumption of alcohol and the incidence of alcohol-related disease declined markedly during Prohibition. Those problems have mounted steadily since its repeal. If the lesson of Prohibition is that it "didn't solve the problem," the lesson of repeal is that it "made the problem worse."

The current dissonance about the status of the nation's "drug problem" is an obstacle to building a consensus that children develop best in a drug-free climate, which includes drug-free schools. Drug advocates and opponents alike too often cast aside logic, evidence, and historical perspective in their zeal to carry a point.

Recently, a number of large-circulation newspapers reprinted a feature article from the *St. Petersburg Times* that took the Partnership for a Drug-Free America to task for conveying conjecture as fact. The article criticized many of the group's nationally televised antidrug ads. It quoted a physician (therefore, an "expert") to the effect that such ads represent "chemical McCarthyism." The article then moved on to discredit one of the Partnership's statistical claims: that the average age of first-time drug experimenters is 11 1/2. The statistic was revealed to be ill-founded and, in the Partnership director's own word, "soft." The valid figure seemed to be age 13.

The overall effect of the article was to cast the Partnership for a Drug-Free America in a dubious light. But the fact is that worrisome numbers of children enrolled in junior high schools—whether sixth-graders or eighth-graders—are experimenting with drugs. *That* is the problem. Comparing champions of drug-free youth to Senator [Joseph] McCarthy does not contribute to a solution. The *St. Petersburg Times* writer offered no solution, but he did contribute to the dissonance.

Because intoxicating chemicals impair the healthy functioning of the nervous system and because the nervous system is the organ of learning, growing children should be drug free. Maturing nervous systems are more critically impaired by intoxicants than mature ones are; childhood losses in learning are lifelong and profound. Moreover, children grow chemically dependent more quickly than adults, and their record of recovery is depressingly poor.

Diagnosing and treating drug-impaired children is a necessary therapeutic gesture, but it is a woefully insufficient approach to the youthful drug problem. As Nahas told his PRIDE conferees and any others who would listen, "medicalization" is not the solution. Unless the climate for experimenting with and using drugs is changed, medical treatment will become an appendage and support of the drug culture. A booming proliferation of drug-abuse professionals and new treatment centers is not, in the long run, good news.

If the solution to the drug problem is not medicalization, or at least not medicalization by itself, what is? The answer is to renorm society's response to illicit drug use. Here Johnston, O'Malley, and Bachman's findings offer some encouragement. Their surveys have found that growing numbers of high school students perceive that it is harmful to try or to use illicit drugs. For example, in 1975 about 18% of the students polled believed that occasional marijuana smoking posed a "great risk"; in 1989 more than twice as many perceived occasional marijuana use as a great risk. Also in 1989, 78% felt that smoking pot regularly is a great risk, and a similarly large majority (71%) perceived the occasional use of cocaine as a great risk. In 18 different drug categories, high school students have reported increasing concern annually about the harmfulness of experimentation and use.

Practically, the evidence suggests that both society at large and individual schools would do well to adopt a "systemic" approach to the prevention of drug abuse. In other words, the supply, distribution, and use of drugs should *all* be confronted. Educational programs, public health bulletins, and drug treatment should *all* be undertaken. The recent decline in youthful drug use seems attributable to a decline in demand—which, in turn, can be attributed principally to the effectiveness of cautionary educational programs and to a firmer, though still dissonant, social consensus that drugs are harmful. There have been fewer successes to report on the "supply" side, as whole nations are brutally terrorized by powerful drug traffickers. Synthetic "designer drugs," such as "ecstasy" (MDMA) or "ice" (methamphetamine), have also slipped into the marketplace over the past few years, though their use has not yet become epidemic among school-age children.

What the law says and does about drug trafficking and use will have a significant impact on the young. In addition to reducing the available supply of dangerous substances, antidrug laws and policy will resonate agreeably with early childhood cautions to avoid danger, to promote health, and to obey community rules.

Plato and Aristotle stressed that children must become practiced in life-enhancing, community-regarding behavior before they are educated to understand intellectually the value of such actions. This developmental necessity is too easily forgotten. Good habits precede understanding. Children must be enjoined to tell the truth before they understand the moral grounds for doing so. Without the initial habit, later intellectual understanding will be mere sophistry.

Schools must be prescriptive *and* descriptive about the "drug problem." But they must be prescriptive first. Superintendents, principals, and teachers must be in accord. Policy and practice must be in accord. They must be in accord that drug-involved children are destructive to themselves, potentially destructive to other children, and destructive of school business generally.

A clear consensus, firm policy, and decisive action will move the nation rapidly toward the goal of drug-free schools. Doing so requires little specialized knowledge and, really, no money at all. Primary emphasis should be placed on *threshold decisions*: decisions to try a dangerous substance for the first time. This means clear messages in elementary and middle school classrooms. Tobacco and alcohol have traditionally been the "gateway" drugs for children; they are followed by marijuana, inhalants, and household medicines—then, the rest.

Schools are ideally structured to prescribe and to describe

important health measures, and schoolchildren are invariably responsive, provided the matter at hand is real and tangible, not abstract and remote. Schools can no longer be said to lack the resources to confront youthful drug use. However, some of them do lack the will.

Drug-free schools are possible by the year 2000. Many schools are substantially drug free today. A systemic approach to the prevention of drug abuse, however, will require clear and forceful measures in other arenas as well: in the workplace, on the highways, in public spaces (parks, concert halls, sports stadiums), and in households. Progress in these arenas, too, will require a strong social consensus.

How badly do Americans want drug-free schools? How do they feel about the schools they have? If Johnston, O'Malley, and Bachman's findings for seniors apply to the American high school population at large, then the typical high school of a thousand students now enrolls 437 who will smoke pot, 103 who will try cocaine, 83 who will try LSD, and 13 who will use heroin. One hundred sixty-seven will have smoked pot recently, and 28 will have used cocaine recently. By the time they are seniors, more than 90% of the student body will have tried alcohol, 66% will drink with some regularity, and one in three will be frequently drunk. Two hundred eighty-six students will smoke cigarettes, and 189 of them will smoke daily.

The drug-saturated years have been a worrisome, dismal period in the history of American schooling. What do we need to produce drug-free schools? What do we need to produce good schools? We need only the national will to do so. Do we have that will? The public must decide.

1 *"Monitoring the Future" is a 15-year, running survey, by Lloyd D. Johnston, Patrick M. O'Malley, and Jerald G. Bachman, of approximately 17,000 high school seniors (and more recently college students and other young adults) from public and private schools in every region of the country. The study's findings are drawn from self-reporting questionnaires administered in the schools by the research team. The research has been carried out under the auspices of the*

University of Michigan Institute for Social Research, supported by a series of grants from the National Institute on Drug Abuse (NIDA). A report by Johnston, O'Malley, and Bachman, titled Drug Use, Drinking, and Smoking: National Survey Results from High School, College, and Young Adults Populations, 1975-1988 *(Rockville, Md.: NIDA, 1989), is available from NIDA, 5600 Fishers Lane, Rockville, MD 20857.*

PART TWO

LOOKING AFTER THE CHILDREN

Looking After The Children

It is almost impossible to work among developing children and not, at least at moments, be hopeful. With children, however difficult they or their circumstances may seem, so much is still possible. Any teacher knows this who has guided a child from non-reading to reading, from tentative exploration of music or science to mastery, from reflexive self-centeredness to a thoughtful regard for others.

The following essays suggest that it is just possible we might discover the rudiments of a society we can stand by in the schooling process rightly conceived: in what and how we read, in what and how we teach, in the purposeful, variegated, and often exasperating process of transforming children into productive adults.

11

Read for Your Life!

A writer friend wrote recently to ask who, really, reads anymore. She did not mean who reads to pass time on buses or to avert self-consciousness during solitary lunches or, at day's end, to hasten weariness into sleep. She did not mean who reads to get a jolt of sexual arousal or a stimulating dose of danger or bloodshed or scandal. She wanted to know whether there are still people who read in order to transform, and possibly to save, their lives.

We must remember that people have actually read in this spirit. Some of them are still afoot. Moreover, their orientation to books (and to films and to stories generally) is unique. Real readers do not believe a story is great and true because it is like real life. They believe real life is occasionally great and true because it is like a story. These readers know that years, that whole decades of one's life can pass without rising to story quality. During these spells it is common to feel less than fully awake, although such passages may also give rise to longing. The purpose of stories is to remind us of what we long for.

Consider how we actually respond to great stories. If, for instance, we find ourselves powerfully moved as Thomas More steps to the executioner's gibbet at the conclusion of *A Man for All Seasons*, it is almost certainly *not* because we have experienced—much less desired—anything remotely like it in our waking lives. More's heroic integrity is not what personal experience has taught us; it is what, in our deep interiors, we recognize and long for. Nor is it necessary to comb past centuries in search of canonized martyrs to make the point.

Millions of ordinary folks felt their throats constrict and their spirits swell as Rocky Balboa somehow made a fight of it with Apollo Creed in the closing moments of *Rocky*. This scene did not put audiences in mind of similar triumphs of tenacity in their own lives. Instead it reminded them of an overarching tenacity and courage which, if they thought about it at all, seemed to precede them into this world. The *Rocky* story simply made it intelligible and accessible.

Real readers catch such glimpses, gain this access all the time. J.R.R. Tolkien, C.S. Lewis and their circle of Oxford friends composed a metaphysical explanation for the kinds of connections real readers make. They believed that all true, great stories pre-exist. Writers and other storytellers are merely media through whom true stories are conveyed to others. In other words, a writer may be said to discover or even to translate a true story, but he or she does not make it up. Tolkien himself was likely to get testy with anyone who said he made up his *Hobbit* or *Ring* characters; he insisted, rather, that he had conveyed them whole from the realm where he found them.

It is obviously possible to invent a story. The great mass of stories are invented—watch any sitcom, read almost any thriller or, to borrow a vivid phrase from another writer friend, a "crotch novel." Some invented stories are endurable. They may build up and discharge a degree of tension, but they are not transforming. They are disposable and, in actual practice, are disposed of immediately after use.

In a lucid but little-known book, *An Experiment in Criticism*, C.S. Lewis suggested that durability is an essential quality of true reading. A true story truly read will be, after a suitable period of refreshment, a renewable pleasure. By their very natures, real readers are rereaders.

I am a schoolteacher by trade, and I can always count on a spirited response when I ask my students what books they like to reread and what films they like to rewatch. Nearly everyone has something to report. Sometimes they are a little sheepish, surprised themselves that treasured stories from their private pasts feel so important to them. Grimm tales, Arthurian legends and classical myths are invariably mentioned, sometimes in such streamlined updates as *Star Wars* or the Indiana Jones sagas. Resurrection stories always come up: Dickens' *A*

Christmas Carol, Shel Silverstein's *The Giving Tree,* Frank Capra's *It's a Wonderful Life.* Tolkien readers reread him, many of them throughout their lives. Devotees of Lewis's *Narnia* stories admit to doing the same.

It does not take long before my students are able to identify a common feature of their personal "repeatables": the stories are invariably about transcending the waking world. Great stories make transcendence look natural, feel possible. It is probably for this reason that virtually all of my students (and family and friends, for that matter) find the movie version of *The Wizard of Oz* an infinitely renewable experience. The genius of the film is to convince us that Kansas and Oz are simultaneously in different realms and yet somehow part of the same realm.

Here it might be said, guardedly, that the depth psychology of Carl Jung may contribute to our understanding of real reading. The Jungian notion of trans-personal symbols and myths can be seen as a variation on Tolkien and Lewis's realm of pre-existing stories. The problem with the Jungians is that in their zeal to identify "archetypes" revealed in the world's myths and stories, they tend to devalue the particular, distinctive impact of each one. At their worst, Jungian writers want to reduce such magnificent achievements as Norse mythology, Arthurian legends and Christian gospels to useful pieces in a vast unification scheme.

Unification schemes do not transform people, but durable stories do. As suggested already, aligning one's life and work with great stories is personally transforming and thrilling. Casting around for stories that happen to resemble our own lives is, by contrast, deadening.

Real reading, like real immersion in any art, extends consciousness outward from the self to some otherness. To be assumed into the contours of a great and durable story is unlike any other pleasure in the world.

Can you imagine extending yourself, without reserve, into the exquisite miniature otherness of Beatrix Potter's books; or into the cozy hearths and pastoral sweetness of *Wind in the*

Willows; into the gorgeous, deadly chambers of *Romeo and Juliet;* into the jeweled light of Keats's "Eve of St. Agnes"; into the white light of St. John's Gospel?

Of course, this is not your list; it's mine. But take your list. Go ahead, try it.

12

Mr. Chips Redux

It is now possible to get foundation money to prove what is already well known: that teachers "burn out." Of course they do. They are not, as a class, venerated by the communities they serve, by either parents or students. The latter pose professional problems not heretofore encountered in schools and for which training and experience have prepared few practicing teachers. Today's students take drugs which obliterate, or retard, the capacity for arousal, attention, concentration, and memory. They typically watch TV more than they engage in any other single thing except sleep. Most of them, no matter how hostile, impaired, or distracted, are required by law to attend classes until they are at least sixteen, and cannot be removed unless they represent a danger to the teacher and their classmates. Corporal punishment, except in a few die-hard parochial schools, is not allowed (and good riddance), but teachers are increasingly being knocked about and, in the city where I live, seriously assaulted and even killed. All of this is stressful and makes teaching often less than grand.

But not all teachers are so beleaguered. And while it is safe to say that the stress level in teaching is up, and tolerance for it down, some of the factors involved in burning out cannot be blamed solely on an inadequate and ungrateful clientele. If the truth be told, teachers themselves can hardly be counted as boosters of the profession. He who is burning out may never have had a sure sense of his mission. He or she may not have much of a head for complexity or much of a heart for battle. There may simply be an insufficient love of learners—"love" is, I think, the right word—to encourage a love of learning. And since the process works only in that order, teaching is not likely to be very satisfying or, again, publicly appreciated, failing that necessary professional love. That love can be trained and directed, but it cannot be taught. So where does it come from?

It may come from God, but the very notion raises issues inconveniently big and not directly to the point under consideration. More directly, that necessary love comes from parents and other nurturers, then from school and the larger society. We get a taste of it, the feel of it, from those who have a bit extra. Not all teachers can be counted among this number, but some can, and these help to keep the young alive.

Recent social science has taught us to call people with identifiable roles, such as teachers, "models"—a dreadful term. "Model" suggests an approximation of a person rather than a person. Worse, we are often exhorted to be the right sort of "model" to the young, a vague notion which amounts to imitating conventional propriety, so that our charges will in turn imitate us. But we can't, and they don't. The right sort of teaching behavior is radically others-directed; it depends on love, which cannot simply be willed.

This is not to say that teachers "either have it or they don't," although I believe something like this is nearer the case than we professionally acknowledge. For even assuming that one is lucky enough to possess some of this enabling, enriching capacity for love, it is by no means foregone that one is going to express it to the fullest. Unbeckoned, the love might lie dormant or, in certain decadent historical moments, turn inward upon its bearer. But if the capacity is there, if one really *has* some, then it may be elicited by others, by attractive "models." All of us in teaching have known and appreciated at least one, and all of us are looking about forlornly for more. Given the dearth, we might look to literature. There, I contend, we will find what we are looking for, although there will be plenty of resistance to recognizing it.

The light and the way out of the contemporary teaching malaise is James Hilton's Chipping, better known as Mr. Chips, in *Good-bye, Mr. Chips*. Most teachers I have spoken to have an opinion about Mr. Chips, but almost none of them has read James Hilton's story or seen the classic film version with Robert Donat in the title role; a few acknowledge having seen the latest movie version, a syrupy musical starring Peter O'Toole and Petula Clark. The real thing is a straightforward and compelling account of a life given wholeheartedly to teaching. In so giving, the teacher, Chips, is thoroughly and transcendentally fulfilled. The very idea smacks of mawkish sentimentality these days, which may tell us something about the climate of the times, but tells us nothing about the teaching vocation.

In spite of the particularities of having been born into a snug Victorian world and having taught classical languages at a British public (private) school for boys, Mr. Chips is, vocationally speaking, Everyman. He is by no means extraordinary, gifted, or even especially eccentric. He is modestly paid and lives close to the margin. He attains no celebrity outside the world of his school, and he holds a specially responsible position there only once, and then owing to wartime emergency. His school, Brookfield, is barely second line among British public schools, and Chips himself is barely up to its standards.

> His degree, for instance, was not particularly good, and his discipline, though good enough and improving, was not absolutely reliable under all conditions. . . .

His very modest mastery of the classics was "to him a kind of secret and valued freemasonry."

In short, Chips would not be able to put together a very impressive résumé. Nor would he shine at faculty workshops or regional education conferences. Yet he manages to emerge in maturity as a fine teacher and, more important, as an incomparably fine schoolman—a *model*, even. He is able to do so in part because, even as a very young man, Chips is an adult. Whatever his adolescence was, it is over by the time he commences teaching. Because his personal identity is not "in crisis," he is able to *be* an identity to his students: to be considered, accepted, rejected, feared, ridiculed, or obeyed.

Because Chips, limitations and all, is so sure of what he is, his students and colleagues can be sure also. He is therefore effortlessly reliable and calming. And once his capacity for love is tapped, he becomes *enabling.*

As it happens, love—romantic love—comes to Chip in mature years. When he is approaching fifty, he meets and marries Katherine, a warm, spirited young woman who is as taken by his old-shoe conservatism as he is by her fresh intellect and vivacity. They thrive together briefly at the school before she dies in childbirth. But as an agent of love, she changes Chips crucially:

> Obedience he had secured, and honor had been granted him; but only now came love, the sudden love of boys for a man who was kind without being soft, who understood them well enough, but not too much, and whose private happiness linked them with their own.

And whose private happiness linked them with their own: that's it. It is that private happiness, observable and available, which makes a teacher's work credible and appealing. The appeal does not, for most students in most subjects, lie in the business itself—in Latin or in chemistry or even in great literature. Rather, it lies in the experience of encountering someone attractive who has made Latin or chemistry or great literature a part of his or her life and whose profession is to demonstrate that relationship. Without the love, without the private happiness, the demonstration is a sham—however great one's talent, or good one's intentions, or streamlined the structure of one's school.

Love also enables one to minister to the young as both judge and counselor. Current counseling theory largely holds that such a dual role is inadvisable, but this theory is nonsense. Every teacher is both judge and counselor, evaluator and encourager. To refuse to judge is to fail to demonstrate a culturally necessary commitment to ideals and standards. It is also a denial of what the "nonjudgmental" party feels, which is phony and often cowardly. To refuse to serve as a sympathetic advocate of learners as persons is a waste of a great personal resource. Chips knew this. Katherine taught him. When some of his charges had clearly blown it and had come to trouble, she advised loving ambivalence:

> "Chips, dear, I'd let them off if I were you. After all, it's nothing very serious."
> "I know. I'd like to let them off, but if I do I'm afraid they'll do it again."
> "Try telling them that, frankly, and give them the chance."

Simple enough, but by no means soft-headed. Wrong is not forgiven, but the wrongdoer may be, and if there are misgivings and doubts, let the forgiven be aware of these, too. It is instructive that the very idea of forgiveness seems alien to contemporary school process. But if we find it too old-fashioned and moralistic to forgive, we eliminate the traditional basis for truthful admission of fault—and perhaps begin to consider the very idea of "fault" old-fashioned and moralistic. We tend to find ourselves presiding over a powerful cycle of infraction and prosecution, feeling uncomfortably ineffectual, feeling certain that, with respect to discipline, "things are getting worse." Not Chips.

When one is loved—is "privately happy"—defenses tend to fall away; they no longer serve a purpose. The walls we construct between ourselves and our students are often fortified by such defenses. But if the defenses fall away, school becomes immediate, which means highly personal. A certain kind of teacher talks about his or her work in terms of names and incidents and is only secondarily alert to Issues. Such souls are easily ignored by educational hierarchies. They only teach. But they tend to last, tend not to "burn out." Chips lasted.

> He had won, by seniority and ripeness, an uncharted no-man's-land of privilege; he had acquired the right to those gentle eccentricities that so often attack schoolmasters and parsons.

The privilege of accrued service and commitment is *personali-*

ty, which is a long way from a model.

Personality is the medium for imparting the culture to other persons; other media do not, by themselves, satisfy. The teaching personality is most authentic and credible when it has endured over time. This is an uncomfortable point to stress in a historical climate obsessed as is ours by youth. Meteoric rises—in politics, in the arts, in sports, in corporate and professional hierarchies— claim national attention, while productive tenure is typically regarded as a failure of imagination. Nothing could be more obviously destructive to the social fabric. Experience, if not the fastest teacher, is incontestably the surest, but those lessons take time; vocationally they may take a lifetime.

> Chips lived through it all. He sat in the headmaster's study every morning, handling problems, dealing with plaints and requests. Out of vast experience had emerged a kindly, gentle confidence in himself. To keep a sense of proportion, that was the main thing. So much of the world was losing it. . . .

A sense of proportion is always shaped by specific vocational, institutional, and historical experience; the more experience, the surer the sense. The building and sharing of such experience can make a life, a life radically directed to others.

It is no mere coincidence that the same historical climate which has lost or rejected traditional reasons for lives in service has also conditioned us to regard the glorification of such lives as "sentimental." The octogenarian Chips lies on his deathbed, dreamily recalling a roll of long-departed students:

> And then the chorus sang in his ears in final harmony, more grandly and sweetly than he had ever heard it before, and more comfortingly too . . . Pettifer, Pollett, Porson, Potts, Pullman, Purvis, Pym-Wilson. Radlett, Rapson, Reade, Reaper, Reddy Primus . . . come round me now, all of you, for a last word and a joke. . . .

It sounds awfully sentimental, but it also sounds like love. Can you imagine?

13

Teaching as Failing

Whenever a teacher enters a classroom to engage students in the process of increasing their understanding of some subject, some process, some created thing, some event—that is, whenever a teacher enters a classroom to teach—he or she risks great failure and, regardless of his or her gifts, *experiences* that failure to a significant extent. Teachers know this, know exactly how it feels. Yet if there is a universal aspect of the teaching experience that is discussed less, one wonders what it is. It is always disturbing to think about failing, but the personal and educational costs of denying the failure are considerable.

Of course the risk and realization of failure are present in the practice of any profession, but because education's aims are inherently less precise, failure is more completely realized in teaching than it is in medicine, law, business, and many other occupations. Although researchers still try to measure such things, the intensity and quantity of a teacher's work are impossible to measure exactly; and since unknown quantities are hardest to love, teachers have been held in overall guarded esteem throughout Western history: ill or moderately paid, of negligible status. A woman employed in the business office of the school where I work used to say, it seems to me daily, "If you can't work, teach. If you can't teach, teach teachers." What bothered us most when she said it was not the intentional effrontery, but, I sincerely believe, the possibility that she was telling the truth.

What is said to reassure us is typically not very reassuring. There seems to be no end to homiletics, whether from podium or journal, about the loftiness of our mission, and there is always a cheery stream of in-classroom how-to's and "breakthroughs" in the psychology of learning/not learning. Apparently instructive, generally inapplicable. The truth of the matter is that what can be said about teaching amounts to reconstructing, with more or less eloquence and timeliness, the archetypal dilemmas posed by our art. It is good to behold and to mull over these reconstructions once in a while, but when we meet our next class, those dilemmas will be fresh and just possibly, despite erudition derived from our journals and conferences, overwhelming. Numerous luminaries have spoken well on teaching. Great practitioners like Socrates and Jesus were especially shrewd in discussing its limitations. Some a few places lower in the pantheon, like Jacques Barzun (in *Teacher in America*) have risked stating clearly what teaching is:

> How then do you pour a little bit of what you feel and think and know into another's mind? In the act of teaching it is done by raising the ghost of an object, idea, or fact, and holding it in full view of the class, turning it this way and that, describing it—demonstrating it like a new car or vacuum cleaner . . . The "subject" should become an "object" present before the class, halfway between them and the teacher, concrete, convincing, unforgettable.

Few people can do this consistently, and no one can do it perfectly; all of us, even at our best, fail considerably.

Human beings generally dread the prospect of speaking authoritatively before a group. The dread is greatest when the group being addressed is not particularly receptive or welcoming, when they do not anticipate being entertained or pleased. Teachers play to tougher houses than actors do. They also play to them in more intimate settings, and the scheduled run is generally longer, regardless of the reviews. An actor, often with reason, may blame a flat performance on his material. Teachers are less able to do this; it is rarely Euclid's or Melville's fault that a class has fallen flat. Teachers move among their audiences, address them, converse with them. Any inattention, boredom, hostility is clearly visible before them. Because there are normally no co-stars or supporting players, the experience of teaching imperfectly is essentially a private matter. And again, because failure is by nature humiliating, we tend to keep it to ourselves. The least successful teachers tend to be those most isolated from colleagues and students.

I once accompanied an English teacher friend to a halting and procedure-ridden meeting of his department in which questions of materials, length of assignments, and curricular timetables predominated. After about an hour of this, my friend, by general reckoning a popular and reasonably effective teacher, startled everyone by exploding, "Can't we talk about what the hell is going on in the classroom? I have a feeling that a lot of the time we're *dying* in there [he had particular colleagues in mind]. Isn't that more pressing business than which term we teach the essay?" He struck a nerve, I think, but one too raw to sustain any more touching. After acknowledging what a good idea it would be to share personal classroom experiences at an unspecified future date, the chairman proceeded gingerly to direct the meeting along its former course. My friend had not interrupted the meeting as a play for attention but rather because he believed that failure in teaching performance could be somehow figured out, adjustments made, superior models imitated. He held the optimistic belief that classroom failure was the result of teaching gone wrong, not of anything integral to the process. One wonders.

Teaching, beyond the teaching of rote operations, is inescapably pretentious—necessary, but nonetheless pretentious. This is not to say that teachers are pretentious people; my personal experience suggests that the opposite is the case, although I suspect everyone savors the memories of one or two stunning exceptions. Teaching is pretentious because of the kinds of knowledge a teacher must possess in order to begin. I am not talking about degrees, examination scores, or any other kind of paper certification, all of which, especially in the United States, are preposterously easy to acquire, but of the bedrock knowledge required to carry on the activity

Barzun described in the passage cited above. First, there are two "practical" spheres of expertise, without which the process is running blind. The first of these is an exhaustive, ordered, clearly articulated knowledge about some subject: politics, calculus, anatomy, African history. The second is a clearly conceived idea of how learners learn. The latter, about which there is no consensus among educational scientists, is of course useless unless it is combined with a sure, possibly intuitive, knack for recognizing the presence or absence of learning when it does or doesn't occur. The futility of acquiring the first kind of expertise is well known to anyone who has set out to do so much as an undergraduate thesis. The futility of acquiring the second kind is perhaps worth laboring a little.

Most of us in teaching have encountered a colleague or visiting expert who for a spell was riding high professionally on the strength of having mastered, for the purposes of explanation, some up-to-date process in learning theory. The rhythm of one's familiar academic jungle may quicken feverishly to such tom-toms before a day or two of classes settle things down. This is not because we resist change or because we are anti-science or because we are dull, but because the new insight invariably fails to translate usefully into the actual world of our classrooms. When exhorted, therefore, to alter the structure of our world in order to accommodate the new breakthrough, it usually comes down to more money, more (possibly different) equipment, more space, more staff, more time, more effort, more care. Except for the specifications of the equipment, we already knew this. Education seems to suffer, perhaps permanently, from a disjunction between learning theory and teaching practices.

Most teachers who stick with it manage to acquire a feel for the modes in which their students learn, and some of them adapt themselves deftly and flexibly to what they find. Not one in a thousand, however, has come to terms with a comprehensive theory of learning, such as Jean Piaget's, although his name certainly does get bandied about. This is not just because Piaget's prose rivals Alfred North Whitehead's for utter opacity; it is also because a structural description of learning does not necessarily inform the more complete, the more various, ordinary language experience in a roomful of children. Committed and caring teachers are constantly restructuring their time and resources so as to increase the capacities of the students in their charge. They are motivated to do this by the palpable failure accompanying existing arrangements. They watch their charges with animal sympathy, the way Piaget watched his. What they tend to watch for is development and mastery and, like Piaget, they are often surprised and delighted when they see it.

So much for the two "practical" prerequisites, mastery of subject and mastery of learning theory. Even if, one strains to imagine, a teacher were to manage both prerequisites, he or she could still fail dismally. Something has to animate this accomplished hulk of a teacher. A "higher faculty," to use an old-fashioned term, has to select some objects of knowledge as important, has to decide on a best style of presentation, has to decide which students and which activities and which ideas deserve the most time and energy and resources. In other words, a teacher sets up as if he knew not only *what* he was doing but the *value* of what he was doing. He had better have an answer to the primordial question, characteristically expressed in a whine, "What are we doing this for?" He had better say, "In the general scheme of things, *this* is important." He will be irritable and restless if he doesn't believe his own answer. Nobody outside the clergy is obligated to be more pretentious.

I have so far avoided mentioning gifts, without which even the most learned, most practiced, most philosophic teacher is lost. No matter how much erudition and principle, little happens without charisma. It helps to be attractive. It helps to have a resonant, easily audible speaking voice. It helps to be appropriately, howlingly funny. I don't know how many of my own high school classmates—although I suspect practically all of us—forfeited a year's worth of first-class historical lessons solely because we were too immature to control our preoccu-

pation with the teacher's bald, shiny, almost gothically pointed head. For my part, I will always treasure the memory of an
exchange I once overheard after a history class I had just given
to a section of ninth-graders. We were studying Rasputin and
the Romanovs, and I, with questionable judgment, had decided to elaborate in some detail about the nature of the tsare-
vich's hemophilia and about the variety of dangers and
tragedies that have befallen famous hemophiliacs throughout
the history. I have something of a reputation for talking too
fast, particularly when animated, and I was extremely animated in this particular discussion. I thought that, despite its overt
sensationalism, the class had gone pretty well.

"Wasn't that *gross?*" inquired a youngster just out of view.

"Who knows? That guy talks like someone put him on the
wrong speed."

So much for the vivid lessons of history.

Teaching is failing—not, obviously, failing utterly, but failing considerably. The business of conveying knowledge, or, as
hedgers from Socrates onward have put it, being "midwife" to
knowledge requires that we recognize knowledge when we see
it and that we be able to distinguish between kinds. These
requirements are elementary, yet they are too demanding.
The poet Edward Arlington Robinson is often remembered
solely for having likened humankind to a "spiritual kindergarten where millions of bewildered infants are trying to spell
'God' with the wrong blocks." We teachers hand out the
blocks. Because most of us are aware that we are doing so and
because of the overwhelming task of dealing with what the
blocks do spell, much if not most of what goes in the name of
teaching is not teaching at all but defenses against teaching.

Defenses comprise all of what we know is awful in teaching
and much that is currently passing as an alternative. We do
not seem to fail if we do not really teach, and we do not teach
if we reduce the educational experience to set procedures
(how old-fashioned!) or if we fail to direct the experience at
all (how trendy!). The eternal pedagogical dilemma has been
how to steer a course between these polar defenses: to order

the process short of petrifaction, to leave room for autonomous development, provided it is the right kind. As I write, the teaching profession is arguing the back-to-basics issue. To what degree should teaching emphasis be placed on enabling skills such as reading, writing, and computing rudiments? How much on activities so engaging that requisite skills will be acquired painlessly along the way? In the present historical climate, "back to basics" has great appeal. Many of us in the profession have experienced directly certain do-your-own-thing excesses. Polemics aside, basics are awfully hard to be against. And if it comes down to one versus the other, the basics, since they are more concrete than themes and meanings and purposes, are relatively easy to teach; this is a point seldom made by the back-to-basics proponents, but one senses it operating. The real problem is that the basics and—what?—the profound should ever have become opposed. The basics may provide a map to the profound; an inkling of the profound persuades one to attempt the journey.

There is something irresistibly noble about the teacher who aims always at the sublime, but it is that teacher who is most likely to despair at the technically flawed, pedestrian works he receives from his students. This teacher, too, is most likely to operate at a level of abstraction inaccessible to certain students and must thus endure their incomprehension—a reaction more disturbing than either boredom or hostility. The higher he reaches, the more he fails. The "basics" champion, on the other hand, may, if successful, point to his students' more competent punctuation or even to higher scores on standardized tests, but he must also share the consequences of those students' inability to integrate trained competencies into their overall personal expression, their disturbing inability to see the point. But of course the middle road—sound fundamentals, with the sublime ever in view—is the way. Were it possible. The teacher who opts for the middle way, if it is precisely the middle way, is deëmphasizing basic skills by half and diluting his potential profundity by half. The middle-roader fails both ways, less. For some reason we tend to honor most in our memories those teachers who consistently aimed high, perhaps too high to recall. The others, the middle-roaders and the taskmasters, are remembered less and less fondly, although I believe personally that the latter have made an invaluable if unremarked contribution to the order of life and letters.

Ideologues are the happiest teachers; they may also be the most effective—most certainly so in the eyes of adolescents. Adhering uncritically to absolute truths, ideologues have grounds to justify the significance and the appropriateness of the subjects they teach and the materials they employ to do it. Whether or not ideologues are very sophisticated, they are attractive for having at least convinced themselves. They *know* and convince us fleetingly that we know, too. We remember them for this. Thousands of more reasonable, more tolerant, more intelligent practitioners retire each year and are quietly forgotten. The ideologue controls his material more surely than does the philosopher. The ideologue gets to the point, while the philosopher stops to consider, to inquire further, even to leave the question open. Ideologues act and inspire action; philosophers are always qualifying and finding out. The philosopher is aware of the limitations of his efforts, fails self-consciously; the ideologue proceeds boldly, suffers the consequences, and fails, whether or not he acknowledges it, tragically.

The ideological teacher and the philosophical teacher are both heroes, the former a martyr to his absolutes, the latter a martyr to his inquiry. Most teachers do neither. Most teachers are busy defending themselves in ways that have become very familiar, although possibly not under the heading of "defenses." Consider the defenses against imputing significance to what is being taught. Whole instructional systems complete with prepackaged materials have evolved to promote the idea that significance is "many points of view taken together"; authorities and texts must not declare significance in order that students may. In American schools and colleges, especially in the humanities, this approach has hardened into the "course." According to this defense, there is no authoritative model to confer significance, there is only *exposure*. Teachers of this persuasion, whether in the primary schools or in the graduate schools, are proud to say that they would not think of imposing their values on their students, as if this statement were not an imposition of value. They may, however, preside over engaging give-and-take, may *clarify* understanding of various opposing positions, may test and grade this understanding. There will be better and worse answers, but there will be no ANSWER. It will not be right or wrong to have dropped the atomic bomb on the civilians of Hiroshima.

Until quite recently it looked as though the disinclination to "impose values" were going to extend into the evaluation of student work. Grading meant being judgmental, meant doing psychological harm, meant promoting competition instead of interest or mastery or growth. There is undeniable truth in all of this—as there is in the fact that, in addition to requiring courage, it is mutually hurtful to inform a student that "I've reviewed your performance carefully, and I find it deficient." This, I think, is what a low grade says. And it must be said, as judgments of student work—grades—form part of the *meaning* of that work. Probably more than any other pedagogical duty, grading demands that teachers declare themselves clearly. Grades are shorthand values. They are not mere quantifications, although mere quantification is a common defense. Eighty percent may be a good or poor grade, depending on how one values the material, the importance of mastering it, the improvement or lack of it that 80% mastery represents.

Other defenses against grading are equally time-worn. Sometimes teachers, out of cowardice, optimism, or egotism, give uniformly high grades, a practice that ceases to delight recipients as they become aware that their efforts have been judged indistinguishable. The practice of conferring uniformly low grades is also a defense against rendering judgment, only here the emphasis is on being thought "very demanding," a familiar form of egotism in academic life—not to be confused with *being* very demanding. An outright refusal to give grades is a sure sign of a teacher's dissatisfaction with the task set before him. Such a refusal is often defended on the ground that one student's progress is not meaningfully comparable to another's. The refusal to grade is really an expression of a teacher's unwillingness to reconcile his values with the institutional and larger social values in which teacher and student are embedded. Embedded as we are, declining judgment means deferring judgment. If a teacher will not judge a student's progress, others must and will, without the illumination the teacher may have provided. So with whatever lights we have, we serve those we teach in part by judging what they do. In so doing we see how much or how little impact our teaching has made. And however lovingly and gracefully we do it, we do hurt students when we grade them. Jesus suggested we judge not lest we be judged almost certainly because he knew how much failure true judgment would reveal.

In some lines of work, particularly in monotonously routinized but necessary work, defensive adaptations may contribute positively to a person's well-being. Workers so situated may well maintain their dignity by denying the significance of the job—by claiming to be "above" it, by claiming that the work is only instrumental to unrelated personal necessities and desires. Beyond what is necessary to be punctual and accurate, a clerk is not obligated to be concerned about his ledgers or his entries into them. The product of his labor does not think or feel or talk back. Teachers who employ such defenses can only incapacitate themselves. By relegating their work to a peripheral orbit in their personal constellation, by withholding feeling from the process, a teacher fails to provide the personal intensity necessary to communicate anything beyond instructions and data. This kind of teacher is easily replaced by a tape recording. But teachers who risk revealing personal commitment to their students and to their subject matter are vulnerable, a condition no less acute for being inherent to the teaching process. Teachers set themselves up for passive and active rejection, and they always get it.

There is only one thing to do about the inevitability of failure in teaching: Acknowledge it. Acknowledging failure means recognizing clearly the limits of a teaching situation, or it may mean recognizing a defense for what it is. Only when failure is acknowledged can one begin to play to strengths. What strengths?

Ego is one. In the late sixties a college friend of mine who had decided to live counter to the culture told me he was appalled at my decision to become a teacher. "Is that what you want to be, a big *ego* up there controlling the class?" Oh no, I said, I didn't want that; I wanted to serve —— —. He had me. Nobody was supposed to be a big ego, nobody was supposed to control anything, because control was at that time among my friends supposed to lead to aggression against the people of Vietnam. There certainly was some egotism—plenty of it— in my decision to teach. Moreover, when I imagined myself doing it, I imagined myself rather attractively "up there controlling the class." Prior to feeling guilty about my egotism, I had been feeling anxious on the opposite score: about whether I had *enough* ego to perform as if knowledgeable, to sustain the buffeting due a fledgling teacher. About teaching as failing, my friend had inadvertently hit the nail, although not fully, on the head. Without question egotism, in various ways and at various times, gets in the way of teaching, but it is also fundamental to a teacher's survival.

Egotism prompts a teacher into the classroom and the actor out onto the stage. Egotism also enables the teacher to choose, to begin, to cast aside alternatives and say, occasionally, "This is true. I know it." (Failure, failure.) Egotism pushes itself brashly past ambivalence, but it does not necessarily negate the truth of "many points of view." The artful, intelligent egotist who is also a committed teacher may just irritate those other viewpoints into being among the emerging egotists he is teaching. Good, funny, pointed teaching can be carried out in this manner. Egotism helps.

Being somewhat arrested in one's personal development also helps. My headmaster startled me once by stating candidly that it was his opinion that there was "something wrong" with primary school teachers, especially men. While this was probably an imprudent thing for him to say, there seemed to be, upon reflection, unquestionable truth in the assertion. What, after all, if not "something wrong," motivates a grown-up to dedicate his professional time to supervising an alien, miniature world of colorful implements, gerbils, large rounded letters and numbers? But then what motivates *any* adult to dwell professionally in the sub-adult world? I suspect that all enduring teachers are somewhat arrested at the age level of those they teach. Without such arrests, teaching the young would certainly be a loveless process—and probably futile. I have not yet met the teacher who communicated effectively with his younger students because he had objectively and correctly studied them and therefore knew how they worked. The really brilliant teachers of the adolescent or the 10-year-old are somehow *there*. If we are anywhere else, our judgments, humor, and compassion will find their mark only randomly. When we attend the young we typically, if not consciously, unloose forgiving, supportive feelings for our younger selves. As Claude Fuess put it in *Creed of a Schoolmaster,* "Patience is largely a by-product of sympathy and cannot be maintained unless a teacher recalls his own childhood and artless approaches to knowledge." At our best, we resonate with our own former failures, forgive them, forgive ourselves, carry on.

But what has all of this been about? Would this near-essay conclude after having suggested that teachers are destined to "fail considerably," although they may be fortified by two commonly acknowledged personality flaws, egotism and arrested development? And even if there are grains of truth in the thesis, why put it that way?

I have decided to put it this way because of the emptiness, the futility, and the costs of putting it the other way. Failure—real failure—is palpable everywhere in the teaching process. We need to name it and to face it, so that we may continue. If we insulate ourselves sufficiently with defenses, we may go unhurt, but we will teach nothing, while providing students models of flight and disengagement. Acknowledging failure and acknowledging defenses, we may come to know as much about our business as the medieval scholastics knew about God: what he is not and that he is necessary. Now off to class.

14

Odds and Sods—
To Those who March to the Beat
of a Different Drummer, if Any

"I was often, when a boy," writes Montaigne in 1575, "wonderfully concerned to see, in the Italian farces, a pedant always brought in for the fool of the play." Here, as elsewhere, the great essayist speaks to us across the span of centuries. Any boy or girl at school, or done with it, recognizes the sentiment, warms to it, for it is practically impossible to have had so little as a year of schooling without having to some degree experienced the person in charge as "the fool of the play." But far from merely giving voice to a lightweight antipathy on behalf of the world's students, Montaigne has touched on something much more crucial to the pedagogical situation: the inevitability—indeed the necessity—of teachers, at least some of them, as fools. 'Fool' of course is too harsh, just as 'eccentric' is too cozy, but, again, one's school experience easily fills the semantic gap.

All teachers are *poseurs*. They can't help it. They are supposed to represent knowledge and authority, but they are given insufficient props. Elementary school students quickly discover the limits of a teacher's 'knowledge': it may extend to certain rudimentary operations at the blackboard or in books or to do with the classification of leaves, but it is emphatically *finite*. This finitude, while a commonplace to adults of reasonably balanced disposition, is profoundly interesting—at first even upsetting—to the young, until their idealization of 'teacher' becomes altered to fit the reality of school. In that reality teachers never know enough, and in some critical areas—knowing who really caused the trouble, knowing how to get along, how to be funny, how to be graceful or otherwise pleasing to the eye—they may be much less adept than the pupils in their charge. As students grow older, as their intellect and talents begin tentatively to unfurl, the personal and professional limitations of their instructors begin to stand forth in ever bolder relief. Here conflict inevitably begins. Following the primeval pattern, teachers become objects of hostility, are engaged in intellectual and other forms of combat or are withdrawn from passively.

When a teacher's 'knowledge' is thus assailed, he is likely to fall back heavily on his 'authority'—which is futile, because at the most fundamental level, a teacher's knowledge *is* his authority. But the kind of authority generally exercised takes the form of personal and institutional discipline, of the veiled or stark threat, of appeals to conscience, of the deft handling of grades. Pedagogical authority was undoubtedly more imposing when teachers were clergy whose business was assumed to be God's business, but as Montaigne's observation attests, such an assumption has not been universally held for a long time. Far from being agents of divinity, modern teachers are more likely to be members of unions: examples, as truck drivers, miners, and seamstresses are examples, of 'labor'—an affiliation which works against teachers in curious ways. To the offspring of parents proudly identified as 'labor' themselves, teachers similarly affiliated are regarded as 'no better than us' (and perhaps worse paid), a viewpoint which runs directly counter to pedagogical necessity. And it is hardly better that the children of professionals and 'management' find it easy, once they have reached a certain level of social awareness, to regard teachers as 'worse than us' (and worse paid). And so it has happened in the West that teachers, who if anything are relied upon *increasingly* to convey what is known and what is right, are made to stand beneath such lofty banners while everything else about them is providing a good example of what can happen in life if you don't get down to business.

Yet teachers are not always despised, and schools are not always purgatories of boredom or infernos of hostility. That this is so has almost nothing to do with superior schemes for the organization of schools, with any heretofore unmentioned virtues of teachers, or with some postulated 'basic niceness' of kids. That school keeps has a great deal to do with the maintenance of a delicate, subtle, and usually unintentional process, one which is typically moving darkly at the periphery of school life. Of course I am speaking of true eccentricity—that is, of revealed personal traits so arrestingly odd that they become focal and marvelous for their own sake.

Much, possibly too much, has been stated already about the inadequacy of teachers, but certain embodiments of that inadequacy are far from harmful in schools; they are rather, in the person of the true eccentric, liberating. The true eccentric, in his own older, preoccupied, perhaps deviant way, speaks directly to the hearts of youth. In order to understand why, it is necessary to come to terms with the real nature of eccentricity, which may mean discarding hackneyed notions of doddering old men who cannot remember what they have just said and cause explosions in the lab.

Eccentricity does not reside in a 'type' of person, but rather in the *relationship* between a designated eccentric and an observer. There must, so to speak, be both a transmitter and a receiver; the peculiar qualities of each combine to determine the quality of the broadcast. True eccentrics *do* nothing more than confront—obliquely and by no means effectively—life's adult vicissitudes. As models they provide limitless comfort and delight to students who are never naturally, fully at home amidst the demands and regimentations of school. To students, whose own most urgent impulses academic life is designed to suppress, the eccentric serves symbolically as both sympathetic victim and hero.

The best adolescent psychology tells us that some time between childhood and adulthood everybody undergoes certain common, intensely experienced crises. In the process of rapid physical growth, one fears, and to some extent experiences, physical oddness: blotchy skin, acrid smells, the appearance too early or too late of beards or breasts. Consciously and unconsciously, one arrives at one's sexual orientation in a more or less final manner. In this unavoidably tumultuous seeking after physical, sexual, and vocational identity, one is always on the brink, or beyond it, of being "out of control."

On all three of these counts—physical oddness, dubious sexual orientation, and a pronounced lack of personal control—the eccentric is likely to arouse sympathetic and other interest from youth. No such 'psychological' explanation is required to *appreciate* the eccentric, although such explanation helps to point up his necessity. The Canadian novelist Robertson Davies understood the necessity uncommonly well, when, in the first volume of his *Deptford Trilogy*, he had his schoolmaster-protagonist reflect:

> I liked the company of most of my colleagues, who were about equally divided among good men who were good teachers, awful men who were awful teachers, and the grotesques and misfits who drift into teaching and are so often the most educative influences a boy meets in school. If a boy can't have a good teacher, give him a psychological cripple or an exotic failure to cope with; don't just give him a bad, dull teacher. This is where the private schools score over the state-run schools; they can accommodate a few cultured madmen on the staff without having to offer explanations.

Dickens, whose appreciation of life's variety led him so often along the back streets of the human city, found occasion to shine his beam into the soul of a schoolman or two. Of these Matthew Pocket, Pip's tutor in *Great Expectations*, is illustrative. His actual tuition is at best indifferent, which in Pip's case matters little as he is not preparing for anything beyond a vague notion of becoming a 'gentleman.' It is Pocket's personality and circumstances that arouse Pip's sympathetic interest. An educated, gentle, economically superfluous man, Pocket, when Pip first meets him, has somehow managed to father eight children at rapid intervals by a wife who is indifferent to them all, preoccupied instead with questions of English peerage and the remote prospect that her own family may be in some way connected to it. Two frantic nurses are assigned the actual supervision of the younger Pockets, and there is the suggestion, given the location of the family dwelling, that these are in periodic danger of rolling into the Thames. This domestic setting, Dickens reveals, has taken a toll on Pocket. "He was a young-looking man, in spite of his perplexities and very grey hair, and his manner seemed quite natural, in the sense of its being unaffected; there was something comic in his distraught way, as though it would have been downright ludicrous but for his own perception that it was very near being so." At the family dinner table the basic attributes of his type are magnificently revealed.

> Mr. Pocket, with the normal perplexity of his face heightened, and his hair rumpled, looked at them [his family] for some minutes, as if he couldn't make out how they came to be boarding and lodging in that establishment, and why they hadn't been billeted by Nature on somebody else. Then, in a distant, Missionary way he asked them certain questions . . . then melted into a paternal tenderness, and gave them a shilling apiece and told them to go ahead and play; and then as they went out, with one very strong effort to lift himself up by the hair he dismissed the hopeless subject.

The penultimate detail—lifting himself up by the hair—refers to a regular, and I believe revealing, habit of Pocket's. Rising to one's feet in this manner clearly indicates a division of will, common to schoolmasters 'out of control' in their particular worlds; similar inhibitions and distortions of movement—with or without puzzling compensations—have been noted among a kind of schoolman throughout the ages.

Habits of speech may also reveal the type. Real eccentrics are rarely remarked for saying intentionally 'funny' things—or, necessarily, for producing any distinct elocutionary effect. More characteristically, they are remembered for the unusual connections they make between ideas, as if in speaking they drew from something other than the common pool of causes and effects, as if criteria known only to them conferred significance on what they had to say. Frederick William Sanderson, the great headmaster of Oundle and H. G. Wells' favorite teacher, spoke in such a manner. So striking was Sanderson's mode of address that Oundle boys, and later Wells, formed the habit of taking down his classroom utterances *verbatim* in order, one suspects, to savor them at a later time. The following is one such transcription from a divinity class given by Sanderson and recorded in Wells' *Story of a Great Headmaster.*

> . . . There are two incidents in the Gospel Narrative which are similar in-er—character and which I have for the moment called Survivals—very characteristic, namely the somewhat surprising narrative of the Temptation of our Lord, and the other the account of the Transfiguration. . . . One remarks that the temptations are always looked at from the personal point of view, which I have put down in my synopsis. Has anybody got my synopsis? Lend it to me a moment. I don't think the personal significance of the Gospel stories has importance nowadays. We needn't consider it. That's what I think about things in general. Personal importance giving way to universal needs. We are not so much interested whether boys do *evil* or not. Of course it annoys me if I find a boy doing evil. Leading others astray. Shockingly annoying. Oughtn't to be. Like continuous mathematics not enabling a boy to pass arithmetic—[mumble, mumble]—screw loose. See what I mean, K_____. Not referring to you my boy (laughter). Hunt me up something in Plato about all these things.

Sanderson generally adhered to this pattern of speech regardless of the setting. Years later, when Wells followed the beloved headmaster on the podium before an audience of the National Union of Scientific Workers, he commented, "It is not always easy to follow Mr. Sanderson, but he is worth following into the remotest corner. He has a style of discourse which I can only compare with some of the modern practices in painting." At this point, Houston Peterson writes, "Sanderson chuckled, slid from his chair, and died almost instantly." This kind of timing, this ability to be, regardless of what is actually said, commandingly focal, is eccentricity in purest form.

It should by no means be assumed on the basis of the examples cited so far that real eccentricity is a predominately European or British phenomenon. Almost as soon as there was a national literature—or more precisely, as soon as we had schools—the eccentric would take his place at the head of the American schoolroom. By 1820 it is possible to detect in Washington Irving's classic, *The Legend of Sleepy Hollow*, a familiar profile, in this instance the rather striking profile of Ichabod Crane:

> The cognomen of Crane was not inapplicable to his person. He was tall, but exceedingly lank, with narrow shoulders, long arms and legs, hands that dangled a mile out of his sleeves, and feet that might have served for shovels, and his whole frame most loosely hung together . . . To see him striding along the profile of a hill on a windy day, with his clothes bagging and fluttering about him, one might have mistaken him for the genius of famine descending upon the earth, or some scarecrow eloped from a corn field.

Irving, an Anglophile, wanted to portray something of a native bumpkin in Ichabod Crane, but American eccentrics cannot fairly be limited by class or region. Nor confined to fiction.

William Armory Gardner, who helped his cousin Endicott Peabody found Groton School in 1884 and then taught classics there until he died in 1930, was very much the real thing. Born into enormous wealth, he was raised, after the early death of his parents, in the unearthly salons of his aunt's colossal Boston mansion, now the Gardner Museum. A bachelor all his life, he was well known for his generosity to the school and to his friends, and he by no means neglected himself. To the great house he built for himself at Groton was appended what he called the Pleasure Dome, which included a little auditorium, a swimming pool, squash court, and a maze. Here, with the assistance of his servants, he would entertain. In Frank Ashburn's biography of Peabody one old Grotonian remembers being assigned to convey a distinguished visiting clergyman to Gardner's house for a courtesy call. No one was on hand to open the door, but a voice from inside beckoned them to come in. As they climbed the stairs, they could hear an animated discussion being carried on, apparently concerning a bridge match. As boy and clergyman entered Gardner's suite, they found him

> . . . standing before the fire naked as he was born except for a voluptuous pair of fur bedroom slippers, toasting his stern and stirring a large plate of porridge as he talked . . . Holding more porridge and unsmiling in a morning coat was his butler and stretched out on the sofa with even less on than Gardner was Bertie.

> "This is Dr. _____," said the boy as solemnly as he could.

> "Of course it is," said Gardner, dropping an elaborate curtsey without spilling the porridge. "How good of you to come. This is Bertie, one of our alumni. You may find us a trifle informal, my dear Sir, but if you will give us a moment until we finish our breakfast, perhaps I can persuade Bertie to put on some clothes more suitable for the day. Do be seated."

Gardner seems to have been an expansive man. Devoted to competitive sailing, riding, food and drink, he also liked to knit socks of lively pattern. Although he might insist on translating the Greek word for alien as 'wop,' he was considered by bright boys to be a fine classicist. But he rarely collected work and was a notorious rambler. He told the boys his grading system was based on "what will give your mothers a suitable degree of joy or sorrow." His cousin Endicott, the Rector, once had cause to admonish him harshly. Gardner took umbrage: "Either my method of teaching is sound or it is not." Peabody replied, "No one is interfering with your teaching. The trouble is you're not teaching. You are demoralizing the entire school."

That Gardner could be so gravely charged and yet successfully maintain an overall reputation as one of the 'grand old men' of the school suggests that he was a person of redeeming parts. Such is not always the case with eccentrics. It was certainly not the case with Captain Grimes, a one-time teaching colleague of Evelyn Waugh's at a very obscure private school and then, name unaltered, a stunningly picaresque figure in Waugh's school novel, *Decline and Fall*. The historical and fictional Grimes appear to be very close in character. Of the real one, Waugh's diary records:

> He was expelled from Wellington, sent down from Oxford and forced to resign his commission in the army. He has left some schools precipitately, three in the middle of the term through his being taken in Sodomy and one through his being drunk six nights in succession. And yet he goes on getting better and better jobs without difficulty.

In *Decline and Fall* the youthful hero, a young teacher, first encounters Grimes as he is attempting to discipline a boy for whistling:

> "What do you mean," said Grimes, "by whistling when I told you to stop?"
> "Everyone was whistling," said the boy.
> "What's that got to do with it?" said Grimes.
> "I should think it had a lot to do with it," said the boy.
> "Well, just do a hundred lines, and next time, remember I shall beat you," said Grimes, "with this," waving his walking stick.
> "That wouldn't hurt much," said the boy, and went out.
> "There's no discipline in this place," said Grimes and then went out too.

The walking stick was no affectation, as Grimes had a false leg, a disability which he allowed students to believe was a war wound but which was in fact the result of his being run over by a tram when he was, in his phrase, "one over the eight." Grimes believed his personal resilience, or at least his survival, was attributable to his being a 'public school man,' the school, for fictional purposes, becoming Harrow. At a pub not far from school, Grimes confides to his younger colleague,

> I'm a public school man. That means everything . . . Not that I stood four or five years of it, mind; I got the push soon after my sixteenth birthday. But my housemaster was a public school man. He knew the system. "Grimes," he said, "I can't keep you in the house after what has happened. I have the other boys to consider. But I don't want to be too hard on you. I want you to start again." So he sat down there and then wrote me a letter of recommendation to any future employer, a corking good letter, too. I've got it still. It's been very useful to me at one time or another. That's the public school system all over. They may kick you out, but they never let you down.

Later, Grimes' military experience would parallel his school experience almost exactly. Rarely sober during the war, he finally committed an offense serious enough that court martial was inevitable. Not wanting to tarnish the reputation of the regiment, his superior officers decided to save a step by talking to Grimes solder-to-soldier, then leaving him alone with a revolver to do the honorable thing. But they unwisely left a decanter of whiskey as well, so that instead of finding him dead, they returned to find him in a state of unrestrained hilarity. The inevitable, and certainly fatal, court martial was avoided when an influential old Harrovian intervened at the last hour and sent him off to Ireland for postal service. "You can't get into the soup in Ireland," claimed Grimes, "do what you like."

Grimes is indomitable, an optimist. However chronically or deeply "in the soup," he never makes any pretense to defend or even to rationalize his behavior. Deviant and inclining ever toward the criminal, he is winsomely open and affable, a state of being Waugh even suggests may have some theological basis. After breakfast at school, still smelling strongly of drink:

> "Funny thing," said Grimes . . . "I don't pretend to be a pious sort of chap, but I've never had any doubts. When you've been

in the soup as often as I have, it gives you the sort of feeling that everything's for the best, really. You know, God's in His heaven; all's right with the world. I can't quite explain it, but I don't believe one can ever be unhappy for long provided one does exactly what one wants to do and when one wants to. The last chap who put me on my feet said I was 'singularly in harmony with the primitive promptings of humanity.'"

Shortly after expressing these sentiments, Grimes slips ignobly out of school, setting up a sham suicide in order to escape an unpromising marriage to the headmaster's daughter. Certain accrued deceptions finally land him in prison where he is reported to have drowned in Egdon Mire in an attempted escape. This report does not convince Waugh's hero, who concludes,

Grimes was of the immortals. He was a life force. Sentenced to death in Flanders, he popped up in Wales. Drowned in Wales, he emerged in South America; engulfed in Egdon Mire, he would arise again somewhere at some time . . . Had he not, like some grease-caked channel swimmer, breasted the waves of the Deluge? Had he not moved unseen when darkness covered the waters?

Pocket, Crane, Gardner, Grimes—all were basically genial souls, but geniality is coincidental, by no means essential, to eccentricity. C.S. Lewis knew none of it in his first headmaster, the Rev. Robert Capron, a fervid sadist. In fact, Lewis may be one of the few alumni to be able to claim attending a completely eccentric school, a condition very unlikely except in establishments as small and as down at heel as the one to which he was sent at age ten by a confused father. In a voice far from letting bygones be bygones, Lewis recalls, in *Surprised by Joy*, his first experience of Faculty:

The teaching staff consisted of the headmaster and proprietor (we called him Oldie), his grown up son (Wee Wee), and an usher. The ushers succeeded one another with great rapidity;

one lasted for less than a week. Another was dismissed in the presence of the boys, with a rider from Oldie to the effect that if he were not in Holy Orders he would kick him downstairs. This curious scene took place in the dormitory, though I cannot remember why.

The location of this man's dismissal becomes less curious if one supposes, as I happen to, that he was Grimes.

Oldie's indignation was usually less righteous. One boy, P., Lewis recalls, was beaten beyond human endurance for being the son of a dentist, although a cause was not always necessary to provoke an assault from Oldie. Lewis: "I have known Oldie to enter the school room after breakfast, cast his eyes round and remark, 'Oh, there you are Rees, you horrid boy. If I'm not too tired I shall give you a good drubbing this afternoon.'" Lewis claims there was no humor or even perverse pleasure in Oldie's exertions: that his awfulness was of a pure and elemental nature.

> Oldie lived in a solitude of power, like a sea captain in the days of sail. No man or woman in that house spoke to him as an equal. No one except Wee Wee initiated conversation with him at all.

> . . . He was a big, bearded man with full lips like an Assyrian king on a monument, immensely strong, physically dirty. Everyone talks of sadism nowadays, but I question whether his cruelty had any erotic element in it.

Oldie's school fell into financial ruin before Lewis could complete its prospectus, but as excruciating as his experience was there, it helped shape his final religious position: "Life at a vile boarding school is in this way a good preparation for the Christian life, that it teaches one to live by hope."

However far from accepted conventions of personal and professional conduct, the true eccentric is hardly strange. Students not only spot him every time, but spot him for what he is. Perhaps then, as Waugh suggests, there *is* something of "immortality," of a Jungian archetype embodied, of a Platonic Form realized, whenever an eccentric takes his appointed place at school. They need not be standing naked at the hearth, nor white-knuckled at their flogging, nor ever 'in the soup' to be appreciated and understood. They may be outwardly ordinary men, even verging on the dull. Such is Le Bas, the superbly drawn housemaster in Anthony Powell's novel sequence, *A Dance to the Music of Time.*

As stressed already, eccentricity exists in relationship, and Powell can certainly be said to hold up his end. Le Bas' house seems to have been modeled somewhat on Powell's own house, Goodhart's, at Eton. In the first volume of his memoirs Powell notes,

> A. M. Goodhart's was not merely a 'bad' house, but universally agreed to be far the 'worst' house in the school. Its record at every branch of sport was unimaginably low; its only silver trophy, the Lower Boy Singing Cup. Tolerant skepticism was the note struck.

This was also the note struck in Le Bas' house, not because Le Bas was in some way irresponsible; on the contrary, he is portrayed, if anything, as overly fastidious, even as a relatively good judge of character, of bad character at any rate. He was ineffectual rather than slack. If Le Bas was a factor at all in the 'badness' of his house, it is because he was, like so many Powell characters, preoccupied with certain concerns of his own to an extent that made his personality comically opaque to those about him. Like Matthew Pocket, Le Bas revealed his inner drama in pronounced physical idiosyncrasies, probably unconscious.

> He was a tall, untidy man, clean-shaven and bald with large, rimless spectacles that gave him a curiously Teutonic appearance: like a German priest.

To Le Bas' various postures, Powell pays especially close attention:

On some occasions, especially when vexed, he had the habit of getting into unusual positions, stretching his legs far apart and putting his hands on his hips; or standing at attention with heels together and feet turned outwards so that it seemed impossible that he should not overbalance and fall flat on his face. Alternatively, especially when in a good humor, he would balance on the fender, with each foot pointing in the same direction. These postures gave him the air of belonging to some highly conventionalized form of graphic art: an oriental god, or knave of playing cards.

Le Bas' verbal utterances were ordinary and faintly remote, but the contortions of his body attempt—decidedly unsuccessfully—to express something coherent of their own. In one instance, agitated by the suspicion that boys have been smoking cigarettes in the house (the narrator's visiting uncle had in fact been responsible), Le Bas "raised his hands from his sides a little way, and clenched his fists, as if he were about to leap high into the air like an athlete, or a ballet dancer." Later, after Powell's narrator has gone up to Oxford, Le Bas pays an unexpected, perhaps random, call. As there had been nothing very warm or cordial in their previous relationship, the narrator is taken by surprise. Le Bas, however, is characteristic: "He came farther into the room, but appeared unwilling to seat himself; standing in one of his characteristic poses, holding up both hands, one a little above the other, like an Egyptian god, or figure from the Bayeux tapestry." Later in the same interview, a chance reference sends Le Bas into a long, silent reverie, during which he "climbed up on the fender, and began to lift himself by the edge of the mantelpiece. I thought for a moment that he might be going to hoist himself right on to the shelf; perhaps lie there." But no, after a painfully halting series of exchanges, during one of which Le Bas unaccountably stresses that "Friendships have to be kept up," he finally, "after several false starts," departs. His valedictory words—"remember one thing—it takes all sorts to make a world"—puzzle the narrator, possibly because they express an interior condition rather than an opinion about the 'world.'

That it was the interior Le Bas, so desperately seeking expression through physical movement, that primarily interested Powell is supported by the fact that the real-life model, unquestionably A. M. Goodhart at Eton, was well-endowed with the ordinary, *external* trappings of eccentricity—yet Powell declines to transpose them into fiction. Powell writes that Goodhart "somewhat resembled Swinburne's friend, Watts-Dunton; the same high forehead, walrus mustache, look of slightly unreliable benevolence, an awareness of being always prepared for the worst, and usually experiencing it." And there were certain personal traits of an almost 'classical' kind: a "curious little purring sound" before speaking, a repertoire of perplexing statements, such as, "Boys come in from football hot, and rather cold." Moreover, although assumed by Powell to be a "repressed bi-sexual"—not a derogatory judgment by the standard of Eton during Powell's day—there was also, writes Powell,

> A touch of kinkiness . . . added by a fervid preoccupation with ladies' shoes (a fancy said to presage masochism), which Goodhart made no attempt to conceal. On the contrary he would from time to time hurry around the house after prayers, bearing with him for the admiration of his mostly indifferent pupils some huge volume illustrating *Feminine Footgear Through the Ages*, or some similar Saga of Boot and Shoe.

Clearly Powell's experience of Goodhart's bold features qualified him to render the rather finer portrait of Le Bas.

Not everyone has Powell's eye. Peter Prescott hasn't. In the turbulent late sixties, Prescott spent some time in residence at his *alma mater*, Choate, went to meetings, interviewed boys, masters and headmaster, and concluded, in *A World of Our Own*, that the school was turbulent in the late sixties manner. He also ventures to discuss school eccentrics and to speak in appreciation of a couple of them he had known as a student: men, he claims, who are no longer possible in the brave new Choate. In support of this thesis he recollects certain attributes and antics of former master Porter Dean "Pete" Caesar, apparently a colorful man. Prescott cites a lot of 'pranks' perpetrated by Caesar, including a kind of anti-fire drill during which a gun would be fired and cannon balls rolled down stairs. There is also reference to wearing frightening masks, casually breaking Ming china, smoking in class in opposition to the rules, wearing sneakers to dinner, and cutting chapel. Another of Prescott's favorites reportedly awakened the boys in his house by loudly playing harpsichord music on the phonograph. And it was said that when it rained, Caesar rode around in a convertible with the top down, but when it did not, he rode around in another convertible with the top up. There is more, all very heavy-handed, embarrassing stuff: affectations which suggest certain personal needs, but which are far from the real thing. One strains to imagine Le Bas or Oldie cutting up in this manner; even a self-conscious showman like Gardner would hardly undress *because* the clergyman was mounting the stairs.

"There are no more such men at Choate," Prescott writes with a perhaps pompous finality. "There will be no more: they are not safe. Arrogant; intolerant; divisive; disloyal; the weakest team man on the faculty . . ." There may or may not be such men as Caesar, as Prescott describes him, at Choate these days, but I would bet that, for those with eyes to see, a real eccentric or two can be found proceeding gingerly about the margins of school life.

Again, what communicates itself with such ruthless accuracy to the soul of youth is the eccentric's inability to manage his circumstances. Regardless of the defenses he throws up, the eccentric is in time unmasked by his charges, who are, so often, unable to manage *their* circumstances. But in this timeless confrontation between their respective inadequacies, the students forever have the upper hand. They have, among other things, numbers on their side. They also have the benefit of collective inertia—while their mentors must, given the nature of their task, address them, move about, command, or at least attempt to command, attention.

Despite some trendy classroom strategies of the past decade, the eccentric is still, like any other teacher, commandingly focal. As performers, however reluctant, teachers are bound to play to each class about 180 times per year. Habits of speech, greasy neckwear, perhaps an unconscious rooting into one's cleavage in search of tissues—all such data are imprinted deep in the student cortex. So stored, this fund of vivid visual and auditory detail provides an engaging and sometimes hilarious subtext to zoölogy or American literature.

And there is no escaping it. The recognition of—indeed as Montaigne suggests, the *need* for—schoolteacher eccentricity in as much a fact of life in the public schools as in the private schools. J. D. Salinger placed Holden Caulfield, with his sure litmus sense of teacher vulnerability, in a prep school. But William Goldman, in *Temple of Gold,* found the same voice serviceable for his Illinois high school protagonists. In Alan Sillitoe's *The Loneliness of the Long Distance Runner,* reform school is the milieu, but the young inmate's observations of those in charge are no less keen.

As the theologian Harvey Cox has pointed out so engagingly, the society of the Middle Ages was enormously refreshed and even sustained by an occasional Feast of Fools. These celebrations were irreverent, vulgar, and raucous. Figures of king and bishop were held up for derision in a festival atmosphere. In the more highly rationalized, more complex, more earnest industrial society that would follow, feasts of fools would not do. They are hard to imagine in Calvin's Geneva or colonial Salem. Among the young and other disenfranchised, the impulse for such feasts is as intense as it ever was; thus Monty Python, "Saturday Night Live," *Animal House.* But the king and bishop—the grown-ups—won't play, and when they are brought into the fray anyway, the confrontation gets serious and even ugly, as it so often did in the Sixties.

But if not a feast, there is still a steady gathering, at least in the schools, of those who in their largely fruitless attempts at responsible pedagogy, relieve all of us from the yoke of our deadly seriousness. For those with eyes to see, a real eccentric or two can be found proceeding gingerly about the margins of any school's life. Cherish them.

15

Miss Dove Rediviva

One spring afternoon in the early 80's, Tallahassee public school teachers and administrators were called together and addressed on the educational implications of youthful drug use. Some chilling words were said about the scale of the drug problem, no longer a novelty in Florida or elsewhere. Untold losses in learning and health were claimed, still worse predicted. The program concluded with a public attorney telling the teachers that, in light of current drug use and exchange on school property, the schools might well be closed as public nuisances.

Public nuisances? O Mann! O Dewey!

Since Sputnik and since whatever the Sixties were, both the educational and social missions of U.S. public schooling have been first questioned and then assailed. Fingers point accusingly in all directions: to the structure of American society (Kozol), to the structure of schools (Holt), to television (Winn *et alia*), to drugs (Nahas *et alia*), to diminished teacher competence (the editorial staff of *Time*). What school fictions we have had lately—television treatments such as *Welcome Back, Kotter* and *White Shadow*, films such as *My Bodyguard*— begin with the premise of the degraded school and carry on from there—typically with a series of small victories in human relations, played out against a backdrop of institutional triviality and silliness.

But as recently as the sleepy 1950's it was possible to locate educational excellence in accessible American fiction. For that excellence to become story and for it to resonate in the collective imaginations of readers, it must somehow have *existed*. But in order to recognize it for what it is, especially in our ornery and alienated present, we must do what problem-solvers and reformers seldom do: keep our minds open to the possibility that the real thing, the desirable thing, may turn out to be nothing like what we are looking for. The right answer, the right filament, the right vaccine might turn out to be something not at all streamlined, complex, or novel. It might have been with us, unused or discarded, all along. Discarding it may even have been the problem. Simply picking it up again, as I pick up a water-spotted copy of Frances Gray Patton's *Good Morning, Miss Dove,* might lead us out of the current malaise of American schooling and toward the light.

For more than four decades Miss Dove was a teacher of elementary school geography. She taught her entire working life in the same school, in the same small town. She taught geography to *all* the town's children, then to their children, then to some of their children. Her influence on the children, on the town, and in some respects on the world beyond the town, she felt to be "formative." She had no college degree. She studied no pedagogy. She was not particularly attractive. She did not "grow" professionally. She was not warm. She exerted what influence she did because of the distinctive and uniform quality of her contact with the young:

> [The children's] imaginations had been nursed on the same sights and sounds and early ideals . . . They had all, for the space of a whole generation, been exposed at a tender and malleable age to the impartial justice, the adamantine regulations, and the gray, calm, neutral eyes of the same teacher— the terrible Miss Dove.

Child psychology since Rousseau, and especially since Freud, has made it clear how dynamic, various, and complex childhood is. Children are not any particular way; they are a present expression of a complicated *process.* Children, especially as conceived of in American educational theories, are seen as almost limitless storehouses of educable potential; the trick in not to "block" that potential. Thus educationists have been working furiously to remove blocks—whether located in the "cognitive side" (assigned these days to the left hemisphere of the brain) or in the "affective side" (right hemisphere). It is amateurish and working class to consider a child dull or stupid; professional and middle class to consider him or her blocked. Similarly, learners are LD (learned disabled), perhaps dyslexic, not muddled; student behavior is hyperactive or hyperkinetic, not inattentive or obnoxious.

Seen in this way children are not scholastically or morally better or worse; they operate on different learning and social "modalities." The kind of setting required by all of these modalities is, *mirabile dictu*, just the sort of school we have been getting: open "learning centers" with "resource stations" here and there, the traffic between directed by "resource persons/facilitators" (teachers), the best of whom can adjust quickly to respond to the myriad learning and behavioral modalities of the highly mobile, infinitely adaptable learners in their charge.

> Miss Dove had no moods. Miss Dove was a certainty. She would be today what she had been yesterday and would be tomorrow. And so, within limits, would they. Single file they would enter her room. Each child would pause on the threshhold as its mother and father had paused, more than likely, and would say—just as the policeman had said—in distinct, formal accents: "Good Morning, Miss Dove." And Miss Dove would look directly at each of them, fixing her eyes directly on theirs, and reply; "Good morning, Jessamine, or Margaret, or Samuel." (Never "Sam," never "Peggy," never "Jess." She eschewed familiarity as she wished others to eschew it.)

Miss Dove was not up front with her students, and there was no rapping.

One thing children, if not always those who study them, know is that a good deal of what they say and think is nonsense. Some of it is playful nonsense, some of it simple misinformation, some of it intentional prevarication. Learning children are constantly checking the stream of what they say and think against authority, in whatever form they find it most credible. Only in this way do they form a notion of what is *really* true, *really* right. Even more crucially, they form a notion, durable long after particular information is accepted or rejected, that *something* is really true, really right. In the absence of authorities whose presence conveys AUTHORITY, all information is democratized, no bit more significant than another, more valuable than another, truer than another. In an age such as ours—which delights in failed authorities, whether incompetent teachers or fallen Presidents—it seems almost authoritarian to suggest that a proposition is no less true for being stated authoritatively.

> . . . on that unassaulted field—in that room where no leeway was given to personality, where a thing was black or white, right or wrong, polite or rude, simply because Miss Dove said it was, there was a curiously soothing quality. The children left it refreshed.

Whatever information or misinformation her students gleaned from Miss Dove about the geography of the world, they left her with the enabling conviction that the world was knowable. Miss Dove was proof.

Too often teachers buy the assumption that firm procedures are a badge of ignorance, a mere defense. After all, what certainties exist in the face of so much that is subtle, complex, and unknown in the learning process? Such thinking tends to divide faculties into camps of curmudgeons and with-its, the tension between them undermining the competence and confidence of all.

But the polarity is wrong. However much or little psychological insight is available to a teacher, the educational and social missions of schooling remain the same. Schools must still pass on the best of the culture (with all the value judgments that entails) to those about to take on the culture and must insist on student behavior appropriate to that process. Any psychological insight that does not serve these missions is educationally useless and may even be something of a hin-

drance. Of this Miss Dove, not a true curmudgeon and certainly not with-it, was well aware:

> She had pondered the new psychology which held that in the
> depths of human nature lay wild-animal instincts of greed,
> anger, idleness, and discourtesy. She could credit that theory.
> She had no rosy concept of human nature. But what did the
> theory prove? The thing that distinguished a man from a
> brute—a gentleman from a savage—was not instinct but per-
> formance.

Performance, yes. How could the profession have drifted so
far away from the concept? Miss Dove was aware that every boy
and girl comes to school with a distinct range of personal performance and of scholastic ability. That is given. The teacher's
job is to lead each student to the highest possible reaches of
his or her range. The morality of teaching lies in the commitment to do this. In a sense teaching does not begin until this
moral obligation is imposed on a teacher's actual routines. At
20 Miss Dove prepared herself to teach by arranging chess
pieces on a board as if they were students, moving them about,
imagining what they would say and do, and working out
responses to them.

> [A]s she talked to the little carven figures on the board, she
> introduced moral value into factual matter. By slight variations
> of tone, compressions of lips, or nods of approval, she made it
> plain that to her certain forces of nature, beasts of the jungle,
> and formations of land were more worthy than others. She was
> partial to the yak which was a "useful" animal; she admired the
> domestic habits of bears and the cleanliness of cat creatures . . .
> (The camel she gave his due. "He is not a pretty beast, either
> in looks or disposition," she told her class, "but he can go many
> days without water.")

Not many practicing teachers or theorists writing in journals over the past two decades have been making a case for
"introducing moral value into factual matter." In fact, the very

idea is anathema, although it may be nonetheless essential to schooling. The great point that has been lost by those who in their seemingly valid but actually quite superficial way have striven not "to impose their own values on their students" is that they are doing so—and *must*—even in their restraint. Few schoolteachers—even parents—can be sure of imposing *particular* values on the children in their care. As every reasonably self-conscious former student knows, most of the particular points of information or conduct received in school have since been forgotten, rejected, or revised. Included among these are the "moral" points. What may not have been forgotten or rejected, however, is the idea of morality itself, the conviction that there are substantial grounds for judgments and preferences. Very often our first conscious encounter with such an idea is the experience of dramatically coming up against it in someone else, someone whose life seems driven by a principle. All of Miss Dove's students came up against it.

> Anything could be taught, of course—fine points of deportment as well as the tributaries of the Nile. By six years of drill and example—forty-five minutes a day, Monday through Friday, September through May—Miss Dove had brought many a child to conform to a code that ran counter to his inclinations.

No harm in that, surely, depending on the code and considering some of the inclinations.

Of course there *is* something a little terrifying about Authority inculcating Morality. But should teachers on that account do otherwise? Religious people have repeatedly documented a kind of terror appropriate to the gods they venerate. And there is an attractive kind of terror some people feel at the prospect of failing to do their best. Miss Dove's terror seems to have been of this sort.

> [T]he terror did not paralyze. It was terror that caused children to flex their moral muscles and dream of enduring, without a whimper, prolonged ordeals of privation and fatigue.

Sometimes, if their ideal of courage was high, it caused them even to dare Miss Dove's disapproval.

Miss Dove, teacher of four decades, did not produce a type. She did not, nor did she try to, turn out children in her own image. To the contrary, she took some pride in understanding the varieties of youthful types in her care, and she was perhaps less surprised than anyone else in Liberty Hill when they grew up into playwrights, policemen, nurses, drunkards, or country club matrons. What she did aim to do was to *shape* her pupils. When students encountered Miss Dove and the perfect invariability of her routines, they encountered something substantial and timeless: a verity rather like extreme heat or cold or the first intimation of mortality. Miss Dove created a schoolroom where responsibilities were clear and meeting them was altogether possible but by no means easy. She created—first on her chessboard, then in her classroom—a world of order, and from that utterly convincing environment, taught about an orderly world.

In the course of *Good Morning, Miss Dove,* Miss Dove becomes, uncharacteristically, ill. A growth on her spine renders her suddenly unable to walk, and a doctor is summoned directly to the school. The doctor, as it happens, is Thomas, a former pupil, bright, sunny, still, to her, "the boy who had wriggled his ears whenever her back was turned." As Thomas is not Miss Dove's regular physician, a clergyman also in attendance attempts to reassure her by citing Thomas's professional training.

> "I know," said Miss Dove. It was she who had begun his training. It was she who, day after unremitting day, had drilled into him respect for industry, desire for exactitude, and the civilizing grace of inhibition.

Inhibition. The word, like repression, has acquired the darkest of connotations, especially when applied to the young. For Miss Dove it is, in appropriate amounts and in appropriate circumstances, a *civilizing grace*. For her, what is most sublime in human character development depends on inhibition.

Miss Dove was a teacher. At 20 she had "embraced her profession with a singleness of purpose that she might, under other circumstances, have bestowed upon matrimony, or foreign travel, or carving in stone." Sure as she was in her calling, she knew it was one calling among many. It was not morally given that Miss Dove should teach, but once she had taken it up, it was morally given that she should carry on. She did not need teaching so much as she knew teaching's need of her. And curiously, this lofty, moral perspective did not stem from, or result in, egotism on Miss Dove's part. When she is visited by another former student Jincey, a girl full grown, married, and pregnant, Miss Dove, though ill and worried, reflects that there is still time to teach the girl's child. Her tuition, given the frivolous if lovable characteristics of the parents-to-be, will be necessary.

> And yet, Miss Dove reflected, possibly all that, along with the shiny hair and silly shoes and pretty smells (for Jincey's agreeable scent still hung in the air), was part of a plan designed by an Authority she did not question. For if everyone lived upon Miss Dove's own lofty plane—if everyone perceived with perfect clarity the hard truths of human life—then there would be no parents and no children. There would only be teachers.

The teacher in Miss Dove coolly accepts such realities. But it is the humanity in Miss Dove that, having accepted them, confirms her in her teaching. Miss Dove's vocation—her whole moral order—is not a defense against real, humane feelings; it is a particular expression of those feelings. Miss Dove is not impaired; she is especially enabled. And she can be touched.

In one affectingly recounted classroom episode, a student haltingly announces that he has received a letter from his soldier brother, in the thick of combat. Miss Dove briskly instructs the boy to read the letter aloud. The boy is overcome with embarrassment and uncertainty, since the letter is a little salty and it includes an appreciation of Miss Dove. Nevertheless he rises to the occasion and reads the letter, in part his brother's explanation of how elementary school geography lessons have prepared him for combat. In closing, the soldier instructs his brother to give Miss Dove a kiss for him. To the boy's horror, Miss Dove steps down from the elevation of her desk, moves to the boy, and matter-of-factly presents a cheek for the decoration. It is duly given. The children sense an epiphany, and some begin to weep. Since this is unscholarly, Miss Dove quickly resumes instruction. Duty returns to duty.

But she is touched. Because she is fully human, she is touched. Because she is fully teacher, she carries on.

Her love flowed out to those children—to those with their pen points poised above their papers and to those in the far places she had helped locate on the map. It did not flow tenderly like a coddling mother's love. It flowed in a fierce rush of hope and pride, the way an old general's heart might follow his men into battle.

She went to the blackboard and picked up a piece of chalk. "Above the fiftieth parallel—" wrote the terrible Miss Dove.

Above the fiftieth parallel there would be order.

16

About Boys' Schools

On trial for his very life, Socrates began his defense by pointing out to the citizens of Athens that it was not really he who stood accused of impiety and of corrupting the city's youth, but rather a vague yet nonetheless popular image of Socrates. The image had been created by his most vocal critics and enemies and was given wide currency in an uproarious stage comedy, *The Clouds*, written by his friend Aristophanes. Socrates was not at all confident that he could assert his reality—and, he believed, his innocence—in the face of such a widespread adherence to an image he himself had never cultivated. His concerns proved to be justified; the image was found guilty, and the man was duly executed.

A similar difficulty tends these days to distort discussions of all-male schools. Contemporary opinion and more than a century's compelling fictions about boys' schools have combined to shroud them in a vaguely dinosaurian aura. Many of the surviving boys' schools are old and steeped in tradition, and this oldness carries with it unexamined negative feelings. Whereas enduring unto oldness often enhances the regard in which institutions or practices are held, the oldness of boys' schools tends, in the popular mind, to make them reactionary, "old-fashioned" in the most pejorative sense. Boys' schools, it is said, hark back to the days when only boys were prepared for universities and for the professions; as such they have been a principal instrument of male domination. To which it might be added: Shame on them and good riddance.

This image of the boys' school as a cultural dinosaur does not, I believe, stand up to objective analysis. Boys' schools of former eras may well have maintained attitudes that today might deservedly be called "sexist" or oppressive, but identical attitudes were also maintained by those eras' boys and girls whether enrolled in coed schools, girls' schools, or no school at all.

It will be argued here that there are no objective data of any kind to support a negative appraisal of boys' schools *qua* boys' schools. The data suggest, if anything, the opposite conclusion. Objective data did not motivate hundreds of colleges and schools to convert from single-sex to coeducational student bodies over the past three decades. The great majority of coeducational conversions were driven by market considerations: Coed schools were believed to attract more, including more qualified, applicants. For some schools on the brink of conversion, the motivating factor was a conviction—largely unexamined—that a coed student body is somehow more egalitarian. Stated simply, the assumption was that boys and girls together in school will be better people than they would be if segregated; they will be more understanding of, and effective with, each other. If that assumption is demonstrably true, schooling boys and girls together is clearly desirable. But *is* it true? A perhaps more important, and certainly more irritating, question is whether the current climate of opinion will allow anybody to find out.

Might there be inherently good, developmentally necessary qualities distinctive to all-boys' schools? That it is now possible to pose this reasonable question to the general public is due in good measure to the rising tide of feminist educational thinking. In their conviction that there truly are innately feminine modes of experience and feminine structures of thought, certain feminist theorists argue that those qualities will be nurtured and exercised best in all-girls' educational settings. The more pervasive the male domination of the larger culture, the more necessary it is to educate girls separately. Structuring schools so that they realize what is deepest and truest and best in females is currently regarded as a progressive educational attitude. Structuring schools so that they realize what is deepest and truest and best in males is not currently regarded as a progressive educational attitude (to put it mildly). This is unreasonable.

Good and various cases can be made that contemporary Western culture is skewed oppressively by male values and preferences. Males have undeniably enjoyed more social mobility, more political rights, and greater compensation for their work than females have. In the twentieth century, gender injustice has been resented and vigorously addressed by both sexes. It is obviously right to oppose gender-based unfairness, but it is a mistake to assume that boys' schools are a contributing cause. If females have been unjustly treated over the past century, and if gender composition of schools is to blame, the principal fault must lie in the dominant type of school: the coeducational school, in which over 90 percent of American school children have been enrolled. Far from being the culprits, single-sex schools, as some feminists have begun to suggest, may be the way out of the trouble.

What is the best school setting for promoting just and humane gender attitudes? This is a serious question. How and if it is answered will depend to a large extent on the climate in which it is discussed. Generous minds are required, minds willing to consider unfamiliar evidence and assumptions. Since serious people who favor single-sex or coeducational schools are likely to be motivated by a concern for the welfare and development of children, there is no need to address the issue in punishing, acrimonious tones. It might help, actually, to cultivate a little lighthearted playfulness. Socrates did—and while it did not save his life, it lightened its passing considerably.

Is there an inherent "maleness" to boys and men? Are the distinctive biological features of males linked to deep psychological structures? If so, then maleness cannot be alienated from males without a fundamental loss of their humanity. If inherent maleness is also susceptible to development, the social structures that bear on that development—especially families and schools—should self-consciously aim to realize its fullest potential.

The American poet and mythologist Robert Bly has not only postulated an inherent deep-maleness; he also argues that its suppression has been the root cause of a current masculine malaise. Drawing on the depth psychology of Freud, Jung, and the contemporary Jungian James Hillman, Bly attempts to document the late twentieth century emergence of a new male type: the "soft man." "Soft man" is not for Bly an altogether pejorative term. Soft men emerged, he believes, in the 1960s in response to feminist breakthroughs. As stereotypes of both genders were held up for critical appraisal, many conventional gender-related views and practices were altered. "As men began to look at women and their concerns," Bly writes, "some men began to see their own feminine side and to pay attention to it." For many this was genuinely liberating: to feel free not to like football if one happened not to, to engage energetically in domestic arts, in the nurture of children. Such men, Bly claimed, found it "wonderful" to be more thoughtful and gentle, less reflexively *macho*. But there was also something wrong with the new condition.[1]

Soft men, while socially nicer and more acceptable to liberated women, are also, Bly has found, enervated and depressed: "They are life-preserving, but not exactly *life-giving*."[2] Forward-looking, sensitive, and intelligent as he may be, the soft man also feels rather a "wimp." He feels he is missing something. Some turn to women to get it back, but the women, whether mothers, sisters, lovers, or friends, do not have it to give back; they did not take it in the first place. The soft man—and indeed every developing male—needs finally to look beyond women for sustenance and direction. Discovering the feminine side of the male self is indeed crucial to self-realization, but it is not the ultimate discovery. For males the ultimate discovery, or rediscovery, is the deep male. The deep male, while necessary to male self-realization, may be a frightening, forbidding presence. He is not, Bly says, "a benign Asian guru" or "a kind young man named Jesus."[3]

The modern male's need to be reconciled with his lost deep-maleness is illuminated, Bly suggests, by the Grimm folk tale "Iron John." To summarize it briefly: A kingdom is troubled by the disappearance of hunters who enter a remote area of the royal forest. A stranger passing through learns of the problem and volunteers to help. When he enters the dangerous region, a great hand arises from out of a pond and pulls the stranger's dog down to the depths. The stranger then returns to the castle for help. With a number of volunteers, he drains the pond, bucketful by bucketful. At the bottom lies a reddish, rust-colored giant, covered with hair from head to toe. The giant, Iron John, is captured and carried back to the castle where he is displayed in a cage. One day soon after, the king's young son is playing nearby with his treasured golden ball. When the ball rolls within Iron John's grasp, he grabs it. To get the ball back, the boy is told he will have to hand over the key to the cage. Since the key lies under the mother's pillow, a deception is required of the boy. He secures the key while his parents are away and releases Iron John, but as the giant heads off to the forrest, the boy calls after him that his parents will be very angry when they realize what has happened. The giant agrees, and the two head off into the wilderness together, presumably forever.

The features of Iron John—hairiness, wetness, redness—are associated with primitive male sexuality; they are not easily acceptable, not nice. The pond, Bly suggests, is the subconscious mind, and emptying it bucket-by-bucket represents a patient, disciplined attempt to discover what lies "at the bottom." The golden ball represents the boy's unity of spirit, positive energy, destiny. The only way to retrieve the boy's imperiled wholeness and destiny is to come to terms with a previously submerged, monstrous reality, and to do this, to make this connection, the liberating key must be stolen from the mother. Indeed, the boy must break with both parents and reconcile himself with the primitive if he is going to make his own way.

What the soft contemporary man is missing, then, is his golden ball. A red, hairy primitive has it. Moreover, this primitive is his own deepest self, deeper than his haphazard childhood identifications, deeper than the expectations the culture has imposed, deeper even than his awareness of an unexpected feminine dimension. To be a man, the boy—each boy—has got to do something very risky and very hard, and he must do it himself. In this regard the "Iron John" tale is consonant with other folk tales and male coming-of-age rituals throughout history and all over the world.

Bly believes the modern male's alienation from his deep-maleness is a consequence of industrialism, which has tended to remove fathers from their sons' company and thus to mystify a man's manner and work. With fathers only erratically present, their work is hard to imagine and harder still to like; sons have a difficult time conceiving their true manhood. The mother-acceptable view of manhood, the "nice" view, does not somehow ring true. Even in—perhaps especially in—the nicest households, the primitive stirs. "In the U.S. there are so many big-muscled high school boys hulking around the kitchen rudely, and I think in a way they're trying to make themselves less attractive to their mothers."[4]

Bly does not advocate male regression to the primitive, nor would he call for a preindustrial economy. The reflexively *macho* man is as alienated as the soft man, only without the soft man's genuine appreciation of women and of the feminine dimension of himself. Bly favors a reconciliation with the primitive, not necessarily a blind surrender to its urges. If males are strong, if they are passionate questers, if they raise their voices sometimes, so be it. This does not mean they must be oppressive and cruel. We must also, he suggests, reverse the tendency to emasculate the male type in the popular culture. From the Dagwood cartoons of the twenties through the television sitcoms of Norman Lear, men, and fathers especially, have tended to be portrayed as hapless buffoons or as benign eunuchs. Persistent denial of authentic masculinity is apt to produce eerie compensations—Rambo and his kind?

"In *The Odyssey*," Bly points out, "Hermes instructs Odysseus, when he is approaching a kind of matriarchal figure, that he is to lift or show Circe his sword. It is difficult for many of the younger males to distinguish between showing the sword and hurting someone."[5] Contemporary culture has by no means made it easy to draw such distinctions. The justifiable feminine imperative "Do not abuse me!" is too easily understood as "Do not be strong enough to abuse me!" Boys and men need to be reassured that the capacity to be forceful and the inclination to be destructive are not the same.

Other voices in depth psychology, particularly those in the field of object relations theory, may help to explain more fully the male's need to discover his deep-maleness. In her new study *Feminism and Psychoanalytic Theory*, Nancy Chodorow considers the developmental implications of the fact that women are the primary nurturers of both male and female infants. Unlike infant girls, infant boys must adapt psychologically to the gender *difference* between themselves and their primary love-object. The mother's femininity is a daunting "otherness"; depending on and ultimately turning away from this otherness will cause a special quality of unease in the infant male psyche. Seen this way, the early (pre-Oedipal) male is launched "negatively" into subsequent development.[6]

This kind of feminist revision of Freudian child development casts mother-son relationships (also mother-daughter relationships) into greater prominence than is allowed by traditional psychoanalysis, with its father-driven Oedipal complex. Both the traditional view and the view offered by Chodorow, however, confirm a deep psychological motivation for males to set out on a distinctive developmental path. According to Freud, following that path entails the need to exceed, to triumph over, the father.[7] In imagination and dream this can be accomplished through satisfying symbolic victories over fathers and other giants—that is, axing down a beanstalk bearing a thundering patriarch or, perhaps, as in oracle-beguiled Oedipus's case, simply bludgeoning one's father to death in a fracas on the open road. In reality, Freud hypothesized, boys overcome the mortal anxiety they feel about their competitor-fathers by identifying with them: an act of psychic "cannibalism." If Chodorow is correct, male children will have begun their journey of individuation before the onset of their Oedipal challenges. In fact, the latter may be a mere extension of an earlier, deeper need to swim free of the feminine "other" and to become a self. The key to self-realization may lie under the mother's pillow, as the tale of "Iron John" suggests.

It is probably not an overgeneralization to state that, throughout the history of civilization up until the First World War, the answer to the question of whether there is an inherent maleness to boys and men would have been laughably obvious. Are males *male*? Is the sky blue? What has raised such questions? Such doubts?

The popular understanding of gender—of both masculinity and femininity—has been traditionally determined by institutions organized by gender: priesthoods, armies, clubs, sororities, scout troops, teams, and, notably, *schools*. Gender-based organizations, whether the National Organization for Women or Eton College, not only risk stating what masculinity or femininity is, but also what a male or female should be. Neither gender has a successful record of making acceptable definitions of the other. There is some concern, however, that the soft man drawn by Bly may be a problematic consequence of males trying to define themselves in conformity to feminist prescriptions. A good, or at least an acceptable, man is thus one who does not attempt date rape; who does not assume that his preferences, activities, and employment are preeminent considerations when making mutual plans; who does not perpetrate gender stereotypes; who would not assume the male always pays the check or that women would not care for boxing, and so forth. No one, of either gender, should be defined negatively.

For better or worse, but probably forever, each gender tends to define its own nature and its aspirations. When the creation and perpetration of those definitions break down, when there is no social structure to affirm them and to pass them on, there is trouble. Gender definition and expectations have traditionally been a responsibility of schools, but schools have increasingly declined to set specific, positive expectations for masculine and feminine conduct. Schools typically define and prescribe good studenthood, good citizenship, but this does not solve a deeper developmental problem. Each student, each citizen, is a boy or a girl. There is that dimension of self-hood to be realized as well, and only a few schools these days are either structured or inclined to address the task. Does it matter?

For nearly all of Western history boys were educated and trained apart from girls. That structural fact, apart from reflecting a number of social assumptions that no longer prevail, was also accompanied by fairly clear conceptions of what a boy should be and do. Some of those conceptions are durably appealing. In the late twentieth century, by contrast, one would be hard-pressed to identify—except in certain boys' schools and other all-male organizations—a clear conception of male adequacy.

Questing, striving, leading, serving, adhering to ideals despite temptations not to—these values have rested at the heart of boys' schools and of boys' stories from the earliest recorded history. Summing up one's wit and wiles and strength in the face of great danger or great adventure is a theme running from Hebrew Scripture through the great Victorian schoolboy sagas such as *Tom Brown's Schooldays*.

Boys schooled together have no trouble seeing the developmental point of teenage David facing the Philistine champion, Goliath. David's story is developmentally important to boys, in fact, exhilarating. It is not unlike Telemachus's story, or even the story of his father, Odysseus. Not all the questing of boy-heroes in the Western tradition is martial or regal. The individuating quests of Jesus and St. Francis are marked by the force and depth of their spirituality. In Peter Abelard's case the quest was intellectual. The Christian chivalry of the Arthurian stories prescribed highly specific expectations for boys and men, expectations that again, despite entailing hardships, personal restraint, and exposure to mortal danger, have for centuries been stirringly attractive to boys. Moreover, the hypermasculinity of the chivalric code was accompanied by an extraordinary veneration of women. Indeed, the women of the Arthurian cycle are more than objects of love and loyalty; they are also intelligent, resourceful, powerful, often formidable adversaries.

The masculine ideal in the West has rarely—and then at its peril—isolated itself from feminine influence. The very object of the masculine quest, as in Romeo's case, may be the love of a girl or woman. But Romeo, like Abelard and Dante before him, arises out of a culture of males to meet the exquisite otherness of his love. Juliet is no school or neighborhood chum. The common thread in the heroic stories of the male guest is the *subordination of the hero's welfare* to the object of the quest. Young David and Romeo and Robin Hood are not selfish. Even now that theme, if vividly evoked, as in *Chariots of Fire* (a semi-documentary film about the Olympic ambitions of two Cambridge athletes, Eric Liddell and Harold Abrahams), resonates with surprising power.

It is well beyond the scope of this article to isolate the precise causes of the break or warp in the tradition of masculine heroism in the West. Undeniably, however, that tradition has been massively countered by the post-World War I emergence of the antihero. Who is the paradigm case? Is it Holden Caulfield, gentle, sensitive, physically and sexually doubtful, on the verge of nervous collapse? Is it Willie Loman's disillusioned boys in *Death of a Salesman?* Is it James Dean's baby-talking portrayal of a conflicted teenager in *Rebel without a Cause?* Conrad Jarrett poised on the brink of suicide in *Ordinary People?* Or is it the lost teenager become middle-aged, as in Jack Nicholson's characterization of Bobby Dupea in *Five Easy Pieces?*

These and legions of other lost boys compose a good part of the cultural backdrop against which boys are now expected to grow up. Whatever dark and worrying messages they collectively convey, the larger point is that they are not conveying enough. They are not conveying how to become a man. Again, very few institutions seem willing to take up this task. An exception is the boys' school.

Boys' schools have not disappeared. Many have not only weathered an era of coeducational conversion, they have thrived in its midst. When their scholastic and extracurricular performance is measured and compared, as Lee and Bryk measured and compared it among parochial school students, boys in boys' schools do better than boys in coed schools—never, apparently, worse.[8] Moreover, boys from boys' schools have not as a body registered special difficulties in adapting to the coeducational conditions of university life. A boys' school can, obviously, be poorly conceived, badly run, and resourceless. Herding boys together under the banner of school is no panacea, but schooling them within a structure designed to realize and to celebrate their distinctive developmental features has resulted in a high count of the most long-standing and most demonstrably effective schools in the world.

There is little mystery in the fact that well-conceived boys' schools have turned out to be good for boys. From their preschool years through their late teens, boys reveal a number of gender-specific contours in their skeletal, motor, and neurological development. Boys develop language skills, the capacity for quantitative analysis, and large- and small-muscle proficiencies at a developmentally different tempo from girls. Child psychologist J. M. Tanner has demonstrated that girls' skeletons and nervous systems are at birth more fully developed than those of boys, and the maturational gap increases somewhat through early childhood.[9]

Gender-based variations in the tempo and pattern of learning can be identified from the pre-kindergarten through the high school years. Primary school girls generally demonstrate reading and writing proficiency earlier than boys do; middle- and high school boys' mathematical-logical capacities accelerate more rapidly than those of girls. Girls develop fine muscle coordination sooner; boys develop large motor coordination sooner. Females reach the peak of their pubertal growth spurt a year or two sooner than boys. Each gender-based physiological difference is accompanied by distinctive psychological and sociological adjustments.

If the learning styles and learning tempos of boys and girls are at variance, a homogeneous school program—whether curricular or extracurricular—will unavoidably miss either the masculine or the feminine mark, if not both. Just as school programs tailored to gender-specific learning patterns should facilitate more learning, teachers adept at teaching boys or girls might reasonably be assumed to be, by virtue of their "specialization," more effective than those who teach (developmentally variegated) boys and girls together. As maturational differences between the sexes level off in the late teens, there are fewer theoretical advantages for educating them separately. Coed colleges would seem to make more educational sense than coed schools, although W. A. Astin's massive 1977 study of 200,000 undergraduates in 300 colleges study suggested otherwise.[10]

From the onset of adolescence, there are new, emotionally vivid gender issues afoot in classroom and corridor. Adult sexual potency is reached, and its attendant urges and manifestations must be managed by the executive capacity of a very recent child. Adolescents must address this demanding and dramatic task while, simultaneously, they are asked to do more, and more difficult kinds of, schoolwork. Middle- and high school students are challenged to progress from concrete to theoretical forms of thought. Higher mathematics is introduced. Students are asked to see and to use language less literally, more symbolically. The performance expectations of athletes and artists and performers are dramatically elevated. Schoolwork and extracurricular performance are increasingly graded and evaluated, and the evaluations are increasingly consequential.

For deep biological reasons, schooling pubescent boys and girls together produces inevitable distractions. Only some of the erotic distraction experienced by boys and girls in school is "active" and visible: flirting, erotic looking, dressing, groom-

ing, posturing for romantic effect. A substantial if not dominant part of the diverted energy goes into suppressing sexual
interests and urges. The flattest adolescent appearances are
likely to express intense arousal neutralized by equally intense
suppression; apparent imperviousness to nubile gender-oppo-
sites comes at some cost. Expressed or suppressed, however,
sexual distraction is an undeniable impediment to focused
activity, to learning and development. This is why Astin attributed the positive effects of single-sex colleges to "restricted
heterosexual activity" and why Valery Lee and Anthony Bryk's
1986 study of coed and single-sex parochial schools invited a
reconsideration of learning environments where adolescent
boys' and girls' "social and academic concerns are separat-
ed."[11] Or, as a colleague of mine put it recently, "I like boys'
schools because the inter-sexual posturing that interferes with
my work goes on somewhere else." That it does go on somewhere else is, of course, crucial to healthy adolescent development, but, despite the predominance of coeducational
schools, there seems to be no demonstrable evidence that the
experience of boys and girls together during school hours
contributes positively either to cross-gender socialization or to
learning.

Here the intuitive advocate of coeducation may well ask,
"But what about the child who simply *prefers* going to school
with the opposite sex?" There is a robustness, an agreeable
weight to this objection, particularly if rounded off with "It's a
coed world after all." It is indeed a coed world—but it is not a
unisexual world. The question of the adolescent's own preference for coeducation deserves to be taken seriously. It will be
an *adolescent* preference, incidentally, not a childhood preference generally. Preadolescent children, given the chance and
mobility to do so, exhibit a powerful tendency to seek out
their own gender for mutual or group activity—despite their
placement in both-gender settings from preschool years
onward. Indeed, possibly the most underexplored feature in
the sociology of education is the persistence of same-sex structures within coed schools. There is, it might be demonstrated,

a shadowy boys' school and girls' school underlying every coed school. Certain members of each make heady forays into the other, and from the rest there is a good deal of gawking, speculating, and general preoccupation with those of the opposite sex who are most proximate.

To return to adolescent preferences: What sort of school program would adolescents, as a body and unguided, prefer? Would they prefer more rigorous and more required courses or fewer? More homework or less? A longer or shorter school day, school year? Required or optional commitments? Classroom exposure to classical culture or to pop culture? Would adolescents prefer to sit through a performance of *As You Like It* or a screening of *Risky Business*? Systematically explore the historical record or discuss the events of the day? Read *Moby Dick* or *Jaws*? If most would opt for the latter alternatives over the former, is there a robustness, an agreeable weight to *these* preferences? It is hard to see why an adolescent preference for coeducation should be regarded as any more substantial than other, highly arguable youthful inclinations.

In the fall of 1989, a delightful bit of anthropological research was carried out by Julia Kennedy, a senior at the Buckingham, Browne and Nichols School, a coed independent school in Cambridge, Massachusetts. On special assignment from her school newspaper, Kennedy donned her brother's clothes, a friend's spectacles, and, in collusion with the editor of the student paper of Boston's Roxbury Latin School, set out to document the ethos of boys' school life from her disguised feminine perspective. Announced to the school as a visiting student journalist, "Justin" Kennedy proceeded through a day of exclusively male camaraderie and a scholastic program that included courses in English, contemporary American history, calculus, art, and chemistry. The day was understandably harrowing for her at times; she initiated, but could not bring herself to complete, a mission to the men's room. She carried with her certain expectations from her own well-established coed college preparatory school, and she reported as many similarities as differences to it in the all-boys setting. The Roxbury Latin School, founded in 1645 by the British divine John Eliot, is an academically rigorous, highly regarded school, and Kennedy knew it. But what about its *boy-ness*? The following is excerpted from her published account of her day.

> The bell rang after about twenty minutes, and we headed for English. During class, the all-male atmosphere became apparent. Here, although the class discussion was quite intelligent, the students seemed more relaxed than at B.B.&N., and ready to joke around.

> While analyzing Wordsworth's poem "Tintern Abbey," [the teacher] inquired, "Does he like his sister?" "I like his sister!" [a student] boasted. Mr. Randall laughed again, shook his head, and remarked, "This is a steamy little class here." Nobody looked at me to see if I was offended. Nobody expected me to be.[12]

While duly impressed, Kennedy was on balance less interested in the caliber of the boys' academic performance than in the behaviors that might bear on their relations with girls. A day in the midst of these boys' school boys seemed to alleviate her concerns that they might be missing something essential in gender-relations:

> I dreaded unbearably crude jokes in class, guys slapping my rear in camaraderie, or else myself nearly getting into a fist fight by the end of the day. However, when none of these horrors happened, I wasn't too surprised.

> [Boys] may spend eight hours each day with hardly a female in sight, but this doesn't mean they don't know how to treat girls. In fact, all-boys' school never [!] produce boys who behave differently from boys with a coed school education.

> They just make for a very interesting day.[13]

An interesting day, and then some. Speaking personally, I too can recall my sudden immersion into boys' school life. While, unlike Julia Kennedy, I entered the school (Cleveland's University School) as a male and as a new member of the faculty, the composition and tone of the school made a vivid contrast to the coeducational high school and college I had attended. I had chosen the school because I needed the job, not for its all-boy composition. I had liked my earlier visits, and was impressed by the directed liveliness in the classes I observed. What I had admired, I thought, was the vigorous, down-to-business tone of the school, which I attributed to the quality of the students enrolled and to an especially effective faculty. I was, if anything, unfavorably disposed to the idea of an all-male student body. Again, boys' schools had played no part in my own (far from exemplary) education, and I wondered whether boys without girls might not evolve into forms of barbarism unfamiliar to me. As it happened, my prejudices were unfounded. I was not unpleasantly surprised by the boys' approach to school life, but I was surprised. In each class, at each baseball practice, at the luncheon table, but most vividly in the continuous stream of light and serious conversation with them in the hallway, after class, or on the way to and from the fields, I was aware of something altogether new to me. There was an unaffected directness, an authenticity I had not experienced before in a school—and that I had not thought possible between students and their teachers. Attempting to describe it to my wife, I used the term "edge." There was a special edge to boys' school life, a positive edge.

Twenty-two years have passed since I registered those initial impressions. I have now dwelled professionally in a boys' school, the same one, so long and so agreeably that I find it hard to imagine deliberately deciding to school children otherwise. I find it continually, renewably inspiring that my colleagues and the boys they teach set such staggeringly high goals for their intellectual, athletic, and artistic performance. The striving after these creates the edge I sensed years ago. Until I observed it in a boys' school, I never saw adolescents so self-directed or so resourceful. Life has never been easy in my school. Challenges are real, consequences are sometimes hard. Even gifted boys are unlikely to succeed without tenacity and courage. It is possible to fail. Despite, and in some respects because of, the fact that their school life poses real challenges, the boys express more straightforward support and affection for one another than I had ever thought possible among schoolchildren.

Whatever I expected from the teaching life in my twenties, I do not think it included a sustained infusion of inspiration and hope, but that is what happened. That is what the edge has produced. I am grateful, but no longer surprised, that I learned this lesson in a boys' school. It is a durable lesson.

[1] *Robert Bly, "What Men Really Want," New Age, September 1982, quotation from page 31.*

[2] *Ibid., p. 32.*

[3] *Ibid., p. 34.*

[4] *Ibid., p. 37.*

[5] *Ibid., p. 33.*

[6] *Nancy J. Chodorow,* Feminism and Psychoanalytic Theory *(New Haven: Yale University Press, 1989).*

[7] *Sigmund Freud,* An Outline of Psychoanalysis *(New York: Norton, 1969), pp. 46-47.*

[8] *Anthony Bryk and Valery Lee, "Effects of Single Secondary Schools on Student Achievement and Attitudes,"* Journal of Educational Psychology *78 (1986): 381-95.*

[9] *J. M. Tanner, "Sequence, Tempo, and Individual Variations in Growth and Development of Boys and Girls Aged Twelve to Sixteen,"* in Twelve to Sixteen: Early Adolescence, *ed. Jerome Kagan (New York: Norton, 1971), pp. 1-24.*

[10] *W. A. Astin,* Four Critical Years: Effects of College and Beliefs, Attitudes and Knowledge *(San Francisco: Jossey-Bass, 1977).*

[11] *Ibid.; and Bryk and Lee, "Effects of Single Secondary Schools on Student Achievement and Attitudes," p. 381.*

[12]*Julia Kennedy, "I Was a Boy for the Vanguard," Roxbury Latin School* Tripod *(Boston 1989), p. 10.*
   [13]*Ibid.*

17

Bring Back Chips

Stephen Gyllenhaal's deftly composed film *Waterland* is about a teacher, and it wants to teach us something about our moment in this century.

Artfully adapted by screenwriter Peter Prince from Graham Swift's 1982 novel, *Waterland* is in its quiet way more ambitious than *Malcolm X*. *Waterland* seeks more than to set the historical record straight; it wants to deny the very intelligibility of that record—to take one final step past theology into pure, terrifying psychology.

The story begins as a rumpled, rheumy-eyed history teacher, Tom Crick (Jeremy Irons), attempts to summarize the thrust of the French Revolution to a classroom full of working-class Pittsburg teenagers.

The students are not engaged. They look cramped and crowded at their desks, their attitudes too casual for learning. Beyond the filmy windows, the Pittsburg sky is gray. The words *Liberté, Fraternité, Égalité* have been chalked onto the blackboard.

Mr. Crick is wanly pumping the class for responses, for anything, when a pallid, hung-over-looking boy at the back of the room asks, "What's the *point?*"

The question is only partly impertinent. From what we are shown of the boy's circumstances and prospects. He could not fairly be expected to see the point of the French Revolution, of history classes, of school or of a grown man teaching in one.

Nor could the boy know when he asks the question that his teacher himself has long since lost track of the point. His bluff called, Mr. Crick slips out from behind his teacherly mask and starts telling the only kind of truth he can: the unvarnished story of his life. The story is neither pretty nor happy, but, due in part to surprisingly frank sexual episodes, it interests the students more than the French Revolution.

Mr. Crick, who grew up in the harsh, majestic fen country—waterland—of Britain's East Anglia, comes of age as England mobilizes for war. While still a schoolboy, he falls into a vigorous carnal relationship with a pretty neighbor girl. The young couple expresses no guilt, no shame, no concern that they are breaking an important convention of their era.

Then Mr. Crick's story takes a turn for the worse. The girl becomes pregnant, and no safe, convenient way to terminate the pregnancy exists. To make matters worse, Crick's retarded brother becomes confused about the paternity of the coming baby and commits a needless murder. The narrative moves relentlessly to a horrifying revelation of what the young lovers do about their conception.

Attentive now, the students are willing to hear more. They are provided background of a previous generation: of something like "history." And here the film forsakes its naturalism and shows Crick touring his charges through the world of his grandparents as if it were a living museum.

But it is not a benign museum. We see ancestral Cricks sink from commercial prosperity to near ruin, and in the process the family patriarch takes his daughter in incest (fast emerging as the preeminent theme in contemporary letters).

So there it is. The *point*. The point of Mr. Crick's life is that his wobbly trajectory into the world has been predetermined by dark, sickening forces that were out of his control.

There is a grim inevitability to Crick's fate. Given the story's existential assumptions, the mature Crick will not reverse his fortunes or gain momentum. He will certainly never teach history again, because, as the film insists, there is no history; there is only one's own story.

This is a very modern point—or more correctly, a very postmodern point. There is no history, only my story; no true and durable values, only my values. There is no common, transpersonal message to be derived from the human record; there is only what has happened and is now happening to me. In such a world both tradition and posterity are hollow impostors. The only politics are the politics of you against me.

In such a world the educational possibilities range from Mr. Crick's hopelessly mouthing canonical verities before the impervious youth of Pittsburgh to Mr. Crick's sharing sad, private reveries before the impervious youth of Pittsburgh. He will fail and burn out either way. There is no happy, improving outcome. There is no inspiration, no progress, no education. There is no history, only my story, and the future is whatever happens next.

We have come to this position fairly recently. In 1934 it was possible for a very different kind of story, James Hilton's *Goodbye, Mr. Chips,* to resonate powerfully throughout the English speaking world. The 1939 film starring Robert Donat made a similar impact. A short novella composed over the course of a few days, *Goodbye, Mr. Chips* is the story of a teacher, and it wants to teach us something.

Hilton's fictional teacher, Chipping, or "Chips," is a loving memorial to an actual teacher who gave his working life to the author's alma mater, the Leys School in Cambridge, England.

Over the course of five decades, Mr.. Chips, a Latin teacher, instructs and otherwise fortifies boys in the same school, celebrates with them, grieves with them, sees the school through policy and structural changes and through one world war. Mr. Chips holds an unimpressive degree, and he is a very shaky classroom instructor at first. He is, if anything, a more dubious teaching prospect than Mr. Crick.

Chips, like Crick, can be assumed to have had a past, even an adolescence, but whatever it was, it is over by the time he takes up his responsibilities as a teacher and as an adult.

Because Chips's adolescence is behind him, he can turn his attention and modest gifts to adolescents—and also to Latin, to the many complexities of a school community he comes to love, and to the larger culture in which that school is embedded. Chips signs on, joins up. By doing so he is enlarged and transformed in ways that surprise him. A tentative teacher becomes an old pro. A slightly priggish young man grows into a wise and generous colleague. A confirmed bachelor becomes—briefly—a loving and lovable husband. A timid soul becomes assertive and strong.

Chips not only accepts history; he emerges as its benevolent custodian. Somehow through sheer durability and service, Chips's ordinary calling in an ordinary place rises into something like, well, *greatness.*

Moreover, it is a greatness storytellers would find renewably appealing. The story does not require the comfortable trappings of an elite private school. Frances Gray Patton's *Miss Dove* novels of the fifties celebrate the same kind of devotion in a New England spinster who teachers geography to three generations of boys and girls in a public elementary school.

The notion that committed teaching sustains not only children but the teachers themselves is by no means limited to fiction. Seemingly whenever a luminous writer takes up his or her pen to document a life dedicated to school life and children—as John McPhee does so gracefully in his *Portrait of a Headmaster,* a biographical essay about Deerfield Academy's legendary Frank Boyden—Mr. Chips comes back to life.

But what has happened to quietly committed souls who keep school and in so doing discover purpose in their lives? What has eclipsed our interest in them and left us instead with beaten Mr. Crick, on the sauce and out of a job? More universally, what has happened to stories about tenacious survivors, problem solvers and strivers?

The answer may lie in a peculiar habit of mind which has now emerged as a cultural norm: We have come to embrace the victim. People increasingly want to see themselves as victims and, when it is convenient, to see others as victims. History can easily be read as the record of victimization, and if particular accounts suggest otherwise, then it must be because they were written by the victimizing forces of oppression.

While it may outwardly seem a restrictive and painful thing to be a victim, emotionally it delivers a terrific payload.

Victims have been done ill by forces beyond their control: class, gender, race, war, crime, institutions of every kind, and—*especially*—parents. Therefore one's trouble, whether it is a disability, an inability, a moral lapse, poor work, unpopularity, loneliness, delinquency, or general unhappiness, is somebody else's fault. The victim is to be consoled and understood, for he or she is not responsible.

At the very core of psychoanalysis lies the proposition that every child is a victim. Fueled by deadly and erotic drives they never asked for, children are pitted in dreadful opposition to their similarly motivated parents. They are said to experience primordial fear of being raped or sexually mutilated by mom and dad. Children's early emotional life is directed by such forbidding complexes as "castration anxiety" and "penis envy."

More and more adult voices are appearing in print or on *Oprah* to say it isn't just a complex; it really happens. And once it happens, victims are "high-risk" candidates to victimize others. To beat and to otherwise abuse their own children, to be dishonest, unfaithful, unreliable, unhappy and unsuccessful. Who can blame them?

It has now become plausible to assert that anyone and everyone is a victim. Even those who somehow miraculously escape the cycle of victimization must know and intermingle with victims; they are thus "co-dependent" victims.

In this evolutionary process, we may have already gone too far. But before we go further, we might pause to consider the absurdity of the notion that being a victim somehow existentially frees one from the responsibility to work hard and to live well.

As it turns out, the culture of victimization has not really thought through this victim business. The reason we pity and console victims is that what happened to them *was not deserved*; it could or should have been otherwise. In other words victims are worthy of our attention because we tacitly agree that *no one should be a victim.*

But in a culture in which everyone is a victim, it becomes hard to care. Victims are starting to seem resistible, even a little boring. In order for us to care, there must be true, inalienable *standards* known implicitly and understood by all human beings everywhere. Such a standard might be "It is wrong to injure children or to use them for sexual gratification." Another might be "It is generally right to tell the truth and to keep commitments."

Such standards—truths—are the only basis for a human community. If there are such standards and thus such a community, then we are able to know a thing or two. We are able to know, for instance, right from wrong, oppressor from victim, victim from mere nurser of wounds.

Communities constituted on shared truths do not always prosper. They do not always win wars or realize a golden age. But they recognize the truth when they see it, and they can discriminate between truth-tellers and liars. Our best accounts of what is true comprise history, which is older and bigger than my personal story.

Moviegoers and readers have become painfully aware, over the course of this quincentennial anniversary of Columbus's first voyage, that we have forgotten how to tell history. Apparently no one knows what to say about Columbus. Certainly the easiest take has been that he imposed his white European-male rapacity, greed, demonic faith and pernicious microorganisms onto an edenic community. He made victims of these good, simple people, and now we are all paying the price.

More thoughtful victimists may object to this kind of thinking and point out that Columbus, too, was a victim, a man in the grip of terrible social forces and pernicious microorganisms.

The contemporary problem is bigger than a botched movie, or even a disturbingly effective one, like *Waterland*. The problem lies in a dangerous public mood, a mood that is at once cynical, timid and lazy. However grand the names for it—postmodernism, deconstruction, relativism—it is basically a bad mood.

The mood is also parasitic, as it uses our language, symbols and other conventions of meaning to persuade us that there is no meaning. It unashamedly distorts and outright fabricates history in order to say in effect: Look, you can express whatever you like and call it history. History it whatever writers in a certain mood write down.

And in the end, as *Waterland* urges us to consider, there is no history. There are only personal stories. But if persons are understood to be victims and only victims, the stories of their lives will be so grim and pointless as to be unendurable. Circumstances victimize Mr. Crick past all hope of living well and teaching well, and besides, there is nothing worth teaching.

An unexamined, but to me fascinating, implication of *Waterland* is that the students in Mr. Crick's class go uninstructed and uninspired. They will have learned nothing, not even about the *Liberté, Fraternité, Égalité* that somehow captured the attention of a younger Mr. Crick. *Waterland* tells us that this non-schooling, this voiding of the cultural record, is inevitable—that it doesn't matter.

It is hard to work with actual children and to accept this view, although I speak as a person steeped in the lore, and also in the company, of Mr. Chipses and Miss Doves.

What would Mr. Chips or Miss Dove say to Mr. Crick over the faculty coffee urn? I think they would say, "If you are as ill as you look, go see a doctor." Or perhaps: "Wash your face and snap out of it—the children are waiting."

PART THREE

TRUE STORIES

True Stories

Theodore Sizer, a lifelong and distinguished educational theorist, once told an assembly of school teachers among whom I sat that next to theology, educational theory is the dullest subject in the world. Personally I am not sure, but there is evidence.

If there is merit in my contention that school life has something important to tell us about the larger culture that contains it, it is certainly true that these good lessons will not likely be conveyed in any comprehensive theory of education. It will be conveyed, rather, in highly particular accounts of what really happens, and what occasionally goes well, in practice. The pieces that follow are tales told out of school, and they are, not incidentally, true.

18

Seeing Things

The prairie—we called it the Fields—was an early confirmation of divinity-on-earth.

Backing on the convent
Was a prairie full of pale green hay,
Green in April, otherwise
Tufted up in wheat-bleached whirls
Like twisted tops of brooms
Brushed over the flat expanse
Skirting farms with weathered barns
Highway streaked, cracked by creeks,
Mouse tickled and pheasant scratched
For a thousand prairie miles
Beyond the skyline's hazy edge.

Hiking, crawling, bellying under and over the fields of high grass, the creek banks, the marshy thickets of sumac and scrub, I understood the primitive impulse to *map out* turf. The retreading of familiar steps, especially in a wilderness, serves to imprint that turf in the brain. External geography is not real until it becomes internal geography. I charted an intricate expanse which covered miles of fields beyond the town's edge, knew every thicket, every tractor path, the depth and feel of each bend in the creek, knew which of the slender scrub trees would support a climber's weight and which tangle of bush and branch was waste and which was likely to give up a crazed rabbit.

And there were those breathtaking stands of poplars (planted in such straight lines to demarcate property?) against deep blue late afternoon skies—or, sometimes, against orange-pink sunset, which, when it happens, is pure holiness.

The fields beyond the edge of town were glutted with animals—not deer, which the farmers had cajoled and herded into Forest Preserves regulated by the state of Illinois. But the animals which are part of the texture of the prairie itself are indomitable: buckwheat-colored rabbits, squirrels, chucks, muskrats, possum, skunk, shaggy rats, river rats, chipmunks, field mice, black snakes, garter snakes, and corn snakes. Because our fields were not farmed or cut, they would, on hot, dry, July mornings, shiver and hiss with snakes starting and twisting away from our footsteps: a glimpse only of their khaki and stripes through the bleached swirls of grass. Khaki and stripes—they all wore the same clothes: chipmunk, garter snake, toad, grasshopper, badger, beaver, even the forgotten fawn.

No chart, no labeled spectrum can convey the scarlet of a scarlet tanager nor the orange of an oriole, nor the yellow of a finch, nor the blue of a bluebird. (Whereas cardinals and jays are flashy, if a little vulgar, the jays just a rank or two above khaki and stripes.)

They—bee, bird, badger, and boy—bake in the same sun-blue medium, on the mat of a prairie. The boy alone is unsatisfied, charging from the generative bake of the fields to the still damp of thicket, creek, and pool.

At his—at my—core the boy is, like Narcissus at his pool, trying to get back to something, trying to join it, merge with it. Spring thaws the impulse; July excites it to boiling. Boy's eye meets bird's eye with an inarticulate thrill, moves to it, would hold it in his hands if he could. He would—and this is true—kill it.

Killing is a little-investigated expression of the impulse to have. Thoreau knew about it. He said he would never trust a pacifist who had not evolved through his urge to hunt. Every boy at his core knows the urge. I am not sure that girls know it.

Killing is an extension of sweet desire, of a primal love—which sounds wretched, perverse. Moreover, it *is* wretched and perverse, the impulse spoiled the instant it becomes understood: when it becomes a conscious intention. Only in deep alienation, in the most depressed illnesses, and in the cheapest "art" is the *self-conscious* killing of the beloved celebrated as profound. But for boys, for a spell in their time, the desire for animals and the desire to kill them are fused. So sweet and so deeply pulsing is the fusion that civilized restraints on its expression (while very important for civilization) do not diminish it in the least. The drive overpowers restraint, overpower gentler affections. It spills over its bearer, and it spoils over the living objects of desire. It can so overcome the killer that even the means of killing—the dagger, the bow, the arrow, the rifle—become charged with it. Men even now, stalled at this point in their development, make idols of their weapons. They oil stocks. They sift bullets through their fingers like coins. They feel, and even dully express, that the sweetness, the power is somehow *in the gun*. Potential slaughter lies this way, and it has always lain this way.

The boy's eye instantly closes the distance between self and the bird on the wire. The rabbit hounded out of bramble and zig-zagging wildly out of reach is frozen in the boy's mind's eye. There is a furry fold between the shoulder and the neck, a soft vulnerability, a target.

Imaginary hunts preoccupy the boy at rest. Simulated hunts fill his play. Halting, hopeless, half-understood hunts direct his wandering through prairie and thicket. There may be a gun, toy or not. There may be a longing for a gun.

I dreamed of rifles
On the wall, ownable, heft in my hands,
The shoulder fit of the oiled stock,
An eye down the dull blue barrel.

Cocking one with a clink I could feel it
Tense inside, over-ready.
Finger joint cool on the trigger's curve,
Fondling, refitting itself,

A certain tickle of control:
The firm pull would be final.

Once there was a rifle, a toy.
A blue tin facsimile.
But I could cock it,
Set a spring and shoot
Hard corks across the living room
Or at the line of plastic crows
Clipped upon a wire rack.
Cork-struck, they dropped
And clicked like plastic on the hardwood,
A slight recognition
In each tinny kill.

So few guns would shoot.
Lightweight pistols lined with flimsy springs
Launched plunger-headed plastic darts
Puckering onto a pane of glass.
Maybe. Maybe at first.
Then the flash and bone of western guns,
Rhinestone holstered handfuls—

One wide morning in a summer field,
I draw suddenly on something in the treeline
And shoot: a cap cracks the clearness.
The sweet char of its powder
Reminds me of something.

And I pass between the sun and form
Of an old mythic bird,
Dead again in the grass.
Again its stillness startles—

Bone-beaked, feather edges fine as snakeskin:
Prey. I am pre-Indian
Standing over pre-Eagle.

Before the bison or the bow
I was sinew and spear,
A sense of skull, of flank, of tender throat,
The cat's night eye,
A pounce.

Before the rifle (smuggled against permission into the garage) there was a year of the bow and arrow. *Father—what a lapse!* The bow was as tall as I was, and I could string it only with arm-trembling exertions. The four blue-feathered, silver-tipped arrows I quickly lost, shot past all finding in the fields, and replacements were purchased at the hardware store in town. *Merchants—where did you imagine those arrows would fly?* Into straw-backed targets? Into cardboard boxes? No, they were fired dreamily up into the undersides of eagles, dead into the swollen guts of bears. Rabbits, foxes, and weasels were stuck clear through, dead instantly, as if frozen by the arrow shafts.

There were never enough arrows. Two or three were bounty. A shot into the Fields, if it was a shot of any distance, was almost certainly a lost arrow. Yet every afternoon of a late, cold, darkening autumn a friend and I, equally entranced by the lure of the kill, padded over the frosty tufts of prairie grass, our toes, fingertips, noses raw with the cold. The lower the sun behind the poplars and behind the ravaged stalks of corn, the creamier the grassy way before us. In that light the swirls of spent grasses were transformed from tans to peach to rose. Only a few times did I see the full cycle into soft grays and blues as night fell. (These outings entailed, besides the loss of supper, angry reprisals and promised confinements.)

What were we expecting with our numbing fingers wrapped around the varnished curve of our bows, our two or three mangy arrows rattling over our backs in their makeshift quivers? We expected deer. We expected a majestic buck. He would step unexcitedly out of a thicket and pause before us, the hoof of one foreleg raised slightly above the turf. He would see us but look beyond us. Then our arrows would pierce him, would make him ours. We could know this passionately, relegating the knowledge of forest preserves to the insubstantial realm of common sense and recent history.

There is a margin of time at dusk on a prairie—the hour when tans blur into rose—when a deer, when even a lion, could emerge before a boy. But in spite of this knowledge we were frightened almost senseless when, in the course of stalking noisily over some spent corn rows, not one, not two, but three pheasants, pheasants rampant, roared up out of the stubble right in front of us. I knew as I drew back my arrow (far too late) that I was no match for the pheasants' magnificence. I might just as well have thrown my arrows at them or made a face. Once projected up into the darkening blue, the pheasants became pure silhouette and glided off in a great arc. Far behind them, far too low, our arrows rose, wobbled, and fell back to earth, lost in a thick stand of scrub. Waves of feeling—reverence and loss—silenced us. We made a show of looking for our lost arrows, but it was rapidly darkening, and it was very cold. My friend said he had to go home; we were both inexcusably late.

I would not go. I was near tears, and I could not explain it. I was *there*, I had arrived, I was standing plumb in the middle of rosy, mythic light I had longed for. Three magnificent fowl, shimmering like honey, in green, in deep red, had risen like flags to confirm it, and I had failed even to touch it.

Another great bird arose. Before I reached for my last arrow, I knew how futile my "shot" would be; the very realization weakened my arms and my trembling fingers. Once again my arrow arched feebly below the trajectory of the pheasant. *If I could not touch these things,* I cried out loud, *why was I there?*

That night I could not sleep for the obsessive reconstruction of the first pheasants' rising. Even in imagination, I could not hold the bow still, could not hold the birds still against the stained glass sky and propel my loving shot through the bones of their breasts. I had been there, but I was just a boy with a boy's bow and two cheap arrows.

I hardened against that hurt. Not far from our house there

was a houseful of brothers who had guns, big boys, who shot to kill. Their talk was all of killing, that and the other secrets. There was something hard, something dead about their company. Even their laughter was deadening—it was more like shouting than laughing. They stole from stores. They kept a large, greasy envelope of obscene photographs in which the naked men and women thrust their exposed parts defiantly toward each other or in the direction of the viewer. They were angry pictures. The naked men and women had the same eyes as the brothers who owned the photographs. They all seemed to have a hunch about me. Would I like to drive their old man's car? (I was nine.) Would I dare fire a .38 calibre pistol up into a streetlight?

One bitingly cold November afternoon I followed their hunched shoulders into the Fields. Wedged carelessly under their arms were rifles, gas compression pellet guns, and .22s. I wanted guns like that, I dreamed of guns like that, and the big boys knew it. The prairie was dead, but a rabbit might be scared up, a pheasant might rise up into the soot-and-steel sky.

There was nothing. Nose and chin, lips and jaw became as numb as a drunk's. Fingers stiffened, the rim of each ear burning with the cold. Then somebody spotted a few gray birds—wrens—perched on the prickly twig-fingers of a stand of trees along the creek. They were so remote and so insubstantial that they might have been bits of dead leaf. One of the dead-eyed boys took aim with his pellet rifle and fired a muffled pop into the treeline. Even to his surprise, one of the leaf-bit-birds dropped off its branch and zigzagged sickeningly downward into the grass.

We ran to it. Incredibly tiny, batlike, its legs drove its injured torso around in a circle. There was a dark red hole at the base of the bird's neck, in which a glimpse of metal pellet could be seen. The gray bird seemed to be skewered to the earth by the pellet in its neck. Its bright black eye saw nothing. The bald little legs would grow still, then start spasmodically, driving the damaged torso around the hub of its pain. That tiny bird charged the whole prairie—perhaps the whole cosmos—with terror and pain.

"Your turn," a dead-eyes said to me. "Kill it." He pumped the rifle and handed it to me. He had never let me fire it before.

He guided the barrel of the rifle so it rested on the bird's pulsing head.

"Kill it."

I looked off into the treeline and squeezed the trigger.

"Bye, bird." Their laughter hung in the cold like pain. One of them made a show of crushing the spent little carcass underfoot, and they moved on, toward home. They let me carry the rifle. All the tractor path home, then into the night, then into other nights, still into this night, I am pulsing with the wounded bird, my eyes following the unnatural circuitry of its pain, its neurons, its vessels, its spine, its connectedness to air and tree and prairie smashed and severed by a small shard of lead. I am still on the brink of firing the shot I fired then.

Soon after the shooting, the world stopped presenting itself to me as being continually alive: a living fabric of earth and grass, at times crawling with, at times concealing, an amplitude of animals. The *continuous* impression stopped, but there would be—and still are—powerful reminders. It can be a reminder frozen in a painting, as in Breughel's *Hunters in the Snow*. People of Illinois know that weather and that light, I know; I learned the numb-footed, numb-lipped return from the hunt over dead, snow-patched turf. I know the green in the gray of winter skies, how the cold penetrates every layer, how it can freeze and emphasize distances yet to walk. No one would waste a word in that weather, walking that ground.

But one midsummer afternoon in the north of Michigan it all came back to me. My family had taken a vacation cottage on a clear, cold lake. I had reached an age, twelve, where Michigan no longer *meant* the tug of pike far beneath the glassy surface of gold-brown water. The sharp-sweet pine, the tang of which, mixed with earth, damp, and cooking, rose up and tantalized me even inside the cabin. It was in the sheets, in the sofa cushions, in the sink drains. It would emanate from the walls and from the wide planks of the floor.

Other things had come up, unsettlingly, to command my attention: less substantial but more insistent. There were, foremost, the inexhaustible rituals of sport. Each sport—baseball, golf, tennis—held out its own elaborate conventions, its attractive (but always subtly changing) nuances, and its gallery of local, national, and mythic heroes. Not to mention the equipment. Sculptures in oiled leather, miraculously polished wooden shafts and frames, gleaming club-heads, somehow both bulbously heavy and sharp-edged, bottle-handled bats, creamy new baseballs, the cul-de-sacs of the cowhide's red stitches blurring into my concentration just before my air-creasing swing. Every summer morning opened into the swirl and drill and news of sport, but the North Woods was not the place for it: the North Woods suspended the noise.

One still and steamy afternoon there, left alone while the rest of the family fished, I struck out aimlessly on a footpath into the woods. Without looking, eyes on the path, I passed beyond the ring of cottages, through the thick, low pines, even through gradations of terrain hardly noticed onto more open, airier ground. The trees were silver birches, and they flickered their higher leaves like bright coins in the breezes. There was movement now. The ground fell away on one side of the path, dropping into the bed of a fast and forceful stream. The stream pushed itself noisily over and around rocks and fallen timber. In the shallows, dappled tan and white, the stream glossed over smooth stones, then darkened into deeper pools of root beer brown.

Mindlessly hurried along by the steam, I happened onto a wide, sandy flat, where the current splayed out to the width of a little river. Ahead of me the birches and scrub circled around and closed the path, but by fording the sandy shallows, I could cross the stream and proceed into what looked like range after range of pale sand dunes, creamy-looking in the late afternoon light.

There, midstream, the clear water rippling over the soles of

my shoes, something underneath the surface caught my eye.
The floor of the stream bed, seemingly composed of sand and
stones, began to move beneath the water like a slow kaleido-
scope of earth tones. There was a quick intimation of "other
laws" taking hold. I did not resist. I watched with a thrill as a
cluster of mottled rocks before me became sizable crayfish
which, perhaps disturbed by my step, scuttled over the sand
away from me. Then, as if sent to verify my trespass and to file
a report, the lacquered snouts of four or five brown trout
appeared about an invisible circumference perhaps a yard
from where I stood. They hovered there in tense precision like
a line of bombers. Their iridescent browns, honey, and spangles picked up perfectly the camouflage of the crayfish, of the
afternoon light over the rippled surface, and the dappled bottom cover. Next, as if to reveal to the adjusted eye even more
elemental components of stream, dark minnows began shooting like needles through the composition, drawn forward in
delicate parallels, then veering sharply away, as if filings before
an unseen magnet.

Anything seemed possible in that enchanted light, provided
I did not take a step. How long did I stay? A few seconds? An
hour and a half? However long, it was rosy twilight, the water
gone to dark glass, by the time I sloshed onto the dune-side of
the stream. I was half-willing to proceed over the dunes to an
unseen Lake Superior, even, if I could have expressed it, to
the Nile or to Arcady. But I only took a step or two, for out of
the scrub along the stream's edge appeared a lovely doe and
her fawn, mute and regal. Again the imitation: *other laws.*

What happened next would surely have been surprising at
another time. But in this particular procession of events in
which stones had become crustaceans, leaves mantises, the
blacker scars on the birches wizened bats, it seemed inevitable
that other deer, what must have been a herd of deer, would
materialize out of the scrub and take their stately places at the
stream's edge. Even in zoos or when otherwise domesticated,
deer call one fleetingly back to an earlier time. Each wants to
say something, some gentle warning. Like cats, both genders

are profoundly feminine. Deer have been hurt so much and for so long that they can only take flight or implore. There were about forty of them that evening. They were spaced along the curve of the stream. Each would drink silently, then draw back upright and still, alert to twilight signals available only to a deer.

There I stood in the middle of it: a secret open to me—and perhaps opening still. Would wolves come down to drink? Panthers? I could spoil it with a shout, with a stomp of my foot, with a splash. Who would believe it? Who would even share it with me? I walked home.

I wanted to explain it, but got no further than describing the path. I did not know how to begin to tell the truth about it. The facts, the words I knew did not say enough: I saw a lot of crayfish and fish and deer. Not even a photograph would contain what I saw. I said I took a hike and that it was really great.

I deliberated hard about asking my family to return with me to the enchanted spot. Even now I am not sure whether the thing I dreaded most was that when we reached the ford, there would be nothing to see—or that they *would* see what I had seen, and the very fact of so much publicity would disenchant the experience forever. As it happened I did not take anybody to the spot, but I returned a few days later, alone.

I took off on this second solitary hike just after bright noon and wondered whether this would alter everything. The walk seemed longer. The path was muggy and buggy, but the gusts which brushed through the birches and the pines stirred up enough sense of deep solitude that another powerful transformation seemed at least possible. Would it be the same? Did I really want it to be the same?

Just at the point where the path terminated and, around a bench of scrub, the stream splayed out into the sandy flat, I stopped. Had it ever really happened? Had I dreamed all that life? The answer came crackling noisily from my left. A large doe shouldered her way out of the thick scrub and stopped still about ten yards ahead of me on the path. With the calm of a cow, she swung her head in my direction and appeared to consider me thoughtfully. Satisfied of something, she turned away and stepped unhurried around the bend to the rushing water. Satisfied myself, I ran home.

19

Boys' Stories

Smart lad, to slip betimes away
From fields where glory does not stay
And early though the laurel grows
It withers quicker than the rose.

And round that early-laurelled head
Will flock to gaze the strengthless dead
And find unwithered on its curls
The garland briefer than a girl's.

A.E. Housman,
To An Athlete Dying Young

When I was twenty-three years old, I took a job teaching in a boys' college preparatory school. At the time it seemed an expedient, and probably temporary, thing to do. I had been a graduate student, I had no money, and I was engaged to be married. The school, as I assessed it, was solid enough; its all-boys composition did not figure much into my deliberations.

I had known graduates of such schools in college: "prep school" boys who, despite clear individual differences, seemed also, in some way I had not bothered to define, to bear a common stamp. If I had examined that impression further, I suppose I would have concluded that this boys' school "mark" derived from wealth and class, also perhaps from the experience of living together in a kind of spartan intimacy. When my prep school friends talked about their school lives, there was a depth of feeling that was foreign to me. Some of them were affectionately wistful about alma mater, and some seemed strangely dependent on former friends and faculty. Many were openly hostile to the schools they had left, resentful of remembered restrictions, bruised by discipline or low appraisals of their abilities.

As a graduate of midwestern public schools, I shared no such feelings. My schooling had been coeducational from kindergarten onward. School life seemed a seamless continuation of life in the town where I lived. The school buildings were solidly made, brightly lit, spacious, and clean. The faculty, until junior high school nearly all of them women, were on balance competent and professional. Although more than half of the graduates of my high school went on to college, I recall no one who felt especially engaged or inspired or intellectually directed by the school. The high school was large— more than twice the size of the liberal arts college I attended—and of necessity highly routinized and, I suppose, a little impersonal. The social agenda of my "set"—both friendships and amorous arrangements—seemed to me infinitely engaging, seemed actually to provide the energy and the emotional substance of the school enterprise. It would never have dawned on me to call my schooling "good" or "important."

By contrast, my undergraduate experience, while hardly distinguished by disciplined achievement on my part, was intellectually thrilling. Teachers seemed eccentric, hard-edged, personable, many of them brilliant. Great cultural figures— Plato, Machiavelli, Keats—came vividly alive through the explication of their work. But returning to a school, a boys' prep school, to teach—I really did not know what I could fairly expect.

My first and most vivid impression was of how thoroughly male a boys' school felt. The presence of so many boys and men was not at all repellent. The absence of girls and the scarcity of women was harder to get used to, especially at first. I remember being fascinated by how much the relative absence of females intensified my awareness of the few who did pass through my perceptual field in the course of the school day: an elderly librarian, the office receptionist, the art teacher, some older boy's girlfriend on the football sidelines. This was no simple erotic arousal; it was a heightened awareness of the otherness, of seemingly every feature of these women and girls. I believe this period of my life advanced me a long way toward seeing and appreciating the astonishing individuality and range of females.

The converse did not occur: the immersion in maleness did not blur or generalize the features of the boys. From the outset, their individuality surfaced in clear, often eccentric relief. As one who had grown up, I had always assumed, a "boy's boy"—from earliest memory moving in packs, then cliques of male friends, crazy about sports, susceptible to the inspiration of questers, swashbucklers, and romantic heroes—I was surprised by much of what I saw in my new school. There were instinctively gracious and even beautifully mannered boys (as well as plenty of noble savages), but there were no "regular," "average," what used to be called "all-American" boys. No one seemed to me merely well-rounded. Their talents, introversions, extroversions, even their occasional pathologies were vividly realized. To me at twenty-three and newly married, they seemed surprisingly far along in the realization of what was distinctive about them. They seemed older and bolder than my boyhood friends in the things they would risk saying or taking on. They also seemed younger in their absence of inhibition; the toughest and most worldly-wise among them seemed to me more vulnerable than the warier and thus blander companions of my schooldays.

This was of course a college preparatory school, and most of the boys threw themselves into their school work with an almost worrying lack of perspective. From the outset, my students accomplished things beyond my highest expectations, often failing, and failing devastatingly, to realize their own. Working among them, I found it impossible to maintain my own detachment, "adult" perspective, critical distance. I remember struggling to find words to describe the school climate to my wife and being able only to come up with: "There's such an edge to the place." It was a stimulating edge. To my surprise, I found that for the first time in my life I was wholly engaged in the task before me: on a kind of train with no clear plan or desire to get off.

To some extent, every new teacher begins his or her work as something of an impostor. Before we can really do it—introduce, clarify points of knowledge; devise activities that exercise students in such a way that they will master them—we play at teaching, strike teacherly poses, hope we are credible. The younger the teacher, the more effortful the debut. Perhaps a carefully designed system of teacher-training in which a master teacher initiates an apprentice is the best way to launch a young teacher, but that was not possible in my school; the other teachers were too heavily loaded with responsibilities to ease me through my initiation.

It was a kind of initiation, and even now, after twenty-five years in the classroom, teaching boys still feels a little like initiation. On balance, I believe this has been very good for me. Any progress I have made in the direction of authenticity in my teaching and my other communications with students has been elicited by the boys' own extraordinary authenticity. And that lesson is continuing. However one assesses its emotional charge or moral value, the social climate of boys together is radically authentic. There is not of course a "type" of boy; there are types.

The dramatic realization of these several types tends to confirm and to celebrate a corporate sense of maleness in the community generally. Such communities feel especially alive. Distinctive boys remind every boy of who he is.

Unworldly Boys

In his superbly thoughtful book, *Secret Gardens,* Humphrey Carpenter makes a persuasive case that the profusion of transformingly powerful children's books that appeared in the decades spanning Queen Victoria's reign and the first world war was a kind of collective elegy for a lost world. At the highest level of generality, the lost world is childhood itself, and refinding it fantastically or whimsically as the young heroes and heroines do in *Alice in Wonderland, Peter Pan, Wind in the Willows, The Secret Garden, The Water Babies,* or *Winnie the Pooh* has proved durably appealing to children. Carpenter also suggests that something more specific than childhood passed with the Victorian era. For the writers in question, predominantly men, something arcadian, something pastoral and fine passed as well. The child's spiritual link with the green earth—with water and meadow in particular—seemed forever severed by the ultimate and massive encroachment of city, industry, and internal combustion. From the vantage point of the great children's-story writers, a vernal past they had just managed to glimpse and to savor had been effaced by modernism. The military-industrial ravages of World War I killed it forever.

Carpenter's thesis is that not just the likes of Alice or Peter Pan or Ratty or Mole needed pastoral sweetness—a prior, better time—in order to thrive; so did their creators. So do, my school experience suggests, many boys. Certain boys, even as I write, seem to have emerged into an era that is cruelly inappropriate to their distinctive spirit and gifts.

Donald Merritt was such a boy. He came to us midway through high school when his elegant family was transferred to this city by the corporation which employed his father. There had been many such moves, at least seven or eight of them, in the course of Donald Merritt's schooling, and he had learned to accommodate these dramatic changes of context with a flourish. In fact, Donald Merritt did everything with a flourish.

From the moment he was introduced to the assembled school as a new boy entering mid-year, his classmates were at a loss as to what to make of him. He was tall and willowy, and his longish blond hair fell away from a center part in untidy curls. Whatever complicated shirt and jersey arrangement he happened to be wearing, the effect was always of some kind of buccaneer's blouse. His black woolen cape—quickly to become Donald's trademark in the school—was, the morning he was introduced, draped jauntily over one arm.

His almost ridiculously Byronic demeanor, it turned out, took no inspiration from Lord Byron. When I got to know Donald, I asked him about Byron, and he cheerfully drew a blank. I was not far wrong, however, suspecting there was an historical figure behind Donald's swashbuckling persona. That figure, as it happened, was Rimbaud, the French imagist poet and famous *enfant terrible*. Donald Merritt was encyclopedic about Rimbaud. He could cite whole poems in both English and French. The French was intoned nasally and boldly, the accent wildly inaccurate. In fact, a French teaching colleague claimed that these impromptu recitations were indecipherable as French. But to the ears of his fellow students, Donald's utterances from Rimbaud were sufficiently "foreign" to impress.

Donald also knew seemingly every detail of Rimbaud's dissolute, foreshortened life. In my own classroom, he once reported at length about Rimbaud's troubled love affair with his fellow *imagiste*, Paul Verlaine. When other boys expressed uneasy interest in the lovers' homosexuality or drug-taking, Donald was loftily contemptuous. "That is a very American, very middle class question," he chided one questioner. Rimbaud and Verlaine were, in his words, destructively, brutally true to their art. "The poems more than justify the lives," he would say, then declaim in forceful nasal tones what may have been "The Drunken Boat."

Donald was apparently unfazed in any way by the masculine teenage conventions of his classmates. If his posturing was an act, it was a flawless act. I can still picture him when the bell sounded ending the instructional day: cutting a swashbuckling path through the throngs of boys heading down to pool or gym or mat for afternoon practices. Donald's leonine head of curls would be thrown back, his cape flung back over his shoulder, as the student body coursed past him like weather.

His senior year he expressed some interest in a play I had decided to direct that winter: Edgar Lee Masters' *Spoon River Anthology*. He told me he had acted in the play previously, in

Minneapolis, and that the performance had been staged in an actual cemetery among the graves. "And that," he told me "is how it should really be done." I did not agree, and in any event I could not imagine such a performance in the dead of winter in Cleveland, Ohio. Whatever reservations he felt about participating in a possibly workaday production of the play, Donald surprised me by auditioning. Up to that point, he had made a point of disdaining all of the school's extra-curricular activities. He liked to leave the school at the earliest allowable hour in order, his schoolmates presumed, to get on with whatever Rimbaud-like activity was available beyond our gates.

More surprising than his decision to try out for *Spoon River Anthology* was the quality of his audition. Although he read loudly and clearly, he was a wooden and painfully unnatural presence on stage. To my pleas to act more naturally and to declaim less, he seemed quietly exasperated. "It was very different in Minneapolis," he said more than once. In the course of an extensive audition it became clear to me that Donald would not be able to play a role in *Spoon River*. He read the lines of an unrequited lover, a town drunk, and a severe clergyman in exactly the same strident voice, rather as if he were shouting detailed instructions from a hilltop to faraway listeners.

If Donald was disappointed at not being cast, he did not let on. He did attend the performance, however, and sought me out afterward to tell me, "You really have to see this play in a cemetery."

Donald Merritt was not a very strong student, even in the arts and humanities courses in which his familiarity with artists and writers unknown to his classmates might have been thought to give him a scholastic edge. The consensus of his teachers was that Donald, while reasonably bright, did very little schoolwork. His compositions tended to be surprisingly general, grandiose, thin in substance.

Recommending Donald to college was tricky, because his teachers wanted to stress his individuality and its undeniably stimulating effect on school life, but there was also an honorable reluctance to overpraise a boy of largely unfulfilled promise. Some colleagues felt that Donald was a superficial scholar and at best a kind of eccentric impostor. But whatever doubts the faculty had about his prospects, they were not shared by college admissions officers. His distinctive bearing and turnout, his interest in Rimbaud and the imagists, his extensive travels, and his collection of Venetian glass ornaments combined to make him an irresistibly attractive applicant. His modest SAT scores, 'C' average, and the mild reservations of some of his teachers were cast aside in the face of such a distinctive approach to teenage life.

To the consternation of a few hardworking classmates who were not so chosen, Donald Merritt was admitted to Yale. A veteran admissions officer there told me, almost derisively, that Donald was the first really interesting boy he had interviewed from my school.

I don't know if Donald blazed a distinctive trail through New Haven. I learned only that he left the university after a term. Reports differed as to the reason. Some said he was unhappy at Yale from the start; others that he had done almost no work, had virtually flunked out. Moreover, I heard that Donald did not return to his family, but had taken off, to travel, destination unknown.

For eight years I did not hear another word from or about Donald, and then I learned he had died of AIDS. Before he got ill, he apparently made a substantial reputation for himself as a sculptor. An alumnus of the school who runs a gallery in St. Louis sent me a handsomely printed book-length catalog of Donald's work, exhibits photographed from a posthumous show. I cannot judge the sculptures: large, column-like forms in polished metal. They resembled human torsos, or, some of them, tree trunks. The catalog also included selected writings from a journal Donald kept. From these I learned that he had changed his name to Merritt St. John. About his AIDS symptoms he wrote, "It is true, I feel this way, this no-energy way, but it can't be true! There have been and there continue to be so many beautiful people. Living people. This day and this sky are so clean, so bright, so beautiful. There has got to be something to learn in this sickness, something great, even in this."

Dead Boys

When little boys grow big enough to play in earnest, when they begin to thrust themselves into surrounding space, to try their speed, to see what can be made to roll, to roar, to burn, to explode, when they are at last left alone outdoors, beckoned by water and heights and culverts and caves—parents of necessity stop paying close attention. The truth of the matter is that boys passionate in their play are, like men passionate in their work, both inspiring and terrifying. The best of it is exhilarating, the worst of it unbearable. Some boys die, and many more come close.

Some boys die. They are by their nature at risk, acutely vulnerable. Some settings are safer than others, but none is really safe. The danger is in the boy, not in the neighborhood. The only reliable safeguard against the death of boys is not to conceive them.

Of course the death of a boy I have taught and known undoes me. But there is something distinctive in the aftermath, something like a hook or a message. Perhaps every boy teaches something, but the lessons of dead boys are especially vivid. One feature common to all such lessons is that death does not obliterate them. To the contrary, death fixes a boy's vitality at a single point and holds it there intact. It is not the dead boys but the living ones, the graduates, whose identities blur, who grow unrecognizably beefy and placid and old.

Seth Sampson will never grow old. He is forever a cherub and a clown and an acrobat. I met him when he was in the ninth grade and my student, a poor student then, in ancient history. Never before or since have I met a boy more pessimistic about his academic prospects. The very words, "O.K., take out a clean sheet of paper for a quiz," were enough to paralyze him. At first he would hand in nothing at all.

Working with him outside of class, I would ask him to read a passage of text and explain it to me. I feared the worst, but he surprised me. He could explain, once he got to know me, even very complex and sophisticated material. One day after school in my office I asked him to read a chapter of our ancient Rome text. When he finished, I asked him several pointed questions on its key points. He answered them all clearly and thoroughly. Then I said, "O.K., Seth, I am going to ask you these same questions again, only this time it counts." He stiffened. "What do you mean 'it counts'?" I told him it meant it counted for a grade, that I would grade his answers just as if they were a test. This threw Seth into a muddle, and he was unable to make sense of anything in the chapter.

The following afternoon I had Seth in again and asked him to read the next chapter of the text. "Is it going to count?" he asked. Absolutely not, I told him. He read, and again he revealed a good understanding when we discussed the material afterward. Because we had done so before with no productive effect, I did not bother to point out again that he obviously had the ability to excel in history, that he somehow had to get over his "test" panic. Instead, I took out my grade book and gave him an A on what I decided on the spot was equivalent of a "half test." When Seth reminded me that I said it wasn't going "to count," I told him I had changed my mind. Why shouldn't it count, I asked him; he obviously understood the material.

By assuring Seth repeatedly that, in his case, nothing counted in history, he began doing a little better. He would now answer factual questions, but he would only write tentative little essays, when fully developed ones were required. This turned out to be a far greater challenge than getting him over his test panic. I tried requiring him to fill out a specified number of pages in his exam book, even if he had nothing to say.

At first he was unable to do this, even by repeating himself. In time his essays grew longer, but they never contained more than a simple point or two, never approaching what was expected.

Unsure myself whether Seth was genuinely limited or whether he was somehow "blocked," I tried another trick. I called him in after he had written a typically insubstantial exam and I told him that I thought he had made a breakthrough this time, that he had made some solid points and was beginning to get the hang of writing essays. I gave him a higher grade, a C or C+, than he had gotten on a history test all year. He regarded me warily.

His next test was, if anything, worse than the previous one. I was tempted to abandon my gimmick, but instead decided to give it one more try. No one in the class did particularly well on the exam. There were only a few Bs, and the rest of the grades were lower. I gave Seth one of the Bs. "Definitely a breakthrough," I wrote on his test book. This time, for some reason, he believed me. Slowly, gratifyingly, fact, example, thesis, and extended reflection began to appear in Seth's written work. He became before my eyes a good, an original, a self-directed student of history.

Better than that, a much more energetic, more surprising boy came to life in the school. Seth Sampson turned out to be a phenomenal clown. He had a highly developed athleticism which did not count for much in school sports, except in the annual gymnastics exhibition. Seth could walk on his hands, execute one-armed push-ups, juggle, tumble, and dive. Inspired by the movie comic Chevy Chase, Seth mastered the art of falling down spectacularly. He could trip himself and fall down forwards or backwards in a way that left no doubt that he had broken bones. The school has a wide central staircase broken by two large, carpeted landings. Seth's *tour de force* was losing his footing on the top stair and tumbling head-over-heels, arms akimbo down the stairs, across both landings, to the bottom. He was never hurt.

He loved to fall; that is, he loved the art of seeming to fall.

What he loved was the surprise and the delight. His emergence as a scholar, as a comic sprite, and as a wonderfully generous soul around school seemed almost part of a plan to surprise us. He would pitch in for any kind of service project or school cleanup. If the alumni office staff found themselves short-handed for a big mailing, Seth would volunteer to stuff envelopes after school until he was late for dinner. He was the only boy known to climb the school flag pole. He was rumored to have sneaked onto the school roof at night, pried open a skylight over the pool, and dropped forty feet into the diving well. It was hard to be cautionary or disapproving when Seth toppled or tumbled. I remember feeling once, when he had righted himself at the bottom of the stairs after a spectacular fall, that he was as beamingly happy a boy as I had ever seen.

A year and a day after Seth Sampson graduated from the school, he died. He had completed a successful freshman college year and came home to see some younger boys graduate. When he and his friends drove back to the college campus to retrieve their belongings, they found their dormitory locked. This did not faze Seth. Once before he had entered the building when it had been locked. He lived in a dormered room on the top floor. By holding on to a drain pipe he hoisted himself up from window ledge to window ledge until he reached the roof—which he did to the cheers of his friends on the ground. Balancing like a tightrope walker, arms outstretched, Seth made his way cross a patch of slate roof to reach the dormer window of his own room. This, he had assured his friends, was the easy part. And at that moment it began to rain.

The pitched slate became slippery as ice. His horrified friends then witnessed the unthinkable: Seth falling four floors onto the grass below. The sight and sound of it were sickening. Seth lay in a heap before them, then he rose wide-eyed to his feet. He said he was O.K., then he lay back down again. A friend ran to a phone to call an ambulance. But help arrived too late. The nerves activating his lungs had been severed. No one could clearly explain how, before he died, he had arisen and spoken. Seth loved to fall; that is, he loved the art of seeming to fall. What he loved was the surprise and the delight.

Edward Lee

Edward Lee was a brilliant scholar, one of the most talented young mathematicians in the United States, although I did not know this when I first encountered him at school. A slightly bemused, squinting, thoroughly lost boy, he approached me on New Student Orientation Day and asked me a question which I at first misunderstood: "Could you please tell me where I belong?" The courtesy and calmness of his manner suggested, just for a second, a higher, rather than a lost, being.

Another early impression of Edward was equally unprofessional. He was Korean, and he had an oddly elongated face. The line of his eyes was drawn so tightly that he seemed always to be straining to see. At first glance, he looked prematurely old, a little wizened. His mother, by contrast, looked young and was very beautiful. I wondered, and I know I speculated out loud, how such a beautiful woman could produce so homely a son. But as is so often the case in school, actual experience presents more heavy-handed lessons than any morality play; Edward Lee became beautiful before my eyes.

I have never had a better student than Edward Lee; that is, I have never learned more from a student. He wrote eloquently. In fact, it seemed to me, he wrote perfectly, although I faulted him sometimes for writing so little on what I thought were vast, rich topics. He once asked me, "How would I say more?" Although he must have asserted many things in the time I spent with him in and outside the classroom, I can only remember questions.

He was a member of a very bright and fiercely opinionated class—Introduction to Philosophy—my class. One afternoon, argument was raging, not very productively, over the relationship between ethical prescriptions and faith in the *Sermon on the Mount*. How did a maxim like "turn the other cheek" or "consider the lilies" or even "do unto others" derive from a requirement of faith: "Our Father. . .hallowed be thy name." Is the *Sermon on the Mount* saying, one irritated boy asked, that you can only do good things if you acknowledge God—or is it saying that by doing good things you acknowledge God? Something crudely like a faith-versus-works discussion was escalating noisily when I noted Edward's uninsistent raised hand.

"Why are you linking the two things at all?" he asked.

"They're linked in the Bible."

Edward persisted: "They are both discussed, but are they linked? I see references to acknowledging God but not doing good things, and references to doing good things but not acknowledging God. Aren't they separate, different things?"

"But what would God think of good deeds from someone who didn't believe in God?"

"Wouldn't God know they were good?" Edward asked.

"But that's assuming there is a God!" someone blurted out. "Assume there is no God. Aren't good deeds just as good without a God?"

Edward smiled. "I personally think they would be, but does that matter as much as God thinking they were good?"

Until Edward Lee said that, I had not really understood that the subject of the very course I was teaching was: What makes things matter?

Edward Lee was incisive, naturally analytic, brilliant. He was warm-hearted, but not really light-hearted. He was not much like a boy, and I believe this saddened him. Perhaps sensing this, Colin Blount, an irreverent and very eccentric colleague of mine, set himself to locating Edward's lighter side.

Colin looked after the after-school soccer program for boys who elected to play that sport but who were not interested or skilled enough to play on an interscholastic team. These "general soccer" boys met on bracing, sometimes chilly afternoons on the most marginal fields. "Captains" and sides were chosen each session, and there was some energy, but little intensity, in their anarchic pursuit of the ball over the scuffed turf.

When the number of boys showing up made uneven sides, Colin, although nearly fifty and fairly broad of paunch, liked to play for whoever was undermanned, officiating with his whistle as he ambled along with the boys.

Edward Lee was a "general soccer" player, usually taciturn and minimally engaged. One October afternoon when his whistle ended the games, Colin beckoned Edward to his side and asked that he stick around for a while. They had both "played" defense that afternoon, but the action had taken place almost entirely at the offensive end of the field. There was something Colin thought Edward should learn.

Whatever Edward was thinking I can only guess, since I only heard Colin's account of the encounter. Apparently Colin spent the next half hour in the brisk air of the deserted athletic fields teaching Edward Lee an old vaudeville routine. "It'll pass the time the next time we're on defense," Colin said hastily.

"Is it required?" Edward reportedly said.

"Absolutely!" said the swollen-gutted man with the whistle. "Change your whole outlook. Change your life!"

Then they set about it. First the words to a little ditty, then some mincing dance steps while leaning over imaginary canes. When I actually witnessed the routine later, I was stunned. Colin would bellow, and Edward would answer in a deadpan monotone, but right on cadence:

Colin: Say, Mr. Lee!
Edward: Yes, Mr. Blount?
Colin: Say, Mr. Lee!
Edward: Yes, Mr. Blount?
Both: We're the sweetest soccer team in all the world. . .
Colin: On the defense, you and me.
Edward: That's Mr. Blount!
Colin: And Mr. Lee . . .
Edward: Positively, Mr. Blount
Colin: And absolutely, Mr. Lee!

Then off Colin would go into a second identical verse, per-haps raising and shaking an imaginary topper from his head. By this time, Edward would have stopped, regarding Colin impassively, as if awaiting further instructions. The whole busi-ness, or even thinking about it, made Colin shriek with laugh-ter.

For reasons I'm not sure I fully understand, I came gen-uinely to like the routine. When I saw them approaching one another from opposite ends of a crowded corridor or meeting on the school's central staircase after lunch, I was always elat-ed to hear Colin's

Say, Mr. Lee!

and the best-perfect response

Yes, Mr. Blount?

Again, this little improvisation gave me great pleasure. I might have been tempted to say its appeal lay in the goofy incongruity of Colin and Edward together, or of Edward and vaudeville. But that would not quite cover it. The incongruity made it funny, but it was something else, a deep congruity that struck the responsive chord. One day, I hailed Edward on his way out of my philosophy class. "Say, Mr. Lee!" I said. He gave me a little smile. I told him I got a big kick out of his routine with Mr. Blount. His smile broadened. "Yes," he said. "Do you think he's pleased?"

Tim Stout

Because I felt I knew him especially well, I agreed to write Tim Stout's official recommendation to college. I had taught him history, served as his faculty advisor, met with his family, and one afternoon after his father's sudden heart attack, sat with him as he shook with grief. His father, Red Stout, had been a larger-than-life figure among the youth of the city. As a young man, he and his college friends created a day camp so action-packed, so eccentric, and so unforgettable that seemingly every boy in greater Cleveland signed up for the summer. At the breakfast hour and again in late afternoon, from June through August, The Red Star Camp's fire engine-red buses streamed through the city's residential neighborhoods. Red Star songs were sung lustily by middle aged accountants and district managers. Red Star pranks and feats were recounted, were worn proudly as badges, by boys over the course of four decades.

Tim was Red Stout's fifth and final son. Tim's big brothers were old enough to be his father, and Tim himself loved to introduce an older nephew to his friends. His friends—and probably half the youth of the city—knew his father Red and his ever-pretty wife Rocky in a way children rarely know other children's parents. To some extent because of this, when Red Stout's heart failed and he died, Tim felt the loss of not only a particular, personal father, but of Fatherhood.

Tim Stout was fifteen when his father died. He grieved, deepened, and grew before our eyes into an admirable and durable young man. Although I planned to work hard on it, his recommending letter to college would be, I felt, blessedly easy to write. The hard letters are those about boys who, while likable and accomplished enough, have indistinct contours, whose lives so far lack story quality. There would be no such problem with Tim. He had been an underskilled, struggling student when he entered the school, but he had battled and prevailed. His math aptitude was so low that, even with earnest effort, he would never, in his algebra teacher's view, make it through the required program. He failed freshman algebra. He repeated it in his tenth-grade year, and by dint of ferocious effort, passed marginally. Not satisfied with his pass, he forfeited a summer of sport and pleasure to take an accelerated algebra review course: three hours of algebra instruction per day, plus five hours of algebra problem-solving outside of class. Immersed in its rules, Tim internalized algebra, and he mastered it, nearly earning an A.

The same drive and tenacity, given his big-boned, well-muscled body, enabled him also to master the conventions of football—but with more instinctive ease. Tim was a complete player, an all-scholastic standout, unanimous captain, school hero. In one game, now enshrined in school memory, he made every one of the team's tackles: every runner, every pass receiver, every punt returner. He is also remembered for single-handedly converting one certain defeat to a storybook victory.

Ahead by two touchdowns with two minutes to play in the game, the opposing team, an arch rival, set up to punt the ball deep in our territory. Our scoring once was unlikely; twice, unthinkable. But Tim, from his linebacker spot, had so battered the opponents' center that on the fourth down, his mind was more on Tim's coming assault than on his snap. The ball sailed far over the punter's head and a hard-rushing end beat the startled punter to the ball, picked it up, and sprinted into the end zone. Still one touchdown ahead, our rivals executed a slow series of downs, but Tim threw their runners back jarringly for three consecutive losses. The opponents back once more in punt formation, with barely time for another play, Tim again justified the center's fears by knocking him supine—but not before another wildly long snap spiraled up and over the arms of the punter. Like Huns, like Vandals, Tim and his fellow defenders pursued the wobbling ball, took it on the run, and scored. "Tim wouldn't accept a defeat," his awestricken coach told the reporters afterward. "He just wouldn't accept it."

I watched those games, I knew those stories. I remembered the passage through his father's loss, the tenacity in algebra. My recommendation was all but written. Typically, however, we interview our candidates before we write their letters. The interviews invariably reveal usable details, and they are often a handy source of quotable opinions and sentiments. It was always good to talk to Tim. so I arranged a formal appointment.

When I told him I wanted some background information for his college recommendation, Tim winced. He said he was grateful to me for writing on his behalf, but he asked if I would do him a favor, and I assured him I would.

"I would appreciate it," he said, "if you wouldn't make a big deal out of football. Football's all right, and I had fun doing it, but that's something I did, not who I am."

Tim told me he doubted he would play football in college. When I asked why not, he said he thought he would be too busy. He said he wanted to study hard in college, do really well. He decided he had to find a way to work outdoors for a living, preferably in the wild. He had talked it over with his brothers, and forestry management, geology, or agriculture seemed the most promising courses of study. Pursuing these fields might mean selecting a college that was off the typical prep-school graduate's pattern.

I congratulated him on thinking through his future plans so carefully. I didn't admit that I was also surprised.

"I made my mind up last summer. My brother helped me find a job collecting data on wolves for a professor friend of his at Michigan State University. I spent six weeks, alone most of the time, on a big island in Lake Superior. My job was to follow the wolves' migration over the island and to keep records of their movements and their prey, log the weather, and so forth. The Michigan State people taught me what to do; then they left me on my own."

I asked him if he had been scared.

"Of the wolves? No, that's a myth. These were timber wolves, and they have no predatory interest in people at all. It's too bad all that business about Little Red Riding Hood and the Big Bad Wolf ever got started. Wolves in the wild are about as scary as collies.

"I wasn't scared. I wasn't even lonely. I worked pretty hard, I think, I got good data, I cooked and looked after myself, I read two great books, *Heart of Darkness* and *Moby Dick*, and I started writing a journal, which I have kept going.

"I never felt I was working for a minute. I never wanted to

be somewhere else, to be doing something else. I had no sense of the clock, there was no dividing line between working time and free time. I was just there, figuring things out, learning something every minute. I was so wide awake that the way I am right now is like being asleep compared to it. It was indescribable."

I told him it sounded as if he had had a great summer. Compared to what Tim was telling me and the intensity with which he was talking, my response sounded predictable and dull.

"It was a great summer, but the best part was after I finished on the island. My brother took me on a trip to New England to see the Universities of Maine, Vermont, and New Hampshire. While we were in Vermont, we drove to see this guy who makes birch bark canoes for a living. He makes the most beautiful canoes in the world. He produces every part of them himself. He doesn't use any power tools or electricity. He doesn't use nails or anything from a store. He makes all his own glues and finishes. You should see one of his canoes. They're works of art.

"Talking to him is when it all clicked for me this summer. That guy was doing exactly what he wanted, and it worked. He makes enough from selling his canoes to live, and he doesn't need much. The guy is brilliant. Working with his hands didn't make him stupid, and he seemed totally happy.

"He told us his philosophy. He said the point of building canoes wasn't the canoe when it was finished. The point of building a canoe was building it. The process of building it is the canoe. You had to be, your head had to be in the process, not jumping ahead to the conclusion or how much money you were going to make or what to do with it. It's that kind of thinking that gets people all worked up and drives them crazy. But almost everybody lives that way, and they do poor work.

"He said the point of building the canoe is the building. When you're looking for prime birch, your entire attention is on the search for prime birch. If you're doing that, you will never settle for anything other than prime birch. There are no compromises, no short-cuts. When you're milling the boards, you're doing that, that's your whole business, that's every-thing. The only outcome is a perfect board; there's no reason for anything less, and there's all the time in the world to do it right. It seems so basic when I talk about it, but it's amazing. You should see one of his canoes.

"So I made up my mind, that's the way I want to live my life. Nothing else makes any sense. I want to do something fine. I want to be totally involved in the doing. As long as I live, I want that awake feeling. Anything else is just kidding yourself."

After talking to Tim, I changed the thrust of my letter rec-ommending him to college. When I finished, my thoughts were still full of his conversation, his experiences on the island and with the canoe-builder in Vermont. Apart from simply admiring Tim, I felt grateful, grateful to be reminded so ingenuously that I too wanted to do something fine, and that that was all I had ever really wanted.

PART FOUR

A BULLY PULPIT

A Bully Pulpit

Since the great Dr. Thomas Arnold began transforming England's Rugby School more than a hundred and fifty years ago, schools have occasionally come to be seen as "bully pulpits." School leadership has indeed sometimes allowed certain leaders to become bullies. I, however, like to think of "bully" in the sense that Theodore Roosevelt used the term—as in "bully for you" or "a bully good show."

*The fact of the matter is that school heads do have a pulpit of sorts. And in a religiously diffuse, if not secular, age, school leadership is one of the few pulpits going. Moreover, the scholastic congregation— students, parents, colleagues—is considerable: troubled possibly, but often concerned and alert. It would be a shame, at least in schools, to pass up an opportunity to take a stand, to be directive, to—pace, ed. establishment—*impose values. *Because it is the twilight of the twentieth century, I must add that I mean that last statement.*

We had better impose values. Moreover, they had better be the right ones. The Gap, Gangsta rappers, the film industry, secessionist militias, and all manner of other energetic forces and factions are imposing their values without regret. As Aristotle reminded us at the dawn of systematic thinking about human development, values are always imposed on children; values are not coolly and freely selected. When we grow smart and reflective enough to discriminate among values, our own are already in place. A decent person, Aristotle claimed, is one who is imprinted early on with durable virtues and then comes, in maturity, to understand these virtues' social and personal necessity. Without the value foundation—without the imposition—higher order mental capacities, like logic and reason, will only serve lower ones, like self-interested short cuts.

These concluding essays are actual messages from my own bully pulpit. They come with my warm good wishes and highest hopes.

20

Three Hopes For School

Being a good boys' school today is not enough. Members of such schools have not finished the job. They can't wipe their brows and express relief that they are better than or utterly unlike some rival school with a similar price tag. That is not, in my opinion, the value of being even a superb school.

That value—and here it is, the hard part—is that a good boys' school has the rare opportunity to pursue without hesitation or embarrassment the three things that will make it and each boy in it whole and good.

There are three things—I don't know whether to call them ideas or ideals. I think I'll call them hopes. There are three great hopes for schools as they hover on the brink of a new millennium.

School courses—especially, I'm afraid, history—have a way of suggesting that major cultural developments like the religion of Moses or the eruption of Greek theatre and philosophy or the art and architecture of the Renaissance simply arise, leave their huge prints, and then retreat, allowing schools and museums to record the impact. According to this habit of mind, Judaism and Christianity occurred, made an impression, and now we can study them. Renaissance painting evolved, and teachers and curators can now make a living drawing distinctions in the pictures, but whatever happened is assumed to be over; other schools of art and famous "isms" have left the Renaissance behind, made it history.

My real point—and it is an urgent one—is to say this is not the way history or human experience works. In fact, the real developments in the human record, including fairly ancient ones, have barely begun. The best and truest developments in the western world are newly born. The three hopes I need to talk to you about appeared in human consciousness at different times in a kind of blink. In that blink millions of people were dazzled, but only a few could sustain that blink into any kind of vision. Because of that, we have only rumors, only hints of the really great, soul-transforming developments in history.

The first of these (barely begun) hopes for you is Reason. Reason: the accurate matching of thought to the world. Let me repeat the definition: reason is the accurate matching of thought, which is inside our heads, to the world, which is outside our heads. The potential for reason is as ancient as language. There is no reason without language, but language does not insure reasonableness. Reason began with the recognition that what goes on inside your head is not the same thing as what goes on in the world. The interior self and the exterior world are different. With this realization, children at some point in their development shed their narcissism and begin their true intellectual journey. With this realization also, philosophy was born.

In the western world, philosophy came into being between the sixth and third centuries B.C. when the Greek thinkers who preceded and followed Socrates first began setting out how the mind works, how the world works, and how therefore to live. The greatest philosophers, then and now, do not use language in a new, elaborate way to make their points. They use language in the ordinary, simplest way—but with amazing accuracy. The difference between a philosopher and all the other talkers in the world is that, if he were singing, the philosopher would be singing in tune; all the others merely make noise.

While it sounds deceptively simple when you hear it, reason has the transforming power of magic. Reason relies on two essential acts of language: true naming and true relating. Think of it—that is all reasonable thinking does; it names things carefully, and it relates the things it names to each other. A few of the relationships are especially important in philosophy, for instance being and not being, before and after, greater and smaller, ends and means, cause and effect, equal and unequal, good and evil. Truly naming and truly relating things in the world are the ways we crack open the eggshell of ourselves and begin to see and then to live in a real, objective world. Applied sciences based on true relationships are very powerful; they can split atoms, cultivate diseases and their cures, cause heaps of steel to fly, span miles of water with delicate yet powerful bridges, tunnel under the English Channel, copy a living organism from one of its cells, cultivate tomatoes the size of softballs from only water and chemicals. False science—that is, science not based on true relationships—produces nothing. False sciences and false creeds, whether they are sciences of religion or politics or education, may make promises, may have charismatic and popular champions, may attract millions of believers and followers, but false science can do nothing in the world, because it is not based on the true relationships among real things. Reason always sees right through false science.

A moment ago I mentioned that reason has the transforming power of magic. There is a magical, or at least mysterious, side to reason, too, and this is it. Reason requires something beyond reason in order to work. Reason attempts to make sense of the world, but it requires something *out*-of-this world in order to proceed. Reason requires perfection.

You and I have never experienced a perfection, yet without it we cannot know anything. Does this sound a little mysterious to you, possibly annoying? Consider for a minute the relationship between perfection and so-called "reality." Have you ever wondered in an idle moment how an idea like perfection ever entered your head? If you can't find one or see one or make one, where did such a concept ever come from?

Yet the idea of perfection lies at the very heart of our knowing. Very few of you, if you are honest, have met the perfect girl, but I'll bet many of you have high hopes. Similarly, I can teach you in a way that will serve you for life the geometry of circles, which is incidentally the geometry of the perfect circle. Using terms like circumference, 360 degrees, diameter, radius, and a number called pi, I can teach you the absolute truth of circles, yet you and I will never see or be able to draw one. The circle I draw on a blackboard or on a computer screen is a pale imperfection, a *symbol* for what is really true. But the closer the copy to the perfection, the truer and better the circle becomes. Engineering based on such geometry is good enough to build on, to bet your life on. At the mysterious heart of every practical, worldly accomplishment is a perfection.

Or, if you are musically minded, think of the C chord, a pleasing coincidence of three tones we have called C, E, and G. If you stretch cat gut or wire or rubber bands and twang them to make these tones, the air will ring with the pleasing consonance of the C chord. The C chord is a perfection. Mankind—Greeks again—discovered and started thinking systematically about these musical frequencies in the fifth century B.C. But the Greeks did not invent the C chord. No one, God excepted, invented the C chord. The C chord was hanging out in the cosmos as pure potential from the beginning. Mankind discovered but did not invent it. The C chord and all true musical relationships are perfections. Raise or lower any of the tones an iota, and you ruin it. Before a C chord was ever strummed, it was there. After mankind has departed the cosmos, it will be there. All true music, like all true science, like all human knowing, is based on perfection.

Whenever we think, speak, and reason clearly we see this. Eloquent language, logic, and mathematics are the tools of reason. It is often hard to master these tools, especially at first.

Socrates and his heirs celebrated reason because they were spiritually thrilled by the liberation they felt in gaining access to what was really true. But reason never became a fad, it never fully carried the day. Socrates' shrewd verbal maneuvers were dazzling, but they were too much for nearly everybody. Reason embarrasses and humiliates the unreasonable. Reason and the reality it lays bare are often sharply at odds with our most pleasurable and profitable habits. The fact of the matter is that the truth really does hurt, and unreasonable people always want to hurt it back. The people of Athens tried and executed Socrates. Latter day Socrates' tend to get the same treatment: uncountable Hebrew prophets, Christian martyrs, Thomas a Becket, Thomas More, Lincoln, Gandhi, the Rev. Dr. Martin Luther King.

Occasionally an historical era will be charmed by reason. There was a so-called Age of Reason, an Enlightenment, in Europe in the early modern centuries. That age knew a little mathematics and mechanics. It liked to think of the cosmos as a huge benign clock and that reason would provide the ultimate blueprint for the clockwork. Out of that hopeful era grew some remarkable political theory, including the founding principles and the Constitution of the United States.

But the Enlightenment fared little better than Socrates. It was drowned out and ultimately overpowered by what the great art historian Kenneth Clark called the Romantic Rebellion, a huge cultural tidal wave which said in effect that feeling mattered more than thought. The meaning of our lives is revealed not in reason but in emotion. Emotion has always had an easy time smothering reason. Emotion is quick and loud and intense. Reason is cool and unhurried. Emotion is effortless; reason requires training and is often very hard.

In a somewhat more debased form, this is still the condition of reason in the modern world. Reasonable people are looked at guardedly, as unrealistic, over-rarefied people. The western world is not fond of serious thinkers. To know anything is to be a know-it-all. To make a reasonable but unpopular claim and to stick to it makes one a reactionary, a prude, an arrogant person. We must instead, our age tells us, be open to everything—above all to be open to feelings and mood. In our age attitude and poses and fashion are all; reason is barely cultivated.

Indeed, Reason's arch enemies are in the ascendant in our era. Anything that debases language is an enemy of reason. The triumph of visual images over language corrodes reason. And behold: sensational tabloids drive out documentary journalism; the public tolerance for sustained thinking, even for entertaining a few propositions in a row, even for entertaining a single challenging if-then proposition, falls to zero. The pleasing image, the 'look,' the logo, the motto, the sound-byte carry the day. A person who finds himself appalled at this barren and shallow climate is urged to numb those feelings, drug himself, lighten up, mellow down, chill out.

In an age screaming out for reasonable considerations, almost no one is being trained to reason. Reasonable people and their work are considered baffling or too difficult or beside the point. Not much has changed since Socrates' fellow citizens tried and sentenced reason to death.

But Socrates made an amazing start, an amazing blink. Reason haunts us, chides us, draws certain souls in its direction, especially those souls who have an intuition that there will be no life and no livable world without it.

Earlier I said that the beginning of reason in our lives was like breaking out of the egg-shells of our infant narcissism. Perhaps the great mass of humankind prefers the security of the shell, just as, sad to say, the great mass of people may prefer their mirrors to their windows. But it is early. Reason is barely born. Even today certain children are being coaxed into the hard light of reason. They are being trained to it. They are among the few.

So Reason is my first hope for you. My second is nothing at all like reason. My second hope for this school and for each of you is courtesy.

Here I want to use courtesy in its full historical sense; that is, as a code of conduct that would see a promising boy through to a complete manhood. True courtesy was set forth clearly in the late middle ages. It came and went so quickly that its appearance seems almost unreal. True courtesy grew out of chivalry, which was the process by which boys born into the landed class became pages, then squires, then knights. The sole purpose of knights through most of the middle ages was to fight, to fight for land and then to protect the land. For almost all of the middle ages knights, from the royal to the most lowly, were thugs. They were armed, armored, trained in combat and trained to ride. There was no human type stronger or more dangerous than the early knight. He behaved as if his might made him right. He could not read or write. He was a terror to the unarmed and the weak. He raped and killed wherever he had successfully plundered.

But at long, long last, after brutal centuries, after whole human life spans of this boorishness and the suffering it caused, its remedy began to emerge. The remedy began with stories, with legends of a different kind of knight, a knight of utter purity, a knight dedicated to a beloved and undefiable woman, a knight elaborately loyal to his lord and his fellows, a knight questing after a perfection: a holy grail, the rescue of the oppressed, the slaying of evil menaces, whether tyrants or dragons.

And following these marvelous stories—stories of Percival and Arthur and the Round Table knights—a theory of chivalric courtesy emerged, and for a time that theory was actually practiced as a system of education for boys. In that system little boys would train as pages. However well-born or privileged, the young pages would learn to help out. They were literally junior servants on the estate of a noble, whose horses and persons the pages would groom. Pages learned courteous speech and graceful obedience and also to keep quiet. By early adolescence, when they had been trained sufficiently in arms and horsemanship, the pages graduated into squires attached to particular knights, whose character they observed and whose person they waited upon. After perhaps seven years' service, a faithful squire would be singled out and dubbed a knight himself. A true knight under the codes of chivalry swore lifelong allegiance to three ideals: to the service of God, the service of his earthly lord, and to the lady of his heart.

This third idea, the lady of his heart, was something quite new. This wasn't a girl friend. This wasn't someone the knight might hope to marry. In fact, the lady of a knight's heart could never be his wife; she was in fact very frequently someone else's wife. Yet he was to love her for life, to be devoted to her. He would take, if he could, a tress of her hair or a kerchief of her clothing into combat or into contests.

So great, so total was the true knight's commitment to his lady, the lady of his heart, that it extended to all ladies, to girls and women of any kind or condition. Girls and women were to be treated with the deepest respect, whether you knew them or not. If they needed assistance, you gave it without having to be asked, whether it was convenient or not.

There is a story I love, a true story of a late medieval knight, Jean de Meingre, who strove his whole life to achieve the chivalric ideal. Sent by the King of France to Genoa on a courtly mission, he passed two women who curtsied before him. He returned their curtsey with kind words and a deep bow. When he did this, his squire turned to him and said, "Do you know who those women are?" Jean de Meingre said he did not. His squire gasped, "they are harlots." The knight then told his squire, "I would rather have paid my salutations to ten harlots than to have omitted them to one respectable woman."

The courtesy of chivalry has been impatiently dismissed as old fashioned, patriarchal, and condescending to modern women. "Don't idealize me," says the modern woman, "just give me my fair share." But this is actually not a valid criticism of the chivalric code. The courteous knight would *insist* on a woman's fair share, however it was socially understood. Moreover, he would have conferred that fair share with modest, respectful speech and graceful personal behavior. I have a feeling modern feminists would have liked true knights. What they don't like is the non-knight, the modern male who reflexively sees women as vaguely inferior and, in the spheres he is interested in, uninformed and less capable. Sexually, the modern man, the non-knight, sees women as erotic goods to be seduced or used, as his will and skill allow.

Chivalry and its behavioral code, courtesy, far from being an oppressive holdover from an unbearable patriarchal past, may actually have been the way out of the oppression, for both men and women. Chivalry, to my mind, is a more realistic approach to gender relations and sexual psychology than anything the twentieth century has produced, and I would include the sexual psychology of Freud in that company.

Chivalry understood far more openly and honestly than modern psychology does that sexual longing *will* come into play in many men's interaction with women, including girls and women it is inappropriate to pursue. This sexual longing is powerful and inevitable. The romantic longing of men for women is not a biological or a cultural mistake. It is an abiding fact, both a great gift and a great mystery.

The misunderstood genius of chivalry is that it both recognized and valued sexual, romantic longing. Rather than repress that longing, the late medievalist suggested that we use it, that we let it drive us, through a code of courteous respect, toward our desire's pure source, towards a perfection.

The medieval poet Dante held a particular woman of his heart, Beatrice Potinari, as the highest object of his love for as long as he lived. She was not his wife. He married someone else. In Dante's poetic masterpiece, Beatrice appears as a guide leading him from purgatory into heaven, and when he looks up finally to behold her, she, in all her beauty, is not a finite, particular person, but rather a kind of window into even more and greater beauty. She points the way. That's what longing is for.

You might think with the normalization of and easy access to so much explicit sex in our era that we would know all there is to know about it. But ironically, our age seems to be absolutely confused about sex, alternating crazily between lewd excesses and puritanical revulsion. And the style! The language! Think of any stanza of gansta rap. Think of any scene from the seriously praised and Academy awarded *Pulp Fiction.* Think of any HBO mainstream comedy special. We have enshrined disrespect. We have enshrined discourteous speech. We have righteously stood up for lewdness and the most debasing insults to women.

The courtesy of chivalry, although just a blink in history, knew and knows better. It knows how to relate, how to love, how to venerate, and is knights know ecstasies Quentin

Tarentino, the author of *Pulp Fiction*, could never imagine.

Certain stories of knights and their adventures persisted through later ages, but the training in chivalry and courtesy got diluted into mere formulas for good manners and personal style. The personal style of the "gentleman" stressed some of the specific behaviors of chivalry, but not its intensity, not its insight. Today we are clearly obsessed with erotic feeling and physical aggression, but in the age of chivalry, in that miraculous blink, there was a glimpse of what sex and strength were for.

But as with Reason, it was a great blink, a great start. Whenever anything like a true knight appears, whether he wears the outfit of a lonely western gunfighter or the high tech trappings of Luke Skywalker, there is, I believe, an exciting flash of recognition, even now.

My third and final hope for this school and for each of you is love.

It is the love that the great Hebrew patriarchs, heroes, and prophets struggled to understand. It is the love at the very heart of Jesus's teachings. English, somewhat confusingly, employs a single word, love, to indicate the love of one's mother, the love of justice, the love of one's friends, and the love of French salad dressing. The Greeks named these loves more precisely, and the most distinctive and profound of human loves they named agape.

Agape can be defined as the willed concern for the welfare of others. The "willed" in that definition is very important. Agape requires conscious effort, deep and constant trying. The other loves—romantic, sexual love, family love, friendly love—are all wonderful and are all great gifts, but they are radically different from agape. The difference is that the other, pleasurable loves simply happen to you. You never willed or decided to love your parents or your best friend or your girl friend. Those loves just clicked; they happened. If you don't believe me, why not test the claim. Why not try to decide, say at 3 o'clock this afternoon, to be wildly in love with someone you don't happen to care for right now. And please write to me if you succeed.

Agape is the kind of love that sometimes asks you to do just that. Agape is not about liking or approving, or admiring. Agape is not soft and fuzzy. Agape is hard. It is as hard as a diamond. While the other wonderful loves gratify us, agape changes us and others. Agape is what Jesus was talking about when he said to love your neighbor as yourself and when he said to love your enemies. He meant agape when he said to take a slap in the face without a hateful response, and to stand ready, in love, to take another.

It is agape and only agape that reaches out to the unloved, the sick, the abandoned, the unattractive, the repulsive, even to the hateful, even to enemies. And because it does, agape and only agape *transforms* the outcasts and the enemies. Arabs and Israelis love their respective children and their spouses and their friends, but not until they can extend themselves agapeically to one another will there be a durable livable future in the Near East.

Agape changes the human heart. There is an instructive moment in the life of Mahatma Gandhi which illustrates the great difficulty but also the saving power of agape. Gandhi was working to unify and pacify India after the Second World War. All hell had, literally, broken loose. Hindus and Moslems were afraid of each other and hated one another with a murderous intensity that broke out in one atrocity after another. At one point a Hindu man in the course of a bloody riot lost control of himself and murdered a Moslem child. When he did this, something inside him deeper than his fear and hatred for Moslems rose up and said *no!* It said I have committed a sin, a crime that has no end. Wretched beyond relief, the murderer sought out Gandhi who was visiting that city, and confessed his crime. You all know what murder is, and you all know what the murderer of a child deserves and usually gets. This is what Gandhi said to the man. He said you must go out and find a Moslem child whose parents have been killed and you must love that child and bring it up as your own.

Courts and prisons don't respond to murderers this way.

They don't feel they can afford to trust murderers that much. They aren't in the agape business. And therefore courts and prisons do little transforming. But if that man succeeded in doing what Gandhi said, he would have been transformed. A hater would have become a lover. A child killer would have become a dutiful, caring parent. More than that, an orphan child's life would have been transformed; his or her hopelessness would have been transformed into hope. But most important, that Hindu man lovingly looking after his Moslem son or daughter would never again fear and hate Moslems.

Gandhi's "sentence" may have been loving, but it was not comfortable. Agape is not comfortable. Really loving even your friends is often uncomfortable. It means not covering up for them when they do wrong, when they cheat, when they take some other shortcut, when they are cruel. Covering up or allowing a friend to go wrong or to do wrong is often done under the excuse of sympathy or friendship or affection, but this is a self-deception. Friends who stand by as friends go and do wrong are actually afraid. They are afraid of the tension or anger or the rejection they will feel if they confront the wrong. Agape demands that we be braver than this. In this way, too, real love is tough.

The love commandment was a magnificent blink in the human record, but despite such a long tradition of formal religion, it is still a blink.

The great evolutionary theorist Julian Huxley once speculated that with the evolution of human self-consciousness, the next major evolutionary shifts will no longer be unconscious biological adaptations to changing environments. Because with conscious decision making, reason, and science, human beings have the terrifying power to transform themselves and the environment into anything they choose.

In my opinion, agapeic love is that evolutionary next step. It is the only conceivable force that could tell us what to do with our sciences, with our states, and with each other. It transcends even reason and courtesy, because it tells us what to be reasonable and courteous about. If the problem is that it is so hard to do, that it requires a total abandonment of our self-centeredness and of the enormous pride we take in our comfort and personal well-being, the hopeful side is that love has never been found wanting. Never in all the human record has love let us down.

I knew a headmaster candidate once who, when the decision to appoint him or not came down to the wire, was asked, "What do you really want to achieve as a headmaster?" The candidate answered without a blink, "I want to help create a community of love."

In this resolve I believe there is hope. There is certainly hope for that headmaster and his school. In all that lies ahead I wish you the light of reason, the strength of courtesy, and, above all, love.

21

A Good Student

This morning I would like to talk to you for a few minutes about good students. My main reason for doing so is that I find I come dangerously close to forgetting what a good student is. In fact, I think we all do.

At the end of every term we post lists of students who earn academic honors and high honors. These boys are generally high performers; not all of them are good students. This spring we will invest a new class of Cum Laude scholars. In my experience many of these boys are good students, but a few are merely high performers.

Many good students—and most of my own best students—are not terribly high performers or at least consistently high performers. Being a good student involves quite a bit more than being a high performer. But we easily forget this.

A famous educational theorist, Howard Gardner, from the Harvard School of Education, just left Cleveland after giving a series of talks to local educators. Several US teachers heard him. Mr. Gardner's point—and it's an essential point—is that we don't have intelligence; rather, we have intelligences. We have math intelligence, artistic and musical intelligence, we have organizational intelligence, literary intelligence, intelligence in physical movement—multiple intelligences. We obviously don't have the same amount of each, but we have our share, and many of us are loaded with more of one kind than another.

The problem with school people—especially if we forget what we are doing—is that we sometimes call a few of the thinking intelligences—say, mathematical or literary analysis—intelligence itself. But this is obviously a mistake. People with a gift for getting along productively in a wide variety of settings have perhaps the supreme intelligence. The brilliant improviser on guitar or saxophone is expressing a deep intelligence. The gifted skier (himself a kind of improviser) negotiating a difficult slope is expressing another deep, enviable intelligence. These intelligences are obvious and impressive when we experience them naturally. Why do we forget they are all genuine intelligences? Why do we fall into the trap of calling certain academic competencies "intelligence" and the rest something vaguer and more accidental, like "talent" or "coordination"?

This past November I paid a visit to Mr. Fred Hargadon, who, after 20 years at Stanford University, is the new admissions director at Princeton. Many people in the college admissions business think Fred Hargadon is the best and freshest thinker about the admissions process in the United States. He certainly was the morning I talked to him.

I have told a number of the seniors about what he had to say, but I'd like to tell the rest of you. He told me that Princeton now gets about 10 or 11 applications for every place in the entering freshman class. Virtually every applicant is qualified to do the work at Princeton. This you probably know already.

What surprised me was that Fred said that very little in the candidates' files was useful—that is, useful in identifying good students. He had the students' SAT scores—and of course at Princeton they are very high. But life, even college life, rarely presents students with neatly packaged, fully worked out problems, followed by four possible answers to them, one of them correct. These tests measure an aptitude of a kind, and they are also quick and easy to grade, but it is an aptitude for which there is no earthly use.

Also in the Princeton candidates' files are student essays. These recently have become suspect. Many of them imitate essays published in books which tell you how to write college essays "that work." Some of the essays, Mr. Hargadon suggested, are of dubious authorship.

The file also contains grades, but as I have just told you,

these tend to reveal who is a high performer, not necessarily who is a good student.

Moreover, the Princeton faculty, while virtually swimming in high undergraduate aptitude, is starving for good students. They beg Fred Hargadon for genuine students, for young men and women on fire about something they've discovered or read or figured out. He used a memorable expression: "The Princeton faculty want more students with light in their eyes."

Back in the 1970s we sent Princeton a young man with light in his eyes. He was, I believe, a genuinely good student. He loved US, I think, and he liked many things about Princeton. His name is Dave Chollet, and he is one of the most unusual boys ever to attend the School.

He was a chauvinistic Westsider, a passionate Roman Catholic, and a sensational athlete: quarterback of good varsity football teams and an outstanding basketball player; for years he held the School scoring record of 44 points, almost all of them on shots that would be three-pointers today.

But I haven't mentioned the unusual part yet. David was crazy about history—in fact, he still is. He didn't learn his history in school; he learned it on his own, in feverish afternoons and late nights with books. The first books were about the heroes of the American Civil War. Then came books about this century's two great wars. The drama and tragedy of Russia in those wars especially appealed to him. He inhaled history, he talked history, he argued history, and even before we had special fellowships, he taught Civil War history to younger students.

He was, by the way, a weak math student who squeaked by the requirement with modest grades. His foreign language skills were even weaker, and several 60s stood out on his transcript. Later he fought his way into a very competitive Russian program at Princeton, where he did equally badly.

It would be an invasion of privacy to tell you David's SATs, but I will tell you that *none* of you would be impressed. But he was a good student. There was light in his eyes. He loved to tell you paradoxes and ironies he found in the historical record. He claimed the Civil War and First World War produced heroes who really were heroes. He was cheerful, passionate, funny, and infectiously enthusiastic about history. For two years, the pattern of my own reading and thinking changed because Dave Chollet was at US.

His file, except for a few rapturous letters from us, cannot have been conventionally impressive to Princeton.

When he got there, there were some tough times. After a great freshman basketball season, he was released from the varsity, because he liked to play Pete Maravich's way, not Bobby Knight's way. He didn't take to the Princeton history department either. They were interested in things like the nature of historical proof; Dave was interested in what a battlefield looked like and smelled like.

While at Princeton, Dave began writing about the Russian Front in the First World War. I have since read hundreds of his typed pages on the subject; these may now run into the thousands. He has also written a book-length epic poem on what went wrong with Jefferson's democracy. Almost nothing he has written has been published, yet the corpus of his work grows and grows. He continues to correspond with obscure military historians, with widows of generals long dead—and with Mr. McCrea.

David has, I believe, no money. He lives in a garret room on the Westside with his books and plans. He has taken to reading the work of the Russian defector Solzhenitsyn, and he says he feels like Solzhenitsyn: an isolated witness to the possible decline of the west.

We hired David to teach history at US for a couple of years. He deeply inspired a few history buffs, and he puzzled and overwhelmed most of his students. He was late to school, or missing, most days. He was irrationally committed to a used Volvo, which couldn't make the journey reliably from Lakewood. After a bad patch of absences, regretfully we parted company.

David is still in his Westside outpost, writing what he

believes are history's lessons to the west. From the standpoint of his Princeton classmates, he must not seem to have come to much.

I personally think it's too early to say. His life story bears no relationship to the dominant types of his age. Nobody anything like him will ever appear on "thirtysomething." I find myself wondering, "How does he live?" "What does he eat?" "Has he got insurance?"

But the fact of the matter is that while he has not lived a life a late twentieth century, middle class person would likely imitate or even understand, it is nonetheless a life very much like those lived by the few, truly great souls we teach about in schools. It's a life rather like Socrates' or Keats' or Henry David Thoreau's or Emily Dickinson's.

This, at any rate, is what I choose to believe.

One more thing. I will be surprised if there is not a senior speech or two this year critical of the type of person—and I quote—"the school wants you to be."

I realize that students often feel there is a dominant US type or mold. But believe me, your teachers haven't fashioned it. I personally don't want you to be any type, other than your best self.

It is unlikely that many of you will turn out much like Dave Chollet. But if you did, that would be just fine.

He was a very good student.

Good morning.

22

Peaceful Confrontation

Before we all go off to class this morning, I would like to take a few moments to give some consideration to the ideas of the man whose life is being celebrated on Monday.

Martin Luther King's dream of achieving human equality in our lifetime was a challenging, but absolutely appropriate, message to his fellow Americans in the year 1955, when he began his active ministry in Montgomery, Alabama. He pursued this goal without resting until 1968 when he was shot by an assassin in Memphis, Tennessee.

King succeeded remarkably in transforming human relations in this country in the direction of mutual consideration, tolerance, and justice. His success was due certainly to a perfect alignment of the end he sought, human brotherhood, and the means he chose to achieve it, nonviolent resistance to those laws and those people opposed to brotherhood and equality.

King will, I think, be remembered as one of the world's most committed and brilliant practitioners of civil disobedience in the service of social justice, but the idea did not originate with him.

The idea, like so many powerful ideas, is ancient. Twenty-five hundred years ago, one of the great sages of China, Kung-fu-tse, whom Westerners centuries later called Confucius, taught his disciples this maxim: "In an unjust society, the place for the just man is in prison."

This striking doctrine says that the way to transform society for the good is simply to present oneself in evil's face and to stand fast. The underlying idea is that your own harmless, yet committed presence will serve as a kind of human mirror in which the wicked and frightened and bigoted can see themselves for what they are. The peaceful witness to injustice is unlike the warrior in that he or she does not kill or force the enemy to behave differently. The peaceful witness—including those who are hurt or killed in the process—urge their enemies to consider the consequences of their behavior and to change.

Peaceful confrontation aims to transform society; doing this is much harder than fighting—and I think one might argue historically that peaceful confronters have sometimes transformed whole eras in ways that warriors have never done.

This was certainly Jesus of Nazareth's feeling when, 500 years after Confucius and a hemisphere apart, he told his disciples to answer brutality with kindness; if someone demands the coat off your back, give him your shirt as well. If someone forces you to carry his provisions for a mile, carry them for two; if someone strikes you in the face, turn the other cheek.

One hundred and fifty years ago, a flinty New England nonconformist, Henry David Thoreau, could not see the moral point of the Mexican-American War, which he viewed as a cynical and unnecessary land grab. Moreover, he didn't see how any government could implicate him in a moral crime by making him pay for it through a special poll tax. As you U.S. history and literature scholars know, he refused to pay the tax and calmly accepted the consequences, which included jail in Concord, Massachusetts. He found life in jail inexpensive and fairly agreeable; he felt as free to think and write there as he did anywhere else. And while he was in that jail, he conceived one of the greatest manifestos of an individual's need to live by the dictates of his conscience that has ever been written; he titled it *Civil Disobedience.*

Early in this century, Mohandas Gandhi, an educated, upper middle class Indian lawyer living in South Africa, was chucked out of a first-class train compartment because he was colored. He was stunned. Deep in his knowing he realized that what he had experienced was intolerable, not just for him, but for everyone in the world.

He decided to change his life. He threw out his lawyer's

clothes, quit the law, read Henry David Thoreau and the teachings of Jesus, and determined to present himself—and as many like-minded souls as he could gather—in the face of injustice wherever he could find it.

Seven years after Gandhi was shot dead in India, Martin Luther King began his social activism. Mr. Morton mentioned yesterday that Dr. King was a very good student. By 1955 he knew well the Biblical teachings of Jesus, the political theory of the Declaration of Independence and the Federalist papers; the teachings of Gandhi and of a great contemporary theologian Reinhold Niebuhr.

King presented himself in the face of injustice for 13 years before he was killed. Along the way he was threatened and insulted, his family was harassed and abused, his house was destroyed by a bomb, he was stabbed, his mail was tampered with, his phones were bugged, powerful contemporaries like Malcolm X disagreed with him and dismissed him, and he was shot dead at 38 (incidentally, that's the age of Mr. Brennan or Mr. Johnston).

The late American philosopher Allan Bloom wrote a book in 1988 called *The Closing of the American Mind.* In it he made many established college professors furious. He did this by claiming that American higher education had become slick, cynical, uncommitted, and detached from any real position of value.

As proof, or one proof, of this sad state of affairs, Bloom would ask his political philosophy students—and they were good ones, as he taught at places like Cornell and the University of Chicago—if they had any heroes. If they did, he asked his students to name them. His students couldn't do it; they drew a blank.

I don't honestly know if all or any of you have heroes. But if you don't, it's too bad. Because heroes have lived and perhaps still do live among us. Martin Luther king was one. May there be others.

Have a good morning.

23

Inherent Responsibility

Graduation speeches are nice, I suppose. Like hymns, prayers, alma maters, special clothes, and floral decorations, they help establish a sense of occasion, of ritual; they help to say this *is* a big day, nice going!

But, truth be told, graduation speeches are almost always forgettable, at best a kind of mulch to the continuing harvesting schools carry on each year.

But I have to say it: something stubborn in me wants to tell you something unforgettable—or at least something you *ought* not to forget. And, whether I succeed or fail over the next five minutes, I want to tell you something important, something upon which life or death does indeed depend. What I have to tell all of you—and these graduates in particular—is better than nice.

A colleague of mine came very close to stealing my text earlier this week, when in the course of bidding farewell to the Shaker campus, he told the boys to remember to be *good*: that goodness to others, for others, is the point. In spite of so much emphasis on scholarship here, smartness is not the point. Nor is talent the point. Nor is fame or material success the point.

Schools could be a lot clearer about the relationship between those values. All of them are fine—especially smartness and talent. But we must never forget—school people especially—that smartness and talent are *means*, not *ends*. Smart doctors, smart city planners, smart bosses are in a position to do more human good than less smart ones. Similarly, talented people are able to make bigger and more pleasing contributions to the human community than are less talented people.

But it is goodness—to others, for others—that counts.

Unless our own talents and intelligence are drawn, like a compass needle, toward the fixed pull of goodness, those seeming virtues—smartness and talent—are potentially monstrous. The problem with Michael Milken and Ivan Boesky and other cheaters is that they were smart; being smart enabled them to injure the futures of others, perhaps a whole nation, in a big way. This year in the eighth grade speaking contest, Mark Felice gave a chilling talk about the serial killer Ted Bundy. One of the monstrous and most dangerous things about Bundy was that he was really good looking and personally charming; these gifts aided him greatly in making his sickening, deadly conquests. Intelligence, charm, good looks, physical coordination, charisma—all of these things are means, not ends; even at their best, they are second best. At their worst, they are our worst enemy. The last thing the human family needs is a smarter, more attractive Hitler.

As you parents have heard me opine before, I believe that when there is enough love and good will to go around, smartness and achievement tend to take care of themselves. But that fixed point, that ultimate end, that *goodness*—this is what we need to stress. Without it we are asea in a streamlined, comfortable, and mighty expensive boat without a map or a single star to guide our way.

In the minutes remaining I want to focus on a very particular kind of goodness. It is a goodness that US boys ought to feel especially close to. It is standing, literally, over our heads. It is, literally, the centerpiece of our motto: Responsibility.

We probably say it enough. When we're worried about a boy, we urge him to be responsible, to act responsibly. When he fails, we call him irresponsible. But what does it really mean? What does it look like, and feel like, in the practice of our everyday lives?

Thanks to a Boston University professor, Kevin Ryan, I got a vivid reminder of what responsibility means and what it feels like. Writing recently for a journal called *Character,* Professor Ryan tells a brief story about responsibility. The story recounts an event from this century's history that very few ordinary people, even scholars, have even heard of. The story occurred in the course of developing America's atomic bomb. Let Professor Ryan speak for himself:

"Louis Slottin was a physicist working in Los Alamos on the Manhattan Project that led to the development of the atomic bomb. One day in 1946, he was working with his team on a critical experiment that required assembling pieces of plutonium. With minute movements, he was nudging pieces of plutonium toward one another trying to form a mass of plutonium large enough to produce a chain reaction. Through his own error, he made a critical mistake and moved two pieces too close together. A chain reaction began and alarms went off as the room was filled with radioactivity. Without a moment's hesitation, Slottin reached in and pulled the pieces apart with his bare hands. In the blink of an eye, he had signed his own death certificate, since he had exposed himself to a large dose of radioactivity. He then calmly turned to his seven co-workers and told them to mark precisely their position during the accident so that their degree of exposure to radioactivity could be determined. He then apologized to them and predicted what would turn out to be exactly true: he would die and they would recover.

"Slottin's heroic act did not just happen. It was a result of a life lived devoted to the enduring habit of responsibility.

"Responsibility is the quality of realizing and acting upon our obligations: obligations to those with whom we are connected. We are not born with responsibility. We can't buy it. We can't take quickie self-help courses in it. It is, however, essential to a civilized and democratic community."

About this, Professor Ryan could not be closer to the mark.

The challenge of course is to practice responsibility, to extend opportunities for boys to be responsible, to expect it, to note it, to be impatient with its absence.

Let me repeat a passage from that sad, great moment in Louis Slottin's story:

"A chain reaction began and alarms went off as the room was filled with radioactivity. *Without a moment's hesitation,*

Slottin reached in and pulled the pieces apart with his bare hands. . ."

Without a moment's hesitation. Here was a man who didn't have to deliberate on responsibility. He did not weigh selfish options versus generous ones. He did not decide to be responsible; he had already learned that deep lesson. He was able to be good and to do right, without a moment's hesitation.

God alone knows what kind of practice or lessons or trials or parenting or schooling Louis Slottin had in order to act so surely under deadly pressure.

We do know that deep in his understanding he had learned there is no life worth having except the responsible ones. Louis Slottin was a smart and a talented man, and his fellow workers at Los Alamos can be forever grateful than he was better than that. He was responsible; he was good.

So as each of you takes his good gifts and talents into the wonders and drama of high school, I invite you to remember what your schooling is for. It is to be good—to one another, for one another.

Congratulations on your various and remarkable achievements to date. Savor your happiness, which is easy; learn from your lumps, which is hard. Be good. And God bless you.

24

Real Thanksgiving

I am glad that our new academic calendar allows us to assemble to celebrate Thanksgiving. For one thing, I don't think we—or really any Americans—celebrate enough. For another, we are in real danger of losing a shared sense of the *value* of giving thanks. In fact, I believe what is most missing in and wrong with contemporary life is the loss of opportunity to express two very basic things human beings *must* express if they are to live fully and well.

The first of these endangered needs is the admission of sorrow or fault. We need to apologize, to confess, to admit we make mistakes. We need to do this even when we are not accused of anything, when we are not in trouble. This has nothing to do with discipline or getting caught or rules or law courts. This has only to do with honesty. As a society, we have gotten very good at defense strategies, at explanations, at excuses. But we have become almost illiterate in the language of honest admission and apology. Today, it is the rare person, not the typical person, who can say, "I'm sorry." "I was wrong."

Also sadly lacking in the repertoire of the '90s person's expressions is a heartfelt, unrequested "thank you." And that's why this holiday and this whole season might be good for us.

We are used to saying thank you when we get what we expect or what we believe we deserve. We say thank you when someone passes the salt, or gives us a present, or compliments us on a game or performance.

Rarely do we express thanks for the real thing: for the fact that by a miracle beyond our knowing we came to be, that we are alive; that for a time we will be a conscious witness and participant in a universe we neither created nor deserve.

The Italians have a great proverb: *Essere non avere:* "to be, not to have." It is our being, not our cars and toys and clothes, for which we are in enormous, mysterious debt.

We are born in mysterious debt. I mean this, literally. Whoever deserved or *could* deserve the view over this valley I saw when I peered out my bedroom window this morning? Whoever deserved to be loved by somebody, or to be in love? Speaking of being in love, a colleague and friend of mine gave thanks Sunday afternoon in the church we both attend. He has just fathered his first child, a boy, and the boy was two days old. My friend spoke out loud in a voice so unsophisticated and so uncool that, without seeing him, you would have had a hard time believing an adult was talking. He gave thanks for his son. He said, "For the past two days I have just been feeling this huge thing descend on me. I have actually felt myself falling in love with my son."

This seemed to me real gratitude. He was grateful for his son's sheer being and for love. He was not grateful that his son was so talented or exceptional or successful. The baby obviously isn't any of those things, yet, and may never be. My friend was not grateful because he's having so much fun with his child. He isn't, yet, and in fact, he's only had a few hours sleep since the birth.

If you think about it, our ancestors who taught us about giving thanks were likewise not interested in what you should say when someone passes the salt or when you get a terrific gift.

Real thanksgiving, including the first Thanksgiving in the New World, has always been a deep, personal appreciation of sheer being, never about material gains and good luck and advantages.

Probably each of us has in mind some Hallmark card image of the first Thanksgiving. Probably it involves a benign rural setting with autumn colors. High collared Puritans and noble Indians stand about a table heaped with harvest fruits. Somewhere in the mental picture are turkeys, living or roasted; pumpkins, corn, and all manner of agricultural plenty.

The nostalgic image of Thanksgiving is all about comfort, all about a safe, sweet American beginning. And Thanksgiving is indeed a part of American history. The governor of the Plymouth Plantation, William Bradford, declared the first Thanksgiving celebration in the fall of 1621 to mark the passing of the first Puritan winter and the first harvest season. In 1789 the new nation's new president, George Washington, declared Thanksgiving our first national holiday. It was celebrated haphazardly until Abraham Lincoln turned his attention away from Civil War agonies and declared in 1863 that the holiday would be *annual*, and that it would fall on the last Thursday in November. It has fallen on that date every year since, with the exception of 1939, when President Franklin Roosevelt pushed it ahead by a week in order to stimulate holiday shopping, which he believed might accelerate recovery out of the Great Depression.

But when we look back, with a historian's care, at the first Thanksgiving, it is not much like the cozy greeting card version. For one thing, the Puritans were not very cozy people. As it turns out, the Puritans did not know anything about coziness and comfort, but they may have known the truth about giving thanks.

Let's remember who the Puritans were. They were religious fundamentalists who felt the national Church of England was too elaborate, too worldly, too far from the simple, demanding teachings of Jesus.

The Puritans believed in an all-powerful God. They believed the Bible was the sacred word of God. They believed that every person is born into sin, and there is no hope for redemption except by a merciful and undeserved act of God. The Puritans believed in *predestination* and the election of the faithful. This means that God has from the beginning of time selected those who will be saved for eternity and those who will be eternally damned. As the Puritans saw it, no amount of good deeds or prayers or clean living can earn a person's eternal life. God doesn't bargain or change His mind. As Puritans saw it, the way ahead looked doubtful and bleak. If they felt like sinning or if they actually sinned, they knew they were headed for hell If they behaved themselves and lived cleanly and well, they might be going to hell.

This attitude reflected what actually were very grim circumstances for the Puritans. Consider the great Puritan leader, William Bradford, later Governor of the Plymouth colony, its historian, and the founder of Thanksgiving.

Bradford was born to farming people in the north of England. Both his parents died before he was eight. His Puritan relatives had to flee England to Holland, where young William learned the cloth-making trade. After a long hard apprenticeship, he tried to set up his own cotton-making shop, but it failed, and Bradford found himself penniless.

When he heard that some members of his congregation were interested in crossing the Atlantic or trying their luck in a New World, he was willing to go. Not much, or much good, was known about the New World in 1620. There would be land to own, but the land was inhabited by "savages." There was, perhaps, a fifty-fifty chance of surviving the passage.

Bradford's voyage took six weeks—that is, six weeks in an unheated, poorly ventilated sailing boat across the North Atlantic in winter; forty days, forty nights in the cold and stink on the way to God knows where. And on one bleak, cold day, the Mayflower anchored off the wintery coast of what is now Provincetown on the tip of Cape Cod. Of his arrival Bradford wrote:

> Being thus passed the vast ocean and a sea of troubles (our) preparation . . . (we) had now no friends to welcome us nor inns to entertain or refresh our weather-beaten bodies; no houses or towns to repair to. . . And for the season, it was winter . . . sharp and violent. . . Besides, what could (we) see but a hideous and desolate wilderness, full of wild beasts and wild men—and what multitudes of them there be (we) knew not.

Bradford and his Puritan mates edged along the Massachusetts coast till they found a more promising harbor at Plymouth. Here they fashioned two rows of crude houses made out of wooden planks. These led up to a fort they could retreat into for safety.

Within four months half of the 101 people who landed at Plymouth Rock were dead. The Pawtuxet Indians of the region had seen whites before and were relatively friendly, but the Puritans carried their muskets everywhere, even to church.

The Puritans who celebrated their survival and first modest harvest could not have been in a greeting card mood. They were most likely in grief for lost loved ones. They were certainly full of apprehension about their future survival. Each was four thousand miles from everything he or she had ever known.

And yes, they ate wild turkey and venison and pumpkin.

History records that the Puritans were grateful. I am sure they were grateful for a chance to rest. They were also, I am equally sure, grateful they were alive, although the hardness of their lives and the future of their lives must have seemed a complete mystery.

But in the midst of all that discomfort and loss and worry, Bradford and his four dozen companions decided to reaffirm life itself.

The Puritans were simple people. They said and sang simple thank yous. They said thank you for being alive in the world.

And because we are alive in this particular world, we can thank them.

25

A Self Worth Esteeming

I want to talk to you about the relationship between trying very hard and feeling good. And by talking about the relationship between trying very hard and feeling good I hope to clear up in all of your minds the meaning of a most confusing and most unhelpful educational buzz-word of the past 20 years: self-esteem.

There has been a tidal wave of educational thinking about self-esteem. Whole school programs—indeed, whole schools—have been devoted to achieving and maximizing this agreeable sounding condition. Self-esteem, certain educationists have been telling us, is an interior mental condition produced by unqualified love, warm nurture, positive recognition and praise. Or to put it even more simply, by assuring a child he is wonderful, he will come to believe he is wonderful, and thus he will become wonderful. By the same token, children who are less than wonderful, including those who are downright awful, are believed to lack self-esteem. The educational and parental challenge then is to pour in the missing ingredients, so self-esteem can be realized.

As I said before, the self-esteem theory seems agreeable on a number of counts. For one thing, it is easy. Just about anybody has it in herself or himself to nurture, praise and pump up another person. It's just a question of getting yourself in the right mood. In addition, the self-esteem theory takes the awful weight of responsibility for poor performance and bad behavior from the person doing it. One is no longer a poor writer, a weak problem-solver, a selfish, rude, vulgar, unsportsmanlike, bratty or egotistical person; instead, one is a victim, a temporary casualty of low self-esteem.

Looking at poor performance and bad behavior this way is

also a great relief to a certain kind of parent. For just as it's no fun to score poorly on a test, play poorly in a game, to get called to task for rudeness or dishonesty or making others miserable, it is often even *less* fun to be known as the parent of such a person. Therefore parents, at least parents of a certain kind, are also relieved to know that they don't have a problematic, unsatisfactory child. They have instead a potentially wonderful child who has been deprived of his necessary and deserved ration of self-esteem. Such parents are likely to come into the principal's office in the aftermath of poor grade reports or of a cheating or stealing incident and say things like, "So where is the warmth and support and praise when we need it?"

At such moments, for certain students and certain parents, self-esteem seems an inspired and valuable theory. Its only problem, however, is that it is completely wrong. Dead wrong. The theory of self-esteem as recently constructed fundamentally misunderstands the true relationship between effort, mastery and the feeling of personal well-being.

Let me tell you a story, a true story, about a boy who graduated from University School not too long ago and who now is a distinguished wildlife manager and conservationist.

When he entered our ninth grade, he was a big, strong, likable boy, but a *very* modest student. To his credit, he did his work, but his sentences were crude, his memory leaky, and his mathematical ability astoundingly weak. After a few weeks in the School, his mother and father and older brothers wondered if US was the wrong choice for this boy. His teachers, including me, wondered too. At the end of the first term our fears were confirmed: he had low D's and a no-hope F in algebra.

The adults in this boy's world began making inquiries at other schools. Only the boy himself wanted to stay. Rather enterprisingly he sought out extra help on his own, not only from his own math teacher, but from another teacher, so he could get another style, another point of view. But even with after-school sessions, long Saturday morning tutorials, he failed algebra for the spring term and for the year. It certainly did not help that his father died suddenly that spring.

For a number of reasons, it seemed a poor time to change schools, and, as I said, the boy himself very badly wanted to stay. He took a number of math aptitude tests, which showed he had no math aptitude. He took the pre-SAT tests, and scored below 300 on the math section, something we believed was statistically impossible even if one randomly filled in the darkened circles on the answer form.

Interestingly to me, this boy continued to try, in fact to try harder than ever, in math—but with an additional motive. Now he was mad—energetically mad. He was mad at his brain, and at the fate that had wired it in a way that was so impervious to algebraic equations and which ordinary boys on his left and right were able to solve.

Happily, this boy did not get mad at algebra. Nor did he get mad at trying. Stopping just short of being too demanding, he got his next year's math teacher to work with him every day on the failed ninth grade course. At the end of the repeated year he received, lo and behold, a passing *60* for the course. Perhaps, more of us thought, it was a gift. Well, so be it. It was a gift well deserved.

But the boy himself had a different take. He startled his mother by saying he wanted to go off to a tough boarding school summer program. Moreover, he wanted to study only math. Moreover, he wanted to study only algebra.

"You passed algebra," we pointed out.

"I want to ace it," he told us back.

In fact he wanted an A in algebra, even if it was a third try. And he did try, and he did earn a *B*, and we put it on his transcript, right next to his 60.

There is one more bit to this boy's math story I want to add. He also got it into his head his junior year that he could raise his terrible math SAT. We counseled him that sometimes students did, but not typically, and typically not very much.

Once again this boy lined up special coaching sessions, bought SAT review books and pored over practice problem after problem at home. And, I'll have to say it, he raised his math SAT substantially—to 500. I remember the day he got his new scores. He was beaming with pleasure. He had beaten the odds. He had raised his math SAT more than 200 points.

I don't think it would have dampened his elation a bit to know that his triumphant 500 math SAT was the third lowest in his class.

I probably don't have to say much more about his progress after that. That kind of tenacity also made him a very teachable and dedicated outdoor scientist. I have not mentioned, because he would not have, that he was also a bruisingly good football player.

When he left US he told me he felt great about his experience here. He felt great, period. He believed, with reason, that he could do anything. At that moment on that day, you could fairly have said he had ample self-esteem. But if that is what he had, it was the *result*, not the cause, of his effective behavior. Let me say that again, his self-esteem—indeed anybody's self-esteem—is the result of achievement, mastery, strain, pain and best effort, never the reverse.

In fact, with every passing year at the School, I am further convinced that God placed me here for the sole purpose of recognizing and reporting this elemental educational fact.

I would like each of you, parent and child alike, to consider how you would respond to the following challenge. And please take this seriously.

Imagine that a reliable wizard appeared before you and offered you one of two cards. One card would guarantee four years of a high school career filled with every conceivable pleasure. You would understand everything you read or heard. Papers and exams and correct answers would flow almost spontaneously from your pencils and keyboards. If you played a sport you started, you scored, you excelled; if you ran for office, you won; if you liked a girl, she was yours; at high school's end you would be honored, prized and admired above all others, but beyond these magic four years, absolutely no special luck or reward was guaranteed.

The other card would guarantee nothing of the sort. With

the other card you would try, even try hard, and occasionally fail—or only barely succeed. Places on teams, grades you hoped for, certain friendships, certain honors and offices would not come your way, even though you were deserving enough. Sometimes when you had done fairly well, or even your best, the school or a coach or a teacher or a boss would want more from you. With this card, you would have doubts from time to time, you would worry and wonder about what would become of you. You would know that if you didn't try, you would never succeed; if you *did* try, there was no guarantee of a satisfying pay off. But if you chose this card, you would try.

Once again: there are only these two cards. The first card is an easy-success-and-great-pleasure card—but with no assurances of anything after high school. The second is the try-hard-and-take-your-lumps card—with whatever benefits that approach to life holds after high school.

Just those two cards and only those two cards. Eighth graders, which one will you take? Also—is the decision easy? And while I'm at it: parents of eighth graders, which card would you take for your son?

I happen to believe there is a right choice in this matter. Choosing right may be counter-intuitive, as the psychologists say, and it is not likely to feel good in the here and now.

Choosing right may result in no immediate self-esteem—but it might result in the creation of a self *worth* esteeming. It might result in a life you will one day be proud and grateful to have lived.

The fact of the matter is that you will choose, and your choice will make all the difference. Choose well, live well, and accept one more time my admiration and congratulations for so much good work.

Index

A.C.L.U., 11
Abelard, Peter, 177
absolute values, 7-9
adolescence
    dilemma of, 90-1
    and sexual experience, 89
affect, lack of, 35-6, 37, 38-9
affluence, in the sixties, 44
Age of Aquarius, 51
AIDS, 216-17
alcohol
    as drug, 88, 99
    legality, 110
Aliapoulios, Menelaos, 76
Alice in Wonderland, 213
All in the Family, 70
American Pie, 49-50
An Experiment in Criticism, 120
Animal House, 158
aphasia, effects of, 26
Aristophanes, 169
Aristotle, 25, 98-100, 113, 212
Arness, James, 34
Arnold, Thomas, 232
Arthurian legends, 238-9
As You Like It, 182
Astin, W.A., 180
authority
    disrespect for, 33, 109
    and teaching, 165-66
automobiles, and youth, 32
Avatar, 48

Bachman, 103, 112, 114
Barzun, Jacques, 130, 132
Basic Instinct, 40
Beatles, The, 30, 44
Becket, Thomas a, 237
Bejerot, Nils, 97, 98
Bennett, William, 103
Bernstein, Leonard, 57-9
Bettenhausen, Elizabeth, 5
Black Panthers, 44
Bloom, Allan, 42-3, 253
Blue Velvet, 40
Bly,. Robert, 172-5, 176
Body Heat, 40
Boesky, Ivan, 255
Bonfire of the Vanities, The, 64
boys' schools, 169-85
    advantage of, 233
    benefits for boys, 179
    female infiltration into,
      182-4
    qualities fostered in, 177
    teacher's perspective, 181,
      184-5, 209-29
    viability of, 179
Bradford, William, 260, 261-2
Brahms, Johannes, 29
Bundy, Ted, 255
Bush, [President George], 63, 64

Campbell, Malcolm Gordon, 80
Capra, Frank, 17, 121

Carlin, George, 86
Carpenter, Humphrey, 212-13
Carson, Johnny [Show], 74
Chariots of Fire, 178
Cheever, John, 43
Chicago, and the sixties, 44-5
child psychology
        and J.M. Tanner, 179
        and teaching, 161-3
chivalry
        as historic concept, 239-42
        and sexual experience 240-1
Chodorow, Nancy, 175-6
Christian religion, 5, 6
Christmas Carol, A, 121
Civil Disobedience, 252
Clark, Kenneth, 237
Clark, Petula, 125
Clinton, Bill, 61, 63, 64
Closing of the American Mind, 43
Clouds, The, 169
coeducation
        as market-driven, 17
        student preference for, 181-2
Columbus, [Christopher], 192
Coming Home, 41
Communist Party, 57
Confucius, 251
courtesy, code of conduct, 238-42
Cox, Harvey, 158
Creed of a Schoolmaster, 140
crime, and tabloids, ix-xi
culture
        commercial, ix-xii
        diversity, 21-3

Dance to the Music of Time, The,
        154-6
Davies, Robertson, 145
Dean, James, 178
Death of a Salesman, 178
Decline and Fall, 150-2

deer, 207-08
Democratic National Convention
of 1968, 44-5, 48
Democrats, 57
Deptford Trilogy, 145
Dern, Bruce, 41
Diana, Princess, 63
Dickens, [Charles], 145-6
Dickinson, Emily, 250
Dionysus
        and erotic quest, 42
        and Jesus, 46, 48-57
Donahue, [Phil], 62
Donat, Robert, 189, 125
Douglas, Geoff, 63
drug abuse, and high school
dropouts, 103
drug usage,
        and civil liberties, 108-09
        in elementary schools, 111
        in high school, 103-04
        history of, 104-05, 106
        legal consequence, 113
        legalization efforts, 109-10
        pathology of, 107-08
        physical effects, 105-06, 107
        prevalence, 114
        in public schools, 160
        treating children, 112
drugs
        and choice, 96
        drug-free programs, 103-14
        llegal, 95-102
        legalization, 75, 96-102
        and pleasure, 95-6
        popularization of, 97
        remedial action, 112-11, 114
Duke of Deception, The, 63
Duke, David, 8

education, goodness as what
        counts, 253-7

Eliot, John, 183
Enlightenment, 237-8
Erikson, Erik, 89
Essex, David, 56, 57
euphoria, of crowds, 29-30
Eve of St. Agnes, 122
Eye of the Needle, 42
Farrakhan, Louis, 8

Fatal Attraction, 40
Federalist Papers, 10
Feminism and Psychoanalytic Theory,
    175-6
film,
    Animal House, 158
    Chariots of Fire, 178
    Fire and Rain, 46, 178
    Five Easy Pieces, 178
    Good-bye, Mr. Chips, 124-8,
        189-90
    Great Expectations, 145-6
    Henry and June, 42
    It's a Wonderful Life, 17-20,
        121
    Jaws, 182
    Malcolm X, 187
    My Bodyguard, 160
    9-1/2 Weeks, 40
    Ordinary People, 178
    and pornography, 42
    Pulp Fiction, xii, 241-2
    Rebel without a Cause, 178
    Reefer Madness, 76
    Risky Business, 182
    Rocky, 120-1
    sex and death, 40-1
    Sleeping with the Enemy, 40
    Star Wars, 121
    *Unbearable Lightness of Being,
        The*, 42
    Waterland, 187-9, 192-3
    Wizard of Oa, The , 21

Follett, Ken, 42
Fonda, Jane, 41
Fonda, Peter, 74-5
Freud, Sigmund, 14, 41, 161, 172,
    175, 241
Freud, 172
Freud, 175
Freud, 241
Fuess, Claude, 140

Gandhi, Mahatma [Mohandas],
    237, 243-4, 252-3
Gardner, Howard, 246
Gardner, William Armory, 148-52
gender
    and controversy, 171
    gender-based differences,
        179-80
    overall question of, 176
    sexual potency issue, 180-1
geography, internal and external,
    197-208
Gilkeson, Robert, 84, 85
Gnadasan, Aruna, 5
Good Morning, Miss Dove, 161-8
Good-bye, Mr. Chips, 1248, 189
grading, in teaching, 137-8
graduation ceremonies, 254-7
Great Expectations, 145-6
Guthrie, Arlo, 74, 75
Gyllenhaal, Stephen, 187

Hair, 49-53
Hamill, Dorothy, 35
Hamlet, 45
Hargadon, Fred, 247-8
Harmon, J.W., 76, 77
Heart of Darkness, 227
Heath, Robert, 80
Hendrix, Jimi, 48-9
Henry and June, 42
hiking, 204-08, 197-8

Hillman, James, 172
Hilton, James, 124, 125, 189-90
historical record, 20-2
Hitler, [Adolph], 255
Holden Caulfield, 45, 158, 178
Hopper, Dennis, 74-5, 76
Hunting in the Snow, 204
hunting, 199-204
Huxley, Aldous, 3
Huxley, Julian, 244

intelligence, nature of, 246-7
Irving, Washington, 148
Isasi-Diaz, Ada Maria, 5
It's a Wonderful Life, 17-20, 121

Jagger, Mick, 48-9
James at 16, 69-70
James, Clive, 46
Jaws, 182
Jefferson, Thomas, 6, 12, 249
Jesus Christ Superstar, 46, 53-6, 57,
    59
Jesus, 130, 177, 243, 252, 253
    commercial exploitation of,
        46
    evolution of concept, 47-56
    as guide, 46
    modern impact, 56
    as modern myth, 52-6, 57, 59
Johnson, Lyndon, 48
Johnston, Lloyd, 103, 112, 114
Joplin, Janis, 49
journalism, and privacy, 61-4
Judeo-Christian tradition, 4
Jung, Carl, 121, 172

Kaplan, Helen, 84
Keats, [John], 122, 210, 250
Kennedy, Julia, 182-5
killing, of animals, 198-204
King, Martin Luther, 237, 251-3

Kohlberg, Lawrence, 98, 108-09
Kolanski, Harold, 84-5
Kolodny, Robert, 79
Kweskin, Jim, and his Jug Band,
    48
Kyung, Chung Hyun, 5

language
    function of, 27-8
    use in reasoning, 233-8
Last Temptation of Christ, The, 53
Lear, Norman, 70, 174
Legend of Sleepy Hollow, The, 148
Lennon, John, 74
Leuchtenberger, Cecille, 79
Leuchtenberger, Rudolf, 79
Lewis, C.S., 24-5, 120, 121, 152
Lincoln, Abraham, 260, 237
Little House on the Prairie, 69
logic, tool of reason, 236
*Loneliness of the Long Distance
    Runner, The*, 158
long hair, as symbol, 50
love, as concern for others, 242-5
Lyman, Mel, 48
Lynch, David, 40

Machiavelli, 210
Madison, James, 10
Mailer, Norman, 74, 75
Malcolm X, 187, 253
Malcolm X, 253

male values, and boys' schools,
    171
    enumerated, 177
    and their feminine side,
        172-6
    in literature, 177-9
    masculine ideal, 177-
    and the primitive, 172-6
Man for All Season, A, 119

Manhattan Project, and radiation experiment, 256-7
Manilow, Barry, 29
marijuana
    and adolescence, 88, 91
    and anxiety, 90-1
    and avoidance, 87-90
    at concert, 34
    chemistry of, 82
    combating usage, 78, 84
    composition of, 107 (find other reference)
    and effect on learning, 75-6
    effects of, 82-7
    as harmless substance, 74-5
    and legal consequences, 93
    and physical effects, 76, 78-82, 94
    prevalence of, 75, 77-8
    remedial agenda, 91-4, 106-07
    and SATs, 86
    and urban slums, 74
Marx, Karl, 8
Mass
    lyrics, 60 (n)
    music by Leonard Bernstein, 57-9
Masters, Edgar Lee, 214
mathematics, tool of reason, 236-7
Maude, 70
McLean, Don, 49-50
McLuhan, Marshall, 73
Meistersinger, Der, 58
Midler, Bette, 29
Milken, Michael, 255
Moby Dick, 182, 227
Mollenkott, Virginia Ramsey, 5, 6
Moore, William, 84-5
More, Thomas, 119
music, discovery of, 236
My Bodyguard, 160

Nahas, Gabriel, 78, 79, 80, 106, 112
natural rights, 6
Nelligan, Kate, 42
New England Journal of Medicine, 76
Newman, Randy, 71
Nichomachean Ethics, 25
Niebuhr, Reinhold, 253
9-1/2 Weeks, 40
Nixon, Richard, 105

O'Malley, Patrick, 103, 112, 114
O'Toole, Peter, 125
Odyssey, The, 174-5
Ordinary People, 178
Orwell, George, 3

Parents Resource Institute of Drug Education, 97, 106-07, 112
Patton, Frances Gray, 161-8
Peabody, Endicott, 148-9
Perot, [Ross], 63
Peter Pan, 213
philosophy, beginning of, 234
Piaget, Jean, 98, 132-3
Plath, Sylvia, as confessional writer, 62
Plato, 12, 13-15, 19, 108, 109, 113, 210
Playboy, 107
Plug-in Drug, The, 65
political correctness, 3, 4-25
pornography, and Clarence Thomas, 61
pornography, in film, 42
Potter, Beatrix, 122
Powell, Anthony, 154-6
Prescott, Peter, 156-7
PRIDE. See Parents Resource Institute of Drug Education.
Prince, Peter, 187
privacy, and journalism, 61-4

Prohibition, failure of, 100, 110-11
public schools
    drugs in, 160
    teaching in, 161-8
Pulp Fiction, xii, 241-2
Puritans, qualities of, 259-62

Quayle, Dan, 61

reading, as transformation of life,
    119-22
Reagan, Nancy, 106
reason
    and Age of Enlightenment,
      237
    and emotion, 237
    and logic, 236
    and mathematics, 236-7
    phenomenon of human
      beings, 233-8
Rebel without a Cause, 178
Reefer Madness, 76
relativism, 8-10
religion, new, 5-6
Republic, The, 12, 14-17
Republicans, 57
responsibility, as essential quality,
    255-7
Richard, Renee, 67
Rickles, Don, 70-1
right living, an agenda, 23-4
Rimbaud, [Arthur], 214, 215, 216
Risky Business, 182
Robin Hood, 178
Rocky, 119-20, 49
Romeo and Juliet, 122, 178
Roosevelt, Franklin, 260
Roosevelt, Theodore, 232
Rousseau, [Jean-Jacques], 62, 161
Rush, Tom, and spiritual help,
    46-7

Salinger, J.D., 158
Sanderson, Frederick William,
    146-7
SATs, 216, 247, 248
    and marijuana, 86
Saturday Night Live, 66-7, 68, 72,
    158
Schwartz, Stephen, 60 (n)
Secret Gardens, 212
self-esteem, 263-7
seventies
    and emergence of drugs, 74
    and Jesus, 45, 50, 52
sexist attitudes, in boys' schools,
    185-6
Sexton, Anne, as confessional
    writer, 62
sexual experience
    and adolescence, 89
    and chivalry, 240-1
    excess, x, xi
    in films, 40-3
    as idolatry, 6
    and long hair, 50
    and pornography, 8
    and violence, 41-3
Sillitoe, Alan, 158
Silverstein, Shel, 121
sixties, the
    and political system, 44-5
and Skinner, B.F., 3
    and tolerance, 44
    and youth, 44-5
Sleeping with the Enemy, x40
Socrates, 12-13, 17, 64, 130, 134,
    169, 234, 236-7, 238, 250
Solzhenitsyn, [Alexander], 249
Spoon River Anthology, 214, 215
St. Augustine, 62
St. Francis, 177, 178
St. John, 28
standards

for public speaking, 73
universal, 192-3
Star Wars, 121
Stone, Oliver, 20
Story of a Great Headmaster, 147-8
student lives, case studies, 212-9
student types, unworldly boy,
    212-17
students, concept of good student,
    246-50
Supreme Court, 61
Surprised by Joy, 152-3
Swift, Graham, 187

Talbot, John, 84
Tanner, J.M., 179
Tarentino, Quentin, xii, 241-2
Tate [Sharon], murder of, 49
Taylor, James
    audience for, 31-3, 35, 36-8
    a concert, 29-39, 34-5
    and hard rock, 34-5
    and identity crisis, 46
    Teacher in America, 130
teachers
    as a class, 123-41
    role of, 124
teaching
    and authority, 143, 165-6
    in a boys' school, 209-29
    characteristics, 161, 167-8
    charisma, 133-4
    and child psychology, 161-3
    commitment, 133
    contrasting styles, 187-90
    effective, 136-7
    expertise required, 131-3
    and firm procedures, 163-4
    and grading, 137-8
    prescription for, 193
    in public schools, 161-8
    as public speaking, 131

recipe for, 124-8
risks of failure, 129-41
role of eccentricity, 141-59
role of love, 126-8
role of personality, 127-8
and sense of proportion, 128
strengths of, 139-41
and student performance,
    164-5
and teachers' influence, 166
Teague, James, 84
Tebelak, John M, 59
television, 65-73, 68
and values, 137
television
    and anxiety, 70
    and cruelty, 70-1
    and offensive influence,
        65-7, 71-2
    and tolerance, 71
    and trivializatiion, 67
    watched by students, 123
Temple of Gold, 158
Thanksgiving
    as appreciation, 259
    celebration of, 258-62
    Giving Tree, The, 121
    as reminder of thankfulness,
        258-9
    Wizard of Oz, The, 121
This Boy's Life, 63
Thomas, Clarence, 61
Thoreau, Henry David, 250, 252
Titos, Alan, 58
tobacco
    harmful drug, 99
    legality, 110
tolerance
    in the sixties, 44
    and television, 71
Tolkien, J.R.R., 120, 1221
Tom Brown's Schooldays, 176

tradition, in boys' schools, 185
Turner, Carlton, 106

U.S. constitution, 11, 12
Unbearable Lightness of Being, The,
    42
unique qualities, and boys'
    schools, 170-1

values
    imposed, 232
    and schools' teaching, 254
    in the sixties, 44-5
    and teaching, 137
    and television, 68-9
    Verlaine, Paul, 214
victim, as concept, 190-3
violence, and rock groups, 49
Voight, 41
vulgarity, in speech, 26

Waltons, The, 69
Washington, George, 260
Water Babies, The, 213

Waterland, 187-9, 192-3
Waugh, Evelyn, 150-2, 153-4
Welcome Back, Kotter, 160
Wells, H.G., 147
White Shadow, 160
Whitehead, Alfred North, 132
Whore, 40
wildlife, in boyhood eyes, 198
Wind in the Willows, The, 122, 213
Winn, Marie, 65
Winnie the Pooh, 213
Wolfe, Tom, 64
Wolff, Geoffrey, 63
Wood, Frances, 5-6
Woodstock, the experience, 30, 31
World of Our Own, A, 156-7
Wyatt, Jane, 69

Yippies, 48-9
Young, Robert, 69

youth
    and faith in Jesus, 46-7
    youth, obsession with, 44-5